Roman Numerals

Roman Numerals

The Second Art West Adventure

BenWitherington III
and Ann Witherington

PICKWICK *Publications* · Eugene, Oregon

ROMAN NUMERALS
The Second Art West Adventure

Pickwick Publications
A division of Wipf and Stock Publishers
199 W. 8th Ave., Suite 3
Eugene, OR 97401

www.wipfandstock.com

ISBN 13: 978-1-60608-548-6

Cataloging-in-Publication data:

Witherington, Ben, 1951–

    Roman numerals : the second Art West adventure / Ben Witherington III and
    Ann Witherington

    vi + 252 p. ; 23 cm.

    ISBN 13: 978-1-60608-548-6

    1. Archaeology—Fiction. I. Witherington, Ann. II. Title.

PS3605 W55 2009

Manufactured in the U.S.A.

In memento mori:

To Ben's Father,
who loved history and made some of his own
during his 92 years of life.

"Blessed and holy are those who die in the Lord."

1

Desert Storm

T HE FLIGHT FROM CAIRO to Abu Simbel was uneventful. The Air
Egypt jet was worlds better than the old prop jobs he endured the
first time he explored Egypt. While sipping his Coke Zero in the back
of the plane, Art West was left to ponder what had just happened in
Jerusalem. He pushed his seat back, closed his eyes and remembered
the new gleaming white limestone building standing on the west slope
of the Mount of Olives near Bethany.

The Lazarus tomb museum opened with some fanfare, and Art had
been there to cut the ribbon with his colleague and friend Grace Levine,
the mayor of Jerusalem, the prime minister, and various members of
the Israel Antiquities Authority. What started as a celebratory occasion
had ended abruptly with the news of another car bomb explosion, this
time right in front of the Church of All Nations. The explosion, heard
all over town, cut short the ceremony, as various VIPs rushed off to find
out what had happened and what could be done. "It must be next to
impossible to live in a constant state of siege," thought Art. Death and
destruction had a way of punctuating life all too often.

Escalating violence in the Holy Land had shut down all but four
digs, heavily influencing Art's decision to take a season off from archaeological pursuits in Israel. Things had not improved, despite diplomatic
efforts. So this summer Art set his sights on a different quest—exploring
Roman influence in various places in the Empire. The dramatic rise in
interest among New Testament scholars in the subject of the Roman

I

imperial cult and its influence in the Empire during the NT period, had even led to a recent glut of scholarly articles on the critique of the imperial cult found in the NT itself.

Art decided to confine himself to Egypt and Turkey this summer. The first two sites on his hit list were Abu Simbel, the great shrine of Ramses and Nefertari near the border between Egypt and the kingdoms to the south, and the Philae Temple in Aswan. In 1960, Art's elementary school class had collected money after reading in *National Scholastic* about the plight of Abu Simbel. The shrine had to be moved to safety before the building of the high dam in Aswan flooded the area to create Lake Nasser. Now finally he would see this remarkable place. Not really expecting to find any traces of Roman influence at Abu Simbel, he was visiting this shrine as a tourist this morning, but his next stop at Aswan's Philae Temple would be a different matter. Emperors ranging from Augustus to Trajan to Hadrian had buildings erected as part of the Philae complex.

As the plane descended to the small airport at Abu Simbel, Art gazed out the window and could actually see the shrines glistening in the relentless sunlight. "Ramses must have been a megalomaniac to force his workers to build a shrine like this way down here in the middle of the desert," thought Art. "It must be 120°F in the shade today." He was going to receive a warm reception whether or not he wanted one. He hoped to just blend in with the tourists, see the shrine, and then take the flight back to Aswan. Nothing could be simpler, or so he thought.

Across the aisle sat an Egyptian couple wearing traditional garb, the wife all in black, and the husband wearing a flat-topped headdress. "Why would they be on this flight?" wondered Art. Besides the small support community for the tourist trade, very little civilization had developed out in the desert next to Abu Simbel. Perhaps the couple was coming to see some of their traditional Egyptian heritage. Even natives should be tourists sometimes.

The plane touched down, jolting Art's thoughts back to the present moment. Art picked up his luggage and proceeded directly to the shuttle bus provided by Egypt Tours. The guide turned out to be Neffi Mafouz, the daughter of the famous Egyptian writer Nagib Mafouz whom Art had long admired. Neffi had been a tour guide for some twenty years in the southern part of Egypt, and was well known for her lively descriptions of ancient Egyptian life. Today she wore a pith helmet and a lightweight beige jump suit, all to shield her 5'4" frame from the sun. Forty years of southern Egyptian sun had baked Neffi's skin to a deep olive. Though not a beautiful woman, she had a vivacious personality and a winning smile. Art could hardly wait for the tour to begin.

"We are so pleased to have you Dr. West. Please feel free to add any comments as we tour the site. Our group today is small, and I believe all eleven of us are now accounted for," said Neffi, grinning from ear to ear.

"So much for anonymity," muttered Art, pulling his Red Sox baseball cap down over his eyes and preparing to face the heat. As it turned out, his picture had been in the Cairo paper that very morning standing in front of the new museum in Jerusalem. Egyptologists like Neffi had been fascinated by the further evidence in Israel of a strong belief in resurrection and the afterlife, not least because many of them thought the idea originated in Egypt during one of the Middle Period dynasties. Thus anything to do with ossuaries, Lazarus, and resurrection interested Egyptologists.

To gain some perspective on the vast shrine, Neffi gathered her flock near the water's edge under a large palm, one of a precious few in the area. Also under the palm was a man in white leaning on a large silver cart. "It's a bit warm today," he said to the tourists, "over 100°F as the Americans say. Surely I can tempt you with ice cream." The groans were audible as the whole group lined up for ice cream on a stick before braving the march across the sand to the shrine's entrance. Neffi just smiled sheepishly. Art readily devoured a fudgesicle while thinking that Neffi probably got her treats for free. Tour guides were notorious for leading tourists to the venders.

The view from the water's edge was grand. Rising up from the desert floor, a small mountain, nearly one hundred feet high, enveloped the shrine of Ramses II and Nefertari. The whole shrine had been not only moved in the 1960s, after carefully cutting it into blocks and reassembling it at this higher elevation, but also set into an artificial mountain, which looked quite real from this vantage point. Upon close inspection, however, one could see the seams in both the shrine and the mountain itself.

Neffi began her explanation. "Ramses II, known to some of you as the Pharaoh of the Exodus, built many shrines across the land. He had plenty of time to do so since he ruled for nearly sixty-seven years during the Nineteenth Dynasty. This shrine here stood as a sort of sentinel warning travelers up the Nile that they were entering the land of a great ruler at their own peril and had best be prepared to do homage to him. While each of his shrines indicates his power, control, and divinity to even the casual visitor, what is most interesting about this shrine is that the image of his wife, Nefertari (not to be confused with the later Queen Nefertiti) is of the same size as that of the pharaoh himself. This is surprising, since elsewhere Nefertari's statue is much smaller than Ramses II. Indeed, at the Luxor temple, she even appears to be the size of a child standing on Ramses' feet!"

"The dates of Ramses II are debated, but if he was indeed the pharaoh of the Exodus, we know that he must have ruled before and during 1290 BC; however, some Egyptologists now think Ramses' descendent, Merinptah, ruled when the Exodus happened. In any case, this shrine seems to have built somewhere around 1310 BC. Let's walk over now and look at the shrine from a more direct angle."

By now it was close to noon, and Art, looking up, noticed a dark haze in the air to the south. He figured it was just due to the extreme heat.

Standing in the middle of the area in front of the shrine was a jaw dropping experience. Each statue stood almost sixty-seven feet high, and each was carved out of one piece of stone. Both rulers were dressed in full royal regalia and Ramses wore the crowns of both Upper and Lower Egypt. The serene expressions on the faces of Ramses and Nefertari seemed to say, "We are in control here, and you are too small for us to even pay any attention to you. Don't even think about doing anything foolish while you are here in our land." Everyone in the group fanned themselves and guzzled bottled water while Neffi lectured. Suddenly she stopped, looked skyward, and shouted, "Khamsin! Sand storm! It's coming! Everyone run for the shrine!"

Before the tiny group could cross the one hundred yards to the shrine itself, the sand, having moved relentlessly up the river toward Abu Simbel, began to pummel them. It became next to impossible to see, with the grains of sand stinging any exposed piece of skin. Neffi yelled out, "Take each others' hands, and run as quickly as you can." Art had never experienced a sand storm like this before, and it was far more abrupt and deadly than he had imagined. He was at the back of the pack of tourists taking pictures. Movement became difficult as the grit-filled wind gusted close to fifty miles an hour.

Art could hear the people in front of him breathing hard as they raced blindly towards the shrine. Suddenly they stumbled in front of the shrine, tripping over the ledge of the porch. Shielding his eyes with one arm, Art helped the couple in front of him by shoving them in between the statues of the rulers towards the door of the shrine. Now they were crawling toward the entrance, and when Art looked up he could see the door swaying and beginning to close. "Hurry!" cried Art to the couple. With another mighty shove he pushed them through the door. As he yanked the door shut, he felt the rush of cool refrigerated air sweep over him. Inside an artificial mountain, covered with sand but still breathing, he looked up into a steel roof that looked like the inside of a domed football stadium.

2

Tours and Guides

ART STOOD IN AWE of what he was seeing—a totally self-contained workshop hermetically sealed off from the blistering heat and sun of the desert. The pharaohs themselves would have been impressed. Other guides and guests arrived quickly to help the new tourists, most of whom were jabbering excitedly about their unplanned adventure. Neffi was busy cleaning the grit from the Egyptian couple.

"We must remain inside until the storm subsides," informed Neffi calmly. "I'm sure you won't mind catching your breath and having a drink in the canteen over on the left. Then we will show you the inside of this man-made mountain."

A myriad of questions went through Art's mind as he enjoyed his ice cold water. Had the architects of this building learned some things from the way the pharaohs had constructed the passageways and chambers inside the pyramids? What function, other than serving as a large "let the traveler beware" sign, had this shrine served for Ramses and his wife? Was it also a temple at one point?

Turning to Neffi, who was sitting across the table gathering her wits, Art quietly asked, "So, does this place hold some secrets? What's been discovered by the Egyptologists out here in the desert? Do we know anymore than we did before moving these monoliths over forty years ago?"

Neffi wrinkled her forehead. "The answer is yes, we know a good deal more, but no, we don't know as much as we would like. We've learned that southern Nubian pharaohs had more African features than one traditionally associates with Egyptians. It's possible that Ramses placed these statues here partly to stem the tide of immigrants from the south of Africa into Egypt. But that does not explain why Nefertari's statues are as large as Ramses here, but not in Luxor. Perhaps she was from this region, and so her statue represents her as 'big' in this part of the land. But we cannot be sure. Have you any thoughts, Dr. West?"

"Both ideas make considerable sense to me, but I'm no Egyptologist. I do need to ask an easier question, I hope. I'm due to stay in Aswan tonight and visit the Philae tomorrow morning. Do you know a good private guide?"

"Of course," she said, "were I not working, I would be honored to escort you, but my assistant Dori Baioumi can take you for a fee. You will like her. You two have something in common," and Neffi smiled her wide smile again.

"What do you mean?" asked Art.

"Wait and see," said Neffi. "Why spoil the surprise!"

"What I see now," said Art with a wry grin, "is that you enjoy suspense, just like your father with his wonderful stories. Did his tales about ancient Egypt inspire you to study Egyptology?"

"Yes, of course, his writings influenced me. He tried them out on me as bedtime stories sometimes. He is a remarkable person in many ways. You know he is still alive, do you not?"

"Yes, but I hear his health has been frail since he was attacked by some fundamentalists who did not appreciate his love of things non-Islamic."

"Yes," said Neffi dropping her voice to a whisper, "but we must not speak of these things here. We do not know who is listening," she warned. "Another bus was blown up not far from here last week, and nowadays locals are afraid to criticize such people. Did you know that even in the public schools here, the radical Muslims have such control of the curriculum that they forbid the teaching of much of our history, including our Coptic Christian history? Even President Mubarak has been unable to stem their influence."

Art pondered this as Neffi continued the tour inside the mechanical mountain. Clearly even Egypt, a largely moderate Muslim country, had fallen prey to the struggles sweeping through the Middle East in the wake of the rising tide of the Islamic fundamentalist movement.

The tour of the facility, including its enormous computer-controlled air conditioning units, was interesting, but Art longed to go back outside and take some shots of the monoliths.

His wish was soon granted. Workers were busily sweeping the sand out of the shrine by the time the tour slipped back out into the now sunny environs. Art managed some splendid pictures, including one of Neffi standing between the two statues, completely dwarfed by their great height. The rest of the tour went off without interruption and Art soon found himself on a short plane ride from Abu Simbel to Aswan, equipped with a business card for Neffi's tour guide agency along with Dori's number. He would ring her as soon as he checked into his hotel, the Jewel of the Nile.

True to its name, the old but refurbished Victorian building sat right on the famed river. Art relaxed on the back patio, sipping his fruit juice, and eating a few scrumptious dates and olives while he studied a map of the island of Philae. The island was honeycombed with temples from many periods, as the map showed, but the ones in which Art was especially interested were the Roman structures built for Augustus and then much later for Trajan and Hadrian.

Emperor worship had extended as far south as southern Egypt. It was precisely this phenomenon of emperor worship—even of living emperors—by the middle of the first century AD that Art wanted to better understand. Besides Jesus, the only significant first-century historical figures worshipped as a gods were some of the emperors. Art wanted to figure out if this phenomenon helped the spread of Christianity, making the idea of a "god who walks the earth with us" more plausible to Greco-Roman people.

Suddenly Art's cell phone rang. It was Dori from the tourist agency.

"Professor West, shall we come and collect you in the morning? What is your pleasure? It would be better if we go early due to the heat."

That's fine," said Art, "what time?"

"Is eight o'clock too early? It will be cooler and quieter then."

"Eight it is," said Art. "I particularly want to beat the crowds to the Roman ruins." "Very well," Dori said. "Have you any questions?"

On a whim Art asked, "Is it safe for me to take a swim in the Nile here in Aswan?" "No, I'm afraid not," said Dori. "Sadly, raw sewage goes directly into the Nile."

She paused, and then with a sad laugh continued, "We used to say, 'If you drink from the Nile you will always return.' Today we say, 'If you drink from the Nile, you will never leave.'"

Art laughed but promised to stay high and dry.

Dori added, "You can take a felucca down the Nile if you like, which is a pleasant thing to do in the evenings."

"Thanks," said Art. "Perhaps I will try that before I turn in. I'll see you in the morning."

Then surprisingly Dori said, "By God's grace," and hung up. Could this be what Neffi had meant? Was Dori a Coptic Christian?

Art looked again at his map, walked down the terrace to the little dock, and spoke to a small man at a kiosk, asking if he could hire a felucca for an hour. "Most certainly, and my son and I will be your sailors," the man replied. "That will be £20 Egyptian please."

Art removed his shoes and settled onto a cushion inside the traditional wooden boat, having asked the man to sail around to Philae so he could take some pictures. Larger feluccas, holding up to ten passengers, were gracefully catching the evening breezes. As they came around the bend in the river, a remarkable island, complete with temple after temple standing on its acropolis, came into view. The sun was setting between the columns and Art could hardly take enough pictures.

"This morning brought a sand storm. Who knows what mysteries of the Egyptian desert will unfold when I visit Philae in the morning?" Art was content for the moment to sail off into the sunset, happily taking picture after picture, and listening to the water lapping up against the sailboat. Augustus, Trajan, and Hadrian had all left their mark here, though they had never personally visited this part of Egypt. "At least I am one up on them in that regard," mused Art.

3

Philae Revelation

THE SUN HAD ALREADY been up for two hours when Art made his way through the lobby to the front of the hotel. Dori, a petite woman with dark hair and charcoal black eyebrows, leapt from a taxi and waved to Art. He immediately noticed a small fish symbol tattooed on the inside of Dori's right wrist.

Art couldn't resist the impulse to ask, "So, are you a Coptic Christian?" She placed her finger to her lips, but nodded positively. Shifting her eyes toward the cab and its driver, she indicated that now was not the time for this discussion. Deftly, she turned the discussion to a more pressing topic.

"I see that you have a map of Philae. That's good; we will use it. I intend for us to explore the Roman ruins in detail. Can you read the hieroglyphs?"

"Sadly, only a few of them," said Art. "My ancient languages of relevance are Greek and Latin."

"You will perhaps be surprised to learn there are some inscriptions in those languages at the temple. In fact, I have brought one with me that I copied from the kiosk of Trajan that I hope you can puzzle out."

Art took the small scrap of paper from Dori, and looked at the crude letters. "It's two forms of the same riddle in both Greek and Latin:

> He is many men and no man, towering like the sphinx,
> dead and alive, but who knows what he thinks?
> Back from the Styx; 666.

"That's roughly what it says. I've smoothed it out a bit into a sort of poetic form. Was this an inscription or a graffito scratched on a wall?"

Dori paused and answered, "Not an inscription. I'll show you when we get there. Clearly it is an ancient writing, but what do you think it means?"

Art scratched his head. "Give me awhile to think about it—only bits and pieces make sense, but the whole certainly doesn't! Graffiti in the first century was often used to make unofficial and uncensored political or religious comment about something."

The cab dropped them at the dock and they jumped into a small motorboat owned by the agency. Dori cranked up the engine and they headed out into the channel toward the island of Philae.

"We'll have to go around the island to land at the modern dock, but now that we're out here I can answer your question. Yes, I am a Coptic Christian. We don't wear visible crosses or other sorts of Christian symbols, but have the tattoos placed on us when we are small. Did you realize that about 30 percent of the Egyptian population is Coptic Christian?"

"No," said Art. "I had no idea there were that many! I heard about the troubles of Pope Shenouda, and how he was jailed, and then finally released. The Western press made it sound like he was the leader of a tiny minority sect. But that's not what you're saying."

"Exactly, but with the growth of Islamic fundamentalism in this country, it has become very difficult for us. We don't believe in jihad or retaliation for wrongs, so we went underground to some extent. Officially we are tolerated, unofficially we are targeted by extremists. I don't want to leave the wrong impression, however. Many of my best friends in Aswan are Muslims, and some of them are even Sufis, mystics of a sort. So these radicals do not really represent all Muslims by any means. You know the writings of Neffi's father, I gather?"

"Yes," replied Art. "He has a true gift, and is part of that older, more generous and respectful tradition when it comes to other religions. But he too has been targeted." The conversation could have gone on much longer, but the boat had reached its destination.

Climbing up on the dock, Dori asked, "How much do you actually know about the Philae temple complex?"

"Not much," said Art. "Enlighten me, especially about the Roman remains here." They walked up to the center of the temple precincts, and immediately noticed the composite nature of the site. Built over many centuries, involving many styles of architecture, Philae resembled the temple complex in Luxor, with one big difference—the absence of a reflection or purification pool.

"This was the last bastion of ancient Egyptian religion and hiero-glyphic usage," Dori began. "It is also a superb example of a threatened cultural heritage being saved in the face of modern civilization's march to change the environment. Here are a couple of good pictures of the temple so you can see how spectacular it is at night, as well as dur-ing the day." Dori pointed to the tourist sign with the pictures and descriptions.

"When the British erected the first dam at Aswan at the beginning of the twentieth century, they did not calculate the long-term effects on this site. After years of problems, the flooding and water damage got even worse in 1960 with the building of the high dam, and threatened to completely submerge the ruins. Fortunately, in 1977 a small dam was built, the water was pumped from the site, and the stones were first numbered then disassembled. The Philae temple was entirely removed from its original island home, and then reassembled on the nearby higher island of Agilka."

Art interrupted, "Sound much like the ruins of Abu Simbel. So we're not on the original site of the temple, are we?"

"No," said Dori, "it is as you say. Originally this temple was built for Isis, the most popular Egyptian goddess of the Greco-Roman period. The setting and beauty of the temple complex attracted many visitors, and eventually various rulers wanted to add to it. Though it was first built during the Twenty-Sixth Dynasty of Egypt, today most of the ru-ins date from the Roman period, which means construction continued for almost eight hundred years. That is really not long when you con-sider the span of Egyptian history, the oldest continuously inhabited and developing country or civilization."

"Some Persians may debate you on that point," smiled Art.

Dori sighed. "Everyone's entitled to an opinion! In any case, Philae was the last bastion of the old Egyptian culture, but it also bears wit-ness to subsequent Roman and Christian cultures. Did you know," she tactfully continued, "that the Christian emperor Justinian waited until about AD 550 before he finally closed these temples?"

Art nodded in agreement and Dori continued. "Ah, but you are interested in the Roman remains, so let me talk about that for a moment. Hadrian built a wall around the complex with a majestic gateway on the west side of the original island. But since your period of focus is the first century AD, I think you'll find the magnificent structure that Trajan built around 100 AD even more interesting. It became a site for the worship of Emperor Trajan, and of the previous Roman emperors who had been deified."

"I see," said Art. "Even the ones from the Julio-Claudian and Flavian families?"

"Yes, just so, but of course the emphasis is on Trajan and his family. Not only did it come to symbolize the emperor cult in the early Christian era, it is where I found the Greek and Latin inscriptions, including the graffito carved on one of those columns with the striking capitals.

With brow wrinkled, Art prompted, "Show me the place where you found this riddle."

Dori and Art walked through the arch to a corner of the Trajan kiosk. Sure enough, chiseled into the column, about five feet off the ground, stood the elegant letters of the graffito, first in Greek and below it in Latin. Someone wanted these words to be read.

> He is many men and no man, towering like the sphinx,
> dead and alive, but who knows what he thinks?
> Back from the Styx; 666.

Art characteristically rubbed his chin and said, "In the first century, the number 666 in the Christian Book of Revelation probably referred to an emperor from either the Julio-Claudian or Flavian periods, so this must be a Christian inscription from ancient times. But why is it all the way down here in Egypt? Had the Christian influence already spread this far in the early second century?"

Dori was quick to respond. "According to our Coptic tradition, St. Mark brought Christianity here in the first century to Alexandria, but this inscription must postdate the building of the kiosk, so it's surely no older than the second century."

Art was still puzzled. "Yes, but the Book of Revelation was probably not written until the last decade of the first century, and yet here we also have that symbolic number in southern Egypt. Was the Book of Revelation really so popular in the second century that it was read in Aswan? And what is this business about many men and no man and the sphinx? I don't know about you, but I've about had it with this heat. What do you say we go back to Aswan and let me ruminate on this?"

"Certainly," she said, "would you like to have a home-cooked Egyptian meal with my family this evening, instead of the continental fare you're likely to get in the hotel?"

Art's eyes lit up. "I'd be delighted! What time should I be there?"

"How about 7:00 this evening? And we'll invite Neffi as well if she is back in town." The two rode the boat back to shore with Art lost in thought. He could not decide which intrigued him more—the signs of ancient Christianity in this temple, or the evidence of modern Christianity in the form of Dori and the Copts in this place.

4

Living Coptic

L IKE SO MANY EGYPTIANS, Dori lived with her parents in an extended family situation, even though she was in her early thirties.
From what Art could gather, Dori was seen as a woman with too much
education, too many abilities, and too liberal a mindset for any of the
Coptic men in Aswan to marry her, an unfortunate circumstance since
she was both charming and interesting.

Dori met Art at the door and welcomed him into the apartment.
It was small by American standards, but spotless. After the requisite in-
troductions, Art made himself at home, joining the family around a low
table in the living room. He soon learned that Samen, Dori's younger
brother, was named after St. Simon (Arabic, Sama'an) the Tanner, from
the tenth century. Today visitors are attracted from around the world to
visit the monastery dedicated to him in the famous Mokattam hills outside of Cairo where thousands of Copts eke out a living sifting through
the garbage. As they snacked on hummus and pita bread, Dori told Art
that Neffi was unable to come, but that she would continue the story of
the Coptic Church since he was keen to hear more.

"You may not know that the Coptic Orthodox Church remains independent of any other Orthodox church: Syrian, Armenian, Russian,
or Greek. We share some similarities in our forms of worship, our icons,
and the way we relate to the stories and traditions of the saints, but
unlike the other Orthodox churches that ordain bishops, we refer to
our patriarch as Pope. We too believe miracles still happen, and in the

help the saints provide us when we seek a miracle. If you go to St. Simon's Monastery outside Cairo, for example, you'll see the wheelchairs and crutches and other relics of healing, showing the signs of God's grace in that place."

"Tell me how you survive here in Aswan," said Art. "It can't be easy, among the Islamic fundamentalists."

"You're right; it is not. Usually, we meet at unexpected times in the church and sometimes we meet in small groups in our homes to pray and worship. The public does not know our schedule."

"Much like the early Christians, according to Acts."

"Just so," said Dori, taking a moment to translate their conversation to her family who did not speak English.

With only a few words of Arabic at his command, Art waited patiently before asking her to tell him more about the Coptic language. "I'm interested because of all the excitement about the Coptic documents, especially the *Gospel of Philip* found at Nag Hammadi, and now the *Gospel of Judas.*"

"There's a good reason those documents were hidden out in the desert away from St. Pachomius's monastery in the fourth or fifth century. They're filled with anti-Christian ideas and contradicted much of the Coptic tradition. St. Athanasius could not afford to allow the monks to continue to copy and be influenced by these documents. They are filled with idle philosophical speculations, but let me tell you the fuller version of things and about the Coptic language as we dine."

Mrs. Baioumi signaled for Dori and Samen to come and help serve. They returned with large, aromatic platters of steaming shwarma, vegetables, and rice flavored with raisins and cinnamon.

Dori's father, Youseff, a small, wiry man with a little white moustache, stood. "We must now say our blessing, thanking God for the food," Dori explained. After her father prayed in some combination of Arabic and Coptic, Dori translated for Art, who had just managed to make out the naming of the Trinity at the end of the prayer.

As they passed the food Art murmured, "*Shokrun,*" grateful he at least knew enough Arabic to say thank you and understand Samen's "*Afwan,*" or "You're welcome," in return. After a few bites Dori continued her conversation with Art.

"The Coptic language uses Greek letters with a few Egyptian characters to transliterate Demotic or Egyptian sounds and words. You'll also find Greek loan words in Coptic documents, like *koinonos,* which means companion, a term found in the *Gospel of Philip* in reference to St. Mary Magdalene."

"It sounds a bit like Yiddish," replied Art.

"Just so," said Dori. "You may know that St. Mark founded the Coptic Church in Alexandria in the mid-first century AD. Until the second Jewish revolt in the early part of the second century, the church had a low profile, but once Judaism came under suspicion in the Empire, the Christian Church in Egypt began to emerge from the shadows of the synagogue. It seems that originally it consisted mostly of converted Hellenized Jews and some Egyptians. We know there was a large Jewish population in Alexandria, which remained the main center of learning in Egypt at the time thanks to its famous library."

"Didn't the Gnostic believers Basilides and Valentinus send some of their pupils to Egypt to spread their heterodox teachings in the middle of the second century?" asked Art.

"They did," Dori confirmed. "But when the Christian church leaders in Rome, or perhaps in Asia, heard of this, they dispatched Pantaneus to Alexandria to correct any false teaching that might have been being spread around by the disciples of the Gnostics. While Pantaneus expected to find a heretical community of Gnostics in Alexandria, he basically found a healthy orthodox church, with only a few aberrant teachers and disciples. Of course, Alexandria was famous for its pluralistic and cosmopolitan culture, so naturally all sorts of philosophies and religions flourished there."

Quietly, so as not to interrupt Dori and Art, Samen and his mother cleared the table, while Mr. Baioumi watched his daughter with obvious pride. Dori became more passionate about defending her Coptic faith.

"I don't know how familiar you are with the Gnostic documents, but they contain a good deal of Greek philosophy. They often became anti-Jewish and increasingly ascetical—not just promoting celibacy but pushing a very negative view of marriage and sex. True Copts like the Jews of Alexandria believed in the goodness of creation, of marriage, of sex, and family. Pantaneus became the head of the Orthodox Christian Academy in Alexandria and helped set the church on a firm apostolic foundation. In AD 189, St. Demetrius, educated in this academy, became the first Egyptian-born bishop in the Coptic Orthodox Church in Alexandria."

Art stood as Dori's mother and brother reentered the room, grateful for a moment to absorb his guide's passionate tutorial. The smell of rich coffee mingled with the sweet hints of rosewater, nuts, and cinnamon wafted from the tray of ataif, a delectable cross between baklava and pancakes. One small bite and Art wished he knew how to bake, as he imagined he'd never find a dessert like this back in the States.

"Dori, please tell your mother how much I appreciate her cooking, and especially her baking. These are wonderful!" said Art, literally smacking his lips. Mrs. Baioumi beamed at the obvious compliment which overcame language barriers.

"So, where was I?" said Dori, laughing.

"Pantaneus and Demetrius," Art offered.

"Ah, yes. And the two of them set out on a vast mission to convert the Egyptian peasants to Christianity using the Coptic language, which sounded like and used words of the native Demotic, but mostly used a Greek script. About this time, the Bible was translated into Coptic so it could be used to spread the faith throughout Egypt. This is a crucial point, for, as you know, the Gnostic documents appear in Coptic, which surely indicates that they date from the third or fourth century, *after* the Coptic translation of the Bible circulated. These Gnostic documents quote a translation of the Bible that did not exist before the middle of the third century AD. The Orthodox Church in Egypt never officially accepted or sanctioned them. Eventually, when Athanasius found out some monks had been copying and studying them, he banned them in the fourth century, which is probably why they were found buried out in the desert away from St. Pachomius's monastery."

Clearly Dori had a passion for her faith and maintained a definite view on the Gnostics. "I have heard some of the loose talk about Gnostics being Christians, but I must tell you that even going back to the second century the Egyptian Coptic Orthodox Church never considered the Gnostics Christian. The Gnostics didn't base their belief system on the historical Christian faith preached by the apostles, or even in the ministry and teachings of the historical Jesus at all."

By now her eyes had brightened and her gestures took on a new exuberance. "How can anyone call Gnosticism an offshoot of the Coptic Orthodox Church, or a rival or lost form of Christianity to the Coptic Church in Egypt? This wasn't the faith the early saints died for in Egypt! It came from outside Egypt! It was repudiated *within* Egypt!

And even though the remains of the Gnostic documents have almost exclusively been found here, no one has found any evidence of separate Gnostic communities. I think Gnosticism originated in what we now call Turkey, and was heavily influenced by Hellenistic philosophy. It seems to me that Gnostic scholars, especially the American ones, know little or nothing about the origins of the Coptic Church. What do you think?" she asked, finally coming up for air.

"It's hard to say," said Art with a sigh, "but the most popular teachers of Gnosticism in the U.S. today all seem to have become disenchanted with orthodox Christianity in any form in any century, and so they seek to rewrite the history of early Christianity in order to promote these heterodox views as if they were an early and legitimate form of the Christian faith. It's an act of self-justification, if you ask me."

"How sad," said Dori, "but I guess it attests to the fact that fallen human beings have an infinite capacity for rationalization. Gnostics are rewriting history to suit their own preferences."

"Indeed," said Art. "I couldn't have put it better."

"I must plead with you, Dr. Art," said Dori, "Coptic Christianity is very much alive in this country but it is endangered here by the radicals, and its reputation is being sullied overseas by the revisionist historians. I hope you will do your part to set the record straight."

"I will do my best," he promised, taking the last sip of his coffee. "But for now, I'd hate to wear out my welcome. I'd best be on my way back to the hotel." He stood and again offered a round of "*Shokrun*" to the various members of Dori's family.

He politely declined her offer of a ride to the hotel, opting instead to walk the four blocks back to the Jewel of the Nile hotel. He didn't notice the slim figure leaning up against the wall in the shadows across from the Baioumi home, nor did he realize the figure had started to follow him.

Seeing others out enjoying the mild evening, Art thought little of the footsteps he heard behind him. He kept up a steady pace, and could now see the bright lights of the hotel in front of him. Louder came the footsteps. Art turned on his heels, just in time to see a young man coming at him quickly—with a large knife in his right hand!

Art swiveled back and started running as fast as he could! He could hear the man bearing down on him and now yelling wildly, "*Allah acqbar* (God is great)!*" Art picked up the pace and began crossing the street diagonally toward the hotel, narrowly missing a car with no lights on—not unusual for Egyptian drivers. As he was about to reach the far curb, Art heard tires screech, and then a sickening thud.

He turned to see the young man sprawled on the hood of the small car. Not wanting any trouble, Art ran into the hotel straight to the desk, yelling, "Call the ambulance at once! A man was just hit crossing the street!" The clerk responded instantly, while Art walked into the elevator, visibly shaken and upset, the lovely meal he had just eaten lurching violently in his stomach. Thoughts raced through his head: "Who knows I'm here? Was I followed to Dori's house? Should I get out of town now?" A wonderful day had just come to a dark and dangerous end.

5

Amulet Chasers

THE LOUD OPENING CHORDS to the Rolling Stones tune "Start Me Up" startled Art out of a deep but disturbed sleep. It had taken a good while for him to get to sleep after the chase through the streets. Groggy and looking at the alarm clock, which said 6:15 a.m., he groaned and fumbled for his cell phone.

"Hello," he croaked.

"Hello, yourself. What are you doing resting on your laurels at this hour when big things are happening?" said the voice with the feminine New England accent.

"Grace!" said Art. "Sorry, but I had a bad night. Plus, you forget it's an hour earlier here!"

"Sorry! Well, this morning's *Jerusalem Post* has a full-page story you need to read. Seems the old Cairo Museum has been burgled."

"What?" cried Art, sitting up fast. "But they doubled security while they were building the new museum! What was taken, or is it too soon to ask?"

"Well, the pieces of antiquity most of interest to you are the amulets from the New Testament era. Several of them, and some lapis lazuli scarabs."

Art's mind began to rev up into high gear. Mumbling more to himself than to Grace, he began to calculate the importance of the theft. "Amulets are a crucial link with the religion of Egyptian culture," he began.

"The pagan Egyptian priests, as a result of the invasion of the Greek language, found themselves at a disadvantage. Their source of income, as well as the power of their temples, depended a great deal on the sale of magical amulets, which were thought to ward off disease, false gods, and the like. But they seemed to be losing their power in the wake of the Hellenistic and then Roman invasions of Egypt. By the time of Augustus, Egyptian religion had begun to blend with Roman religion in Egypt (and vice versa)."

Grace broke in before Art started a long lecture. "Slow down. The reason I woke you up on this Sabbath morning is that there is a detailed picture in the paper of one of the missing amulets, both front and back images. And on the back of this particular one there is a number."

"A number? Do you mean a modern identification number?"

"No silly, I wouldn't be calling you for that. It's an ancient number, in both Greek and Latin, the latter of which reads 'DCLXVI.'"

"No way! 666?" Art said incredulously.

"Exactly!" Grace wished she could see Art's face.

"But why in the world would 666 be on the back of a first-century amulet from Egypt?"

"Well, since that's your bailiwick, and you're into all things apocalyptic, I was hoping you'd enlighten me." Grace Levine specialized in Aramaic inscriptions from the turn of the era—a specialist in Greek and Latin inscriptions she was not.

By now Art was scratching his head. All vestiges of sleep had left him some minutes ago. Amulets were not just the ancient equivalent of jewelry; they served as talismans or religious objects expected to protect or help or heal the person who wore them. Art visualized in his mind several sorts of amulets.

"Okay, Grace, spill the beans. Which amulet had the numbers on the back of it? Was it a blue scarab?"

"No, but you can try again," teased Grace.

"Right. Was it an amulet shaped like a person?"

"No, and that's two strikes, mister."

"Surely it wasn't an ankh, the Egyptian symbol of life, was it?"

"Yatzy!" praised Grace. "This one was made of solid gold. It could have been worn as a necklace."

"But what kind of person would have been wearing the life symbol with the number 666 on the back?" wondered Art.

"I'm sure you will come up with some sort of ingenious theory," challenged Grace.

"What is so weird about this," continued Art, "is that just yesterday when I was on the little island at Aswan looking at the Philae Temple, I saw a graffito with the number 666 on it and a strange little poem of sorts with it."

"And how did the poem go?"

"He is many men and no man, towering like the sphinx; dead and alive, but who knows what he thinks? Back from the Styx; 666."

"Now that is a poem almost as inscrutable as the sphinx itself," laughed Grace.

"You're no help," moaned Art.

"Oh, and I have one more story to tease your brain into active thought. Have you seen the new issue of *Biblical Artifacts*?" asked Grace.

"Well, no. It wasn't in the newsstands when I left Jerusalem. Why?"

"There's an article by a prominent NT scholar claiming that the World Discoverer translation of the *Gospel of Judas* was a botch job, and that furthermore, Judas, far from being presented as Jesus's bosom buddy, is said to be a demon!"

Art whistled. "Wow, that ought to set the cat amongst the pigeons. And once again, these harmonic convergences are hitting me over the head. Last night I had dinner with a Coptic Christian family and they were bemoaning some of the nonsense coming out of North American scholarship about Gnostic Christianity and the Coptic Gospels in particular."

"Well, here's a thought, Art. Keep in mind that Gnosticism was syncretistic. It tended to blend together Greco-Roman ideas and Christian ones. Suppose it adopted and adapted some Egyptian ideas and symbols as well?"

Art was silent, but the gears had started to turn. "It's an interesting hypothesis," said Art, realizing that this idea would require a lot of research to back it up. "Grace, I'm glad you called. My alarm clock didn't go off and I planned to catch the 7:15 train back to Cairo for my lecture. I'm sure I'll hear all about it there."

"Oh, you need to leave! And I have so much more to tell you. Art, I'm seeing someone! We'll talk soon. Traveling mercies!" said Grace as she hung up.

Art looked at his phone, and his jaw dropped. "What exactly does she mean by 'seeing someone'?"

~

The basement of the famous Cairo Museum of Egyptology was packed to the rafters with artifacts from a variety of periods and regions. Sitting at a desk in a tiny office piled high with papers was Walid Serwassy, a bespectacled man with a long grey handlebar mustache. His skin glowed in the fluorescent light of his basement office as sweat seeped through the front of his khaki shirt.

It was not just that it was a warm day, and the air conditioning in the room was poor at best. Walid was wilting under the enormous pressure from the government: 1) to get the new museum finished, since tourism was the second major industry in Egypt and the country desperately needed the revenue; and 2) to recover the precious amulets. The problem was that this appeared to be an inside job.

This meant that someone Walid had hired and trained betrayed him by stealing the amulets from a storage box in the basement, probably thinking no one would notice in the chaos of crating things for the move to the new museum. But Walid *had* noticed, because he kept a detailed ledger of what was packed in which crate, and thus he'd discovered the theft almost immediately. Further complicating things, the amulet touring exhibit was scheduled to open in Berlin in another week. He'd promised to feature several of the now-stolen amulets since they were particularly good examples of their type and era. Walid longed for a large dose of headache medicine and some cool water right at the moment, but just then someone banged on the door.

A short man poked his head into Walid's office. "Serwassy, you are in deep trouble." It was Khalid Abdul Nasser, the grandson of the former president of Egypt and currently the head of the Supreme Council of Antiquities. "You know perfectly well that the government cannot afford to be publicly shamed in the matter of its great treasures. If you do not recover them soon, it will mean your job, and I mean find them by the time the new museum opens in the fall."

"Yes, Mr. Nasser," Walid meekly replied. "I realize we are having a bit of trouble now, and the government has no funds for a lengthy investigation, but I have a suggestion."

"Yes, make it quick man. I'm needed elsewhere," said Abdul nervously.

"Well, suppose we hire that famous American archaeologist, Art West, who seems good at finding things. He is supposedly honest, and he is in the country. Besides, if something goes wrong, then it will not be the fault of an Egyptian! Naturally, we will give him the aid of a detective and just enough funds to do the necessary snooping around the black market and elsewhere."

"For once you actually have a good idea!" Abdul rushed on with a wave of his hand. "I like this one. It will save face. How soon will you talk to Dr. West?"

"Well, as Allah would have it, he is due here today to give a lecture," smiled Walid triumphantly.

"Excellent, excellent! Send him my greetings!" And Abdul Nasser was gone as quickly as he had come.

"Now if I can just convince Dr. West to take the case," muttered Walid to himself. "I wonder what he charges for finding priceless amulets?"

6

Black Market Bargains

THE RAIN CASCADED DOWN the front windows while the phone rang off the hook at the Amstutz Antiquarian Antiquities shop in Manhattan. Local collectors considered this emporium their triple-A source for all things ancient and interesting. But lately, the shop had been overrun with tourists and merchants. Mr. Johannes Amstutz, proprietor, had been featured on the World Discoverer specials for his collection of ancient manuscripts and genuine, high quality objects, and the spot had done far more for sales than his brief appearance the previous year on *Antiques Roadshow*.

On this day, there was an especially nervous visitor in the shop. Though he carried a very precious parcel, the Moroccan man drew no prolonged or quizzical glances in a room filled with the bizarre and the peculiar—both in its artifacts and in its shoppers. Pretending to browse through the cabinets that contained ancient icons, the man, who called himself El Tigre, bided his time while Mr. Amstutz finished another transaction. Finally, the shopkeeper ushered the Moroccan into the private back office.

"To what do I owe the pleasure of your company in person?" asked Amstutz, who had long known this man.

"Well, sometimes parcels get lost in the post, do they not, and in this case the parcel is too precious to place in the hands of others, though I must admit that the Air Egypt flight taxed me to the limits. I am weary. Shall we get on with what we discussed on the phone?"

Johannes Amstutz had been a famous (but secretly infamous) antiquities dealer for over thirty-five years, and had made tidy sums selling to the various museums in New York, including the Metropolitan Museum of Art. He had had dealings with El Tigre before, and the items the Moroccan brought had always proved to be genuine and worth the price he asked for them. Indeed, only last year, Amstutz had made a cool half-million profit on a particular jade and alabaster object El Tigre had smuggled from Egypt. Thus, while inwardly excited, he needed to maintain a poker face.

"Monsieur Amstutz," said El Tigre in his French African accent, "I have for you this time the *pièce de résistance*. I bring several genuine Egyptian amulets, one of which is made of solid gold and, *mirabile dictu*, is said to have been a personal amulet of one of the Caesars."

"You have proof of this connection?" asked Amstuz.

"*Naturellement*, or I would not be here."

Opening his parcel, El Tigre placed the amulet in the palm of his hand, and then turned it over. "You see these markings on the amulet, on the cross piece? We find the words '*Caesaris . . . Flavianus*' . . ."

"Yes, I see that," said Amstutz, squinting at the amulet, with its tidy but tiny script, "but the last word is smudged and difficult to decipher."

"Of course, you are right, but this is enough to link it to one of the Roman emperors who reigned in the last third of the first century. And now, consider this." El Tigre showed Amstutz another amulet, very much like the first, but with just one word inscribed on the back. "What do you make of this number, a Roman numeral, as you would call it?"

"DCLXVI—666. This wouldn't be the one featured on CNN last night as stolen from the Cairo Museum would it?" challenged the dealer.

"It would not be discrete of me to say, Monsieur Amstutz. Naturally, I must keep my sources private and protected. Confidentiality is the heart of the antiquities market, as you know. Otherwise, precious objects on the market never come to light and land in the laps of greedy private collectors. I only show you this second item as proof that the first is genuine, as they come from the same collection. The second is not for sale just now, but I am here to offer you the first one."

Amstutz wrinkled his already furrowed brow, and swept his hand through what was left of his hair. His mental calculator let him know he could sell it for about $5 million. "You know me to be a fair bargainer who values our ongoing relationship. Let us dispense with unnecessary haggling. I am prepared today to offer you $2.5 million. We can do a wire transfer to your account, as we have before."

El Tigre fidgeted, scowled, and then finally said, "Good will and a good relationship with you are worth much. So, with some hesitation, I accept your offer. I have other items to sell, elsewhere, and am pressed for time."

They concluded their business, the amulet changed hands, and El Tigre watched as Amstutz made the online transfer into his own Swiss account. After closing the drawstrings on the little velvet bag and placing the other amulet back in the passport carrier around his neck, he quietly slipped out the back door into one of Manhattan's many alleys and disappeared into the morning.

Amstutz leaned his 5'8" frame on the door of his office with a smile on his face. Sometimes these deals were too easy, especially when the seller was so eager. Unfortunately, in his smugness he failed to notice that his secretary, Lucy, had heard the whole exchange on the intercom, which Amstutz had inadvertently left on.

7

A Train of Thought

ART LOVED TRAINS. As a child the train that chugged through High Point and on to Greensboro never failed to fascinate him. He could certainly have flown from Aswan to Cairo, but he preferred the space and the pace of the old trains so that he could get some work done. This particular train, the Aswan Express to Cairo, made only one stop in Luxor. Even so, this so-called express could take up to seven hours because of maintenance on the lines, which is why he took the 7:15 a.m. train. Though modern, the Aswan Express still included two passenger cars, leftovers from the British period, with sliding wood and glass doors leading into private compartments. He closed the door to his compartment, but left the shade up.

His sold-out lecture on the Egyptian Gnostic Gospels was not scheduled until five in the afternoon. When he arrived in Cairo, he would have time to check in at the hotel, shower and change, and meet with Sewassy at the Cairo Museum before setting up in its main lecture theater. He was not sure what the meeting was about, but he wanted to cooperate in any way he could. Art suspected that Sewassy's head might well be on the chopping block after the recent heist of the amulets.

Before reviewing his lecture, Art revisited his morning conversation with Grace. She was dating someone! This piece of news temporarily eclipsed the burglary story. "I hope this man, whoever he is, knows from the start he is out of his depth," muttered Art to the four walls. Grace Levine was already full professor of Aramaic language and literature at Hebrew University in Jerusalem, a brilliant scholar and lecturer, and "*la femme formidable.*" She and Art had been friends and colleagues for many years, though outsiders always found them an odd working pair. After all, she was a self proclaimed "Yankee Jewish feminist," whereas Art was an evangelical WASP from North Carolina. On the surface, they could hardly be more different. Art made a mental note to call Grace later in the day.

Suddenly there was a knock on the door, "Tea and toast sir, as requested," said the tall porter with the navy blue uniform.

"*Shokrun!* Just put it right there on the little table," said Art, barely looking up from the images of amulets now appearing on his smartphone. "What in the world is a gematric number doing on the back of an Egyptian amulet? And what was that graffito all about at Philiae?" wondered the professor.

Gematria is the art of creating symbolic numbers that often add up to a name, or even a name and a title. Before the rise of Arabic numbers, many ancient alphabets used alphabetical letters as numbers. So, for example, A = 1, B = 2, and so on. In grade school Art and his friends had passed notes in this simple code.

In Latin, however, the symbols are not as linear. I, II, and III are 1, 2, and 3, but IV is 4, and V is five, with X used for 10, L for 50, C for 100, D for 500 and M for 1,000. Not only did the numbers not simply follow the sequence of the letters of the alphabet letter by letter, the system itself had several peculiarities. While IX = 9, CM stands for 900. In each case the first number is subtracted from the following one, thereby opening DCLXVI to a variety of interpretations, not as a number but as a name or phrase.

Art's favorite gematric ditty was the famous graffito found in the pagan catacombs in Rome: "I love a girl whose name is 143." Since a variety of numbers could add up to 143, figuring out her name from the number becomes very difficult. Going the other way around, once one knew the name, the equivalent numbers were easy.

When it came to apocalyptic numbers, Art was perfectly well aware that 666 had already been deciphered by more than one scholar. First and foremost, this number falls short of 7 or 777, which is the number for perfection, and so would be seen as a symbol for something less than perfection, or even imperfection personified. Historically, 666 had been determined to be the numerical value of a very famous coin inscription: "*NERO CAESAR DIVI FILII AUGUSTI*"—"Nero Caesar the divine son of Augustus." The inscription reflected the rising tide of the imperial cult, suggesting that Nero was a god walking upon the earth, not merely a son of an immortal. But why in the world would such imperial propaganda be inscribed on the back of an amulet?

Though the date when Christians began wearing crosses as symbols around their neck remains uncertain, Art did know that the ankh had a long history as a talisman before the Christian era. At some point, Christians simply adopted the ankh as a Christian symbol and called it the *crux ansata*, meaning the cross with a handle on it. Could the amulet with the 666 be a Christian talisman meant to protect the wearer from the evil influence of the imperial cult and its emperor? It was possible. Talismans, like curses, were used to ward off evil spirits or dark forces. This is why Paul says in 1 Corinthains 12:1–3 that no one who has God's Spirit in them says "Jesus be cursed," attempting to ward off the influence of Jesus. Could the talisman be thought to work like the curse, warding off the evil influence of a false god? The ankh was a symbol of life, indeed the key of life, just as people believed Jesus was the source of life, and the anti-Christ was the emissary of death.

As Art struggled to reconcile the Egyptian ankh and its inscription, he thought of the Revelation 13 reference to people being marked on their right hands or foreheads with a symbol "which is the name of the beast, or the number of his name" and its urging that those who have insight should calculate the number of the beast, "for it is humanity's number. The number is 666" (Rev 13:18).

While this chapter had been debated for two millennia, Art knew that the one being worshipped was the beast who came from the sea "whose fatal wound had been healed," and he saw this as a reference to Nero. Not long after Nero's demise, there arose a legend that Nero, while he may have died, had come back to life, surviving a mortal wound. The legend suggests he went to Parthia (or somewhere in the far east of the Empire) to bide his time until his return. Understandably, after the fire in Rome in AD 64, which led to the martyrdom of various Christians including Peter and Paul, Christians would have seen Nero as the archetypal wicked person, especially with the rise of the emperor cult in the second half of the first century. The "beast from the sea" then represents the emperor, and the land beast, the emperor cult. Throughout the land, the emperor was proclaimed a god who walked upon the earth, fit to be worshipped.

But that was not the end of the tale. In the 90s another emperor, this time a Flavian named Domitian, took over the Empire. He posted inscriptions demanding that he be worshipped as *"Deus et Dominus Noster"*—"Our Lord and Our God." Because he went on to persecute Christians some saw him as the second coming of Nero. Could this ankh then have been a Christian cross meant to ward off the evil influences of the emperor and his demands for worship?

Yes, thought Art, this is possible, but he would need to rethink the graffito he had seen at the Philiae temple in Aswan. Was this ankh evidence that Christians in the 90s saw Domitian as Mr. 666 himself, perhaps even the reincarnation of Nero?

Art had been so engrossed in his work that he didn't realize that the train had stopped at Luxor across from the magnificent temple of Thebes. He gazed out the window and remembered his previous trips there and how much he loved the temple's evening sound and light show. He had a vivid image in his mind of what Luxor must have looked like even in the NT era. Despite the decline of Egyptian religion, the Luxor temple had remained magnificent, not least because the Valley of the Kings and Queens was also in Luxor, and the royal family was still being buried in this region in the NT period.

A veiled woman swathed in a well-worn black abaya carrying a small wicker basket through the corridor of his car momentarily pulled Art out of his reverie. Turning back to his lecture notes, Art missed seeing the slender, tiny asp slip under the door frame of his train compartment. Unconsciously recrossing his ankles under the table, he also missed its silent and stealthy trek across the floor towards his ankles, which were under the little table protruding out from beneath the window in the compartment. He felt only a faint tickle as the snake wound itself around his right ankle. As the porter opened the door, and announced in a loud voice "tickets please!" the startled asp reflexively sank its teeth into Art's ankle. And then there was a deafening scream.

8

Twin Brothers, Singular Mother

THE ARAFAT BOYS FROM Bethlehem were famous all over town. Identical twins—dark, handsome, athletic, and tall, at least by Palestinian standards, topping out at six feet plus—their personalities could hardly be more different. Their mother, a Christian, gave them biblical names. Issah, the Arabic version of the name Jesus, had followed her in the Christian faith. He worked as a freelance cameraman for all the major international networks, most recently the BBC. Ishmael, however, having witnessed at age twelve the shooting death of a schoolmate at an Israeli checkpoint, had become a loyal member of the Hamas party. Today, no one in the general public knew he still associated with Hamas because Ishmael led a double life. By day, he often worked as a courier for Hamas; by night he started as shooting guard for the Macabbee Tel Aviv Elite basketball team, a role that had catapulted him into Michael Jordan-like popularity in Israel.

Within the international operations of Hamas, Ishmael had become an "intersection" for essential messages, parcels, news, and funds. More importantly, he maintained the database of Hamas's human targets, including progress reports about attempts to eliminate them.

The hit list that Ishmael carried in his memory included a Christian professor of New Testament named Arthur James West. A known friend of various important Israelis in the IAA (the Israeli Antiquities Authority) and at Hebrew University (including Dr. Grace Levine), West had made the list for a variety of reasons. Much to the dismay of Hamas, his recent Lazarus tomb discovery had improved Jewish-Christian relationships a bit in Jerusalem. More alarmingly, West was recorded as saying that Jews had a right to be in Israel and to claim Jerusalem as their city. Most egregiously he said, in an overly candid interview, that the Palestinians were not descendents of the Philistines, but rather Arabs of one sort or another, making their claim on the land of Israel much more recent than the ancient claims of the Jews. Though he'd conceded that Palestinians had a right to live in Israel, Hamas considered the comment too little, too late to redeem his initial statement. Hamas had agreements with other Muslim fundamentalist groups to help one another eliminate their enemies.

Strange as it might seem, Art West was more vulnerable in Egypt than in Israel. He had no real support network in Egypt, whereas in Israel he had a wide array of friends who could help him, not only in the government, but even among some "misguided," liberal, peace-loving Muslims. Capitalizing on his exposure, Hamas employed its agreement with other Muslim fundamentalist groups to aid in the elimination of known enemies of their cause. So it wasn't surprising that Ishmael had just received a message: "The package was successfully delivered at Luxor. The professor should soon be sailing West across the Nile on a funeral barge."

Menachem Cohen was in all respects a remarkable man. Sporting dark curly hair, olive complexion, and a huge smile displaying perfect teeth, he stood not just out in the crowd, but above it, at a towering 6'4". With top-drawer degrees in business from both the London School of Economics and Tel Aviv University, he became a multimillionaire by the age of thirty-five. After serving in the Israeli Air Force for two years, he went on to start Cohen Digital, manufacturing computer chips that rivaled Intel's best. At forty he took his company global, and spent his time piloting the corporate jet from plant to plant, continent to continent. Then, at forty-five, looking for a new challenge, he bought the languishing Tel Aviv professional basketball team, infused it with cash and turned it around in just two years. What could possibly be next for the redoubtable Mr. Cohen?

As it turned out, next was Grace Levine. Though charming, Cohen had been married to his career for most of his life, and had hardly dated, despite the constant nagging of his parents and both sets of grandparents. Now, with his business secure and his team in first place, he had resolved to tackle his personal life with the same unrelenting determination that had made him one of the most successful men in Israel. In the two months he'd been secretly wining and dining Grace Levine, he'd discovered that not only was she his intellectual equal, but had remarkable business sense for a person who had spent her life in academia.

The *Jerusalem Post* officially discovered that Grace and Menachem (or Manny as she insisted on calling him, after her favorite Red Sox player, Manny Delcarmen) were an "item" when they showed up together in Cohen's box at a Macabbee game. Grace was dressed to kill, wearing red stiletto heels and a red and black cocktail dress with a sparkling necklace, which somehow complimented her small red glasses and curly dark hair quite nicely. When Manny had told her they were sitting in a luxury box, Grace figured the word *luxury* was the key to her wardrobe choices, having never attended a professional basketball game before. Manny, for his part, rarely appeared in public with anyone other than his business associates or his family, and so the talk in the press booth was more about the couple in the luxury box than the shot clock. In no time, the paparazzi had refocused their lenses, landing the couple on page three of the *Post* and the front page of *Ha'aretz* the next morning.

Grace had wanted to tell Art about Manny before he saw the papers, as well as discuss the Cairo Museum robbery, and was disappointed that his early morning train schedule had interrupted them. But, she had plenty to do at the office, and had no trouble filling several hours before heading to her favorite coffee shop on Ben Yehuda Street. Just as she reached the steps of Solomon's Porch her phone buzzed. "SOS, man down!" read the message, which had come from Art's phone.

9

Man Down

The train porter immediately panicked when he saw the asp, Egypt's most poisonous snake. As the story goes, Cleopatra herself committed suicide by agitating an asp, which obliged and bit her. A member of the cobra family, the asp comes in several shapes, sizes, and colors, including the brown horned sand viper—with its flat head and smooth scales—that had bitten Art. Though somewhat slow acting, the poison of the asp is often fatal—the venom contains a powerful neurotoxin that causes respiratory arrest if not treated quickly. Luckily for Art, his would-be assassins had picked a young specimen, small enough to crawl under the train compartment door but not necessarily mature enough to be fatal without multiple bites.

The porter remembered meeting a doctor a few cars back, and while yelling "Help" in Arabic he bolted back the way he came. Out of breath he yanked open the A compartment door. "Doctor, come quick; a man has been bitten by an asp. We need your help at once!"

Without hesitation, the doctor grabbed his satchel and came running. He knew that the first thirty minutes after the bite would make the difference between life and death. He'd treated snake bite victims before, and all but three of those bitten by a "sand viper," as he called it, had died because he reached them too late. Art lay on his pallet in the compartment, eyes wide open, wondering why he'd sent a message to Grace. What could she do after all? Part of him realized he had typed in panic. The snake, however, had regained its calm and settled under the bed, invisible to the guard returning with the doctor, Shamil al Sheik.

Seeing the red and already swollen marks on Art's ankle, Shamil quickly extracted his knife and suction cup from his bag. Ignoring the patient for the wound, he turned to the porter and instructed him briskly in Arabic "Hold the man down, please, this *will* hurt."

Making an X-shaped cut on Art's ankle, vivisecting the two bite marks, he opened up the wound further. Immediately as the physician applied the suction cup, Art felt like a leech had set out to drain him of his blood. He'd almost acclimated to the sensation when he saw the syringe. He closed his eyes and hoped, as did the doctor, that the antivenom worked. The next ten minutes would tell the tale. Both men knew that if Art began laboring for breath, it was too late—the neurotoxin would have reached its goal.

Shamil began speaking to Art in Arabic, and Art had managed to whisper "English please."

"Sir, the next few minutes are very important. You must try to remain calm. You are a very fortunate man that I was only two compartments away and that the porter came at once, but where is the snake?"

Art nodded in the direction of the floor. The doctor backed up towards the door, and said sharply, "Get a broom handle at once!"

Sweat seeped from every one of Art's pores and the adrenalin surged through his veins. He'd seen the havoc snakes could wreak on a human life, and consequently had an Indiana Jones-like fear of them. He flashed back to an occasion when he was in the desert in Jordan near Petra where he'd seen a child step on a viper. She died within twenty minutes. Fortunately for Art, he was a much bigger person and had been bitten by a much smaller and younger asp.

The doctor said in highly accented English, "What is your name, Sir?"

"Art, Dr. Arthur West. Thank you for coming at once," Art croaked as he grimaced.

"Dr. West, I notice you are breathing rather rapidly, but please tell me if you are having any difficulties breathing?"

"No, not yet." Art then took a deep breath, just to make sure.

"Can you describe the snake?"

"It had to be a very young asp," said Art. "When I looked down at my ankle it looked more like a little coral snake, very small in diameter."

"Then Allah be praised, for your chances of surviving will be much better. I must empty and then reattach the suction cup, and you will feel a little discomfort."

"That's alright, do whatever you must," urged Art.

By now the porter had returned with a broom and was waiting in the door for instructions. "Naturally we must get this snake off the train at once, lest it endanger someone else. What I need you to do," said Shamil in Arabic to the porter, "is gently and quite slowly stick the broom handle under the bed, just here, and the snake should quite readily fasten onto the end of the handle, as long as it does not feel threatened or prodded."

Ever so slowly the porter slid the broom handle under the bed, whilst the doctor stood aside. Most of the handle had disappeared when suddenly he felt movement at the end on the handle. "What do I do now?" he asked anxiously. "I think it has attached itself to the end of the stick."

"Slowly lift the handle off the ground, do not drag it on the floor, or the snake will slither off the handle. Then ever so slowly raise the broom. Keep it level until we throw the whole thing out the train window."

Alerted to the emergency, the conductor had kept the train in the Luxor station The doctor quickly lowered the small window in the compartment and stepped back into the doorway. The porter, as if in slow motion, moved towards the window, quietly poked the end of the broomstick out the window, and hurled it onto the neighboring tracks below. Unconsciously, all three men collectively exhaled.

Art by this point had begun to shiver, but not convulse.

"Tell me how you feel now, Dr. West?" said Shamil.

"Well, other than my ankle is on fire and hurting like a son of a gun, I feel alright. I'm not nauseous but I feel kind of clammy."

The doctor smiled at Art's southern accent and colloquialisms. "Well, that is quite normal, I am pleased to say, and the natural aftermath of the antitoxin shot, which seems to be doing its work. If you do not mind, I am going to sit on the other bed here for the next ten minutes. Porter, you can tell the conductor we will know very shortly if the train can depart or not."

After the porter left, Shamil continued. "Dr. West, this was a very near thing, and surely it did not happen by accident. Do you know of anyone who might want to do you bodily harm?"

Art thought about this and naively replied, "Why I'm just an academic, an American Bible teacher and an archaeologist. I wouldn't harm a fly; in fact, I'm a pacifist."

"Very peculiar," said the doctor. "It is also a good thing that I trained at the American University in Cairo, or else your accent would have been beyond impenetrable. What brings you to the world's oldest civilization, if I may ask?"

"Well, I am scheduled to give a lecture at the Cairo Museum this afternoon on some Gospel texts in Coptic, and I have been doing a bit of exploring down in the southern part of Egypt. I'm just returning from Aswan. My ankle is becoming a bit numb, Doctor, is that normal?"

"Oh yes, the toxin causes paralysis and obviously it affected the nerves and tissue in the immediate area of the bite, but if you stay still, and if you are still not laboring for breath, which I see you are not, you should be alright," said Shamil. "I think the crisis point has passed."

Ten minutes later, the doctor extracted the suction cup from Art's ankle and dressed the wound. Art sucked in a breath quickly as the doctor applied some alcohol, and then some antibiotic cream and a bandage.

"I want you to lie still for the next hour; no blood circulating more than it would in the rest position. I will check back when we are an hour further down the tracks towards Cairo. After I come back, we will get you up and see how you are walking. Is this acceptable?"

"Absolutely," said Art. "And thank God you were here to help me in my hour of need."

"Yes," said Shamil smiling, "it was Allah's will. Nothing good like this happens by chance."

"You are so right, of course," said Art, "but it makes you wonder why he let the snake in here in the first place?"

The doctor laughed and without hesitation answered, "Well perhaps Allah was testing you, but more likely, he wanted you to have the antitoxin in your system so that if this should happen again in the next few months, you will likely have some immunity. I have a suspicion this is not your last close call with a snake, given that archaeological work stirs up the birds and rodents on which they feast."

Art's phone rang yet again. Everyone involved had been ignoring the repeated rings in the last thirty minutes. It was Grace.

"When you send an SOS, I expect you to pick up the phone immediately!"

"Well, I wasn't really myself. In fact, I just nearly made an asp of myself."

Grace groaned. "Well it can't have been too bad if you are making your usual bad puns. What happened?"

Art quickly brought her up to speed then added, "And no, I was not attempting to see if Mark 16:18 ("they will pick up deadly snakes with their hands, and when they drink deadly poison it will not harm them at all") is true. Even you know I don't think that verse was an original part of Mark's Gospel or even Scripture for that matter. But speaking of marks, I have been pondering the Mark of the Beast lately, and now I seem to be a marked man. There have been two attempts to do me harm while I've been in Egypt! And you know, the doctor asked me a funny question: 'Who would want to do me bodily harm?'"

"Who indeed?" mused Grace, letting the question hang in the air for a moment "Well, on another and happier subject, I must tell you about my suitor," she said with a hint of melodrama.

"Yes, please, who is this lucky guy?" said Art, his ears and spirits perking up.

"You're not going to believe it when I tell you."

"Try me anyway," said Art, "I can suspend my disbelief for a moment."

"I've been seeing Menachem Cohen," beamed Grace.

"No way!" shouted Art.

"Yes way!" said Grace. "And you know he has been a perfect gentleman, not to mention he is an observant Jew, which is why he has, as one of his subsidiary companies, an outfit called Kosher Klean, a sort of Molly Maid service for observant Jews. They come in and not only clean the house, but also make sure there are no non-kosher foods, fabrics, clothes in the house, etc. It's as much a consulting firm as a cleaning one, in some ways."

"Well I never! What an ingenious idea," marveled Art.

"Oh this man is full of them," said Grace with pride.

"I'll bet he has your mother's seal of approval," said Art, laughing.

"Oh she's over the moon about this whole deal, and quite prematurely has been talking about a wedding! But we've only had seven dates so far. But getting back to your problem, is there anyone I can notify? Do you need help?"

The throbbing in Art's ankle had let up a bit, but he needed to end the call. "Grace, dear, I think I'm okay. My ankle still hurts and I'm probably still in shock, at least mentally. But, I have to get my act together for the lecture in Cairo before the train pulls into the station. We're already approaching Memphis and Sakkara, so I'd best let you go. But thanks so much for calling. You have no idea how much it meant."

"It's the least a friend can do," said Grace. "*Mazel tov* on your lecture. We'll talk again soon."

Art closed his phone, and once again noticed the lady in black walking up the corridor of the train car. Outside his compartment, she briefly froze, and seemed to stare straight through him despite the black veil.

"Who is that masked woman?" wondered Art, and then she was gone.

10

The Tiger and the Talisman

BERLIN WAS NOT THE city it had been when President Ronald Reagan visited in the early 80s and urged, "Mr. Gorbachev, tear down this wall!" The destruction of the wall and the reuniting of Germany for the first time in almost forty years proved to be one of the first signs that the Soviet empire was indeed crumbling. Though over twenty-five years had now passed since that historic visit, progress had been slow in the renovation and renewal of East Berlin. The city was unsettled. The remains of the old regime still smoldered while the influx of millions of Turks into the reunited Germany, especially into its large cities like Berlin fueled racial tensions, and the mafia, mainly Eastern European, reached its tentacles into all sorts of enterprises, including the sale of precious artifacts and art objects. Berlin had become the perfect place to unload hot property— a perfect place for El Tigre.

When the plane from New York touched down in Berlin, El Tigre used his Blackberry to check the time of his meeting that afternoon with Herr Doctor Geburtstag—doctor of what, he had no clue. El Tigre could always count on the good "doctor," with his lust for artifacts and precious art objects, to pay cash for the goods he brought.

Getting the ankh past security at the Berlin airport had been insanely easy. He simply wore it on a chain around his neck. Security must have thought it some sort of odd cross. Dressed all in black including black gloves, the diminutive Moroccan's ankh stood out around his neck, but no one at the checkpoint ever thought to ask El Tigre if it was contraband.

Since he planned to stay for a while, he'd arranged to rent a small car, which could get around any traffic jam and be parked almost anywhere. Stopping first at baggage claim and then at the Hertz counter, El Tigre quickly found himself behind the wheel of a fire engine red Italian Smart car that looked more like a golf cart. Weaving through traffic jams, El Tigre soon arrived at his hotel, La Grand Dame, just off the center of Berlin.

Despite its name, La Grand Dame was an unobtrusive boutique hotel tucked into a corner on Alexanderplatz. It was neat and tidy, served good food, and by Berlin standards it was relatively inexpensive. No one of note ever stayed there. El Tigre especially liked that he could walk to Karl Marx Alley, the street where Dr. Geburtstag had his office.

It bothered the Moroccan that he knew little about his client. During the war, Herr Geburtstag's father had been a ranking Nazi who, after World War II, joined the Communist ruling group in East Berlin. A portrait of the man in SS uniform hung in the hall leading to the office. Despite growing up Communist, Geburtstag considered himself a legitimate businessman—of what business, El Tigre, who operated on a "don't ask don't tell" policy, had no idea. The Moroccan's modus operandi was to keep the transaction simple and lucrative and maintain plausible deniability. He knew he could pass a polygraph because he genuinely did not know what happened to the objects once sold.

Geburtstag had arisen early, eager for the transaction. El Tigre had clearly implied that he'd brought something special. The doorbell rang, jarring the businessman out of his reverie, and he hastened to answer the call. Though he had hired help, he did not trust anyone but himself on this day.

"*Guten tag,*" said El Tigre, who was fluent in five languages and well-versed in world religions since he specialized in religious artifacts.

"*Guten tag,*" responded Geburtstag, as he ushered the Moroccan into his study.

"I see you wear women's jewelry," said Geburtstag, in a feeble attempt at a joke.

El Tigre stiffened but responded with a smile, "*Naturellement,* since I am part French."

Geburtstag found this amusing, but could not stop staring at the ankh around El Tigre's neck. He knew full well what he was gazing at—a genuine first-century solid gold ankh with an odd inscription. El Tigre continued to smile wryly.

"Perfect," sighed Geburtstag. "Well, before we get down to business, I have a question, and I expect a direct answer. Is this the ankh reported missing from the Cairo Museum?"

"Missing is not the word I would use," said El Tigre, "for two reasons. First, it did not belong to the Cairo Museum, although they might disagree. Secondly, I received the ankh as a gift, shall we say, from a member of the staff. Now, I have only one question for you. Have you seen the internet movie *Zeitgeist*?"

Geburtstag looked surprised and said, "Why, yes, in fact I invested in it. I liked its message, suggesting that all religions are one and have evolved through the centuries. I especially liked the overarching themes of syncretism and mythology and the film's basic claim that Christianity is a hoax, built of elements of Egyptian and other ancient religions, and thus Christianity's claims to uniqueness are false. Why do you ask?"

"Because this ankh may well suggest a different theory altogether."

"How so?" said Geburtstag, furrowing his brow.

"You see, Herr Geburtstag, this ankh has the number 666 inscribed on the back."

"From the Christian book called Revelation?" asked the surprised German. "May I see it? In fact that number apparently was not used as a symbolic number before the Christian movement began." El Tigre held it up for Geburtstag's inspection.

El Tigre then began to explain, "This must be the sign of life for some high-status person, possibly Egyptian, possibly Greco-Roman, a person whom one might think had nothing to fear from Roman authorities, and yet, and yet he wore this ankh. If this person was a Christian, he was a clever one, because the ankh was an already accepted symbol, which would not be seen, on the surface, as a symbol of that new eastern religion, Christianity. And the symbol was apt, not only because it looked like a cross, but also because the ankh was the key or sign of life, and Christ was said to be the source of everlasting life. But here is the most interesting part. As you likely know, ankhs were worn as talismans to preserve good health and ward off evil spirits. Perhaps the number on the back represents the demon that the wearer wanted nothing to do with—the demon at the center of the emperor cult, the emperor himself who posed as a god walking upon the earth."

El Tigre continued to muse, his eyes seeming to stare into the past. "Why would one need such protection, unless one frequented the imperial cult temples which were springing up all over the Roman Empire. Why indeed? Could this ankh have been worn by a high-status Christian convert, a convert from within the upper echelons of Roman society? Even Paul tells us that members of Caesar's own household had been converted. Scholars have shrugged this off and thought it might refer to some of Caesar's slaves, but what if that is underestimating the degree to which Christianity had penetrated Roman high society? Suppose a high ranking elite member of Caesar's household who had converted to Christianity wore this ankh to protect himself while still living in those circles?"

Geburtstag interrupted El Tigre, "Well it's a theory. It suggests that Christians believed they held a distinctive salvation message, a unique revelation from their god, and believed all other gods were false gods, indeed they believed they were '*daemons*,' to use the old Greek term. Yes, maybe the ankh could ward off the evil spirit of the emperor. If that's true, it confirms some of the early Christian records suggesting Christ was the only means of salvation for the world. They certainly weren't pluralists! Such haughty people! I have no sympathies for Christians and their holier-than-thou attitude. Better for the world to think the early Christians were lower-class souls propagating some despised superstition that had no intellectual capital behind it, and no historical or religious merit, than what this ankh suggests: that early Christians had managed to persuade some high and well-educated persons who worked in elite circles, but sought protection from spiritual harm by wearing such objects as this one."

"Exactly," said El Tigre, "shall we get down to business now?"

"Indeed, and what is your bottom-line asking price? I do not like to haggle over such things," said Geburtstag in his most serious tone of voice.

"Because of the rarity of the object, its potentially religious implications, and the purity of its gold, I am asking $5 million U.S."

Geburtstag let out a small exclamation. "Too rich for my blood, but I am prepared to offer you three million."

"You say you do not like to bargain, but Monsieur, if there was ever a moment for bargaining it is now. I doubt you'll ever see another object like this in your lifetime. Nevertheless, I will compromise, as I value your business. Shall we say four million?"

Geburtstag hesitated, sighed, and then agreed. "Alright, with reluctance, four million, because it is important to get this object off the public market and out of sight of those who might use it as yet more Christian propaganda."

"*C'est vrai*," replied El Tigre.

And so it was that El Tigre found himself $4 million richer as he wandered down the Karl Marx Alley whistling a Moroccan tune. Back at Geburtstag's office the old fox, wearing a wry grin, muttered to himself, "That fool should have known this item would bring close to $10 million in some circles. He must have been desperate for the money."

11

Flower Power Revisited

GRAYSON JOHNSON HAD BECOME Art West's friend and associate in the past year. The son of the cult leader Charles Johnson and a graduate of Fruitland Bible Institute in California, he was a blond hippie for Jesus. He sported a nose ring, a tongue stud, and more tattoos than one might think safe. "Israel is real, but Jesus is more real," read his favorite T-shirt, which he wore constantly. He lived in a spartan apartment near the Scottish Presbyterian Church in Jerusalem.

Grayson supported himself by working at the Jerusalem YMCA and a health food store. Whenever he could, he hung out with various conservative Christian groups in the city. He was a vegetarian, a pacifist, and someone profoundly interested in the correlations between archaeology and the Bible. This latter interest had led him to attend worship services at the Garden Tomb not far from the Damascus Gate in the Old City.

An avid reader of *The Left Behind* series by Timothy LaHaye and Jerry Jenkins, Grayson figured the world was coming to an end soon, and he wanted to be in Jerusalem when Jesus came back. Grayson had considerably helped Art with the Lazarus tomb matter, and Art had continued to pay Grayson a small stipend to keep him informed with what was happening on the archaeological front in Israel.

This summer, Grayson had joined a dig at Caesarea Philippi, one of the few northern sites under excavation despite the troubles in Lebanon and on the Syrian border. Built on a promontory, Caesarea Philippi sat next to a river believed to have been a tributary of the river Styx. The city originated with the Greeks, who named it Panyas or Banyas after their god Pan, but in the first century, Herod Philip, the third of Herod the Great's sons, revamped the city and made it his capital. More renovations resulted in the renaming of the city to honor both Philip (hence Philippi) and Caesar (hence Caesarea). Here there were images in niches and statues of Greek and Roman deities, including statues of the Emperor himself. A surprising discovery had been made in the first week of the June digging—an inscription about a priest, providing evidence of the emperor cult being safely ensconced here this close to the Holy Land. Grayson could not wait to tell Art.

The phone rang while Art was disembarking from the train in Cairo, and limping his way across the platform to an awaiting taxi.

"Doc, you for sure will not believe what we have dug up in Caesarea Philippi," gushed Grayson.

"Okay, Grayson, spill the beans. What is it?"

"We've got proof positive that the emperor cult was right here in this city, under the nose of the Jews on the border of the Holy Land during the first century AD."

Art whistled and said, "Go on. What's the evidence; is it an inscription?"

"I just knew you were going to ask that, and so I wrote the inscription down. Now my Latin is skimpy, my Greek is better, so I'm going with the Greek part of the inscription. But you need to come and scope this out for yourself."

"I will indeed," said Art. "Go on."

"It reads, 'Auguries for the Emperor were taken by me, Publianus, the pontifex, and were good. He is our lord and our god."

"Incredible," said Art. "Has Dr. Avner suggested a date for this inscription?"

"Well, he isn't sure except to say it is first century, probably from the middle or latter part, but that is a guess based on when we know the emperor cult was spreading."

"Well, the dating will be all important. If this could be dated to the earlier part of the first century, say during the time of Tiberius or Caligula, it would provide our earliest evidence of the emperor cult, and would show it already existed in the east, perhaps as early as the time of Jesus."

"Yeah, I remember that dude Bishop Wright when he was here in Jerusalem giving a lecture serving up a tasty and memorable line—'Christ was the reality of which the emperor was only the parody.'" said Grayson. "Wouldn't it be far out if already in Jesus's day there were the beginnings of the emperor worship here in Caesarea. What a place for Jesus to ask his disciples who they thought he was!"

"Well Grayson, hold that thought. I will be coming your way in the next week or so hopefully, when I am finished here in Cairo, and we will explore the possibilities together."

"Fantastic," said Grayson, "Wish I could be there to see the pyramids."

"Someday we'll work that out," said Art. "Blessings." And he rang off and ran off to his cab. The Cairo Museum and its treasures were beckoning.

12

The Tale of the Ambulatory Amulets

THE CITY OF CAIRO is one of the world's largest and most crowded cities, especially the closer one gets to the Giza plateau where the pyramids are. Taking its name from the Arabic Al-Qahirah, which means "the Vanquisher," was particularly apt after its eventual triumph over Memphis as the northern capital of Egypt. In ad 969 Cairo began simply as a royal compound of the Fatimid caliphs, later taken over by the Mamaluks, the Ottoman Turks, and even briefly, in 1798, by Napoleon. Most famous in modern times, however, was the long rule of Mohammad Ali (for whom the American boxer was named) from 1805 to 1882, after which the British controlled the city until after World War I in 1922.

By far the largest metropolitan area in all of Africa, Cairo is the sixteenth largest city in the world, with over seventeen million people in the greater metropolitan region, and over eight million living on top of one another in huge high rise apartments just within the old city limits. In terms of the press of humanity, it makes cities like New York or Los Angeles look small.

Though the old train station was conveniently located near the museum, the usual gridlock greeted Art. Inching along slowly toward his destination he remembered that taxis in this town seldom went anywhere quickly, and that their drivers chiefly reacted to the traffic snarls with an over use of the horn and brakes, punctuated by swearing in their native tongue. Art's meeting with Walid should have begun more than ten minutes ago, and while Art hated to be late, he also knew it was futile to press the driver. Ten minutes later, Art paid the taxi driver, grabbed his two bags and hastened up the front steps to the Cairo Museum with its pinky rouge front entrance.

The Museum of Egyptian Antiquities, known commonly as the Egyptian Museum, houses the most extensive collection of genuine Egyptian artifacts in the world. While it has more than 136,000 items on display, it stores hundreds of thousands more in its basement, prompting the need for the new more extensive museum with proper air conditioning and climate control. Long-time visitors have often joked about how the mummy room is the only climate-controlled exhibit— the museum has air conditioning for the dead who don't need it, but not for the living, who do!

Walking quickly through security, and leaving his bags with the coat check person, Art spotted Serwassy in his bright white suit pacing back and forth in the main foyer of the museum anxiously awaiting Art's arrival.

"Ah, Professor West, at last we are seeing you. Did you travel well?"

"In fact it was a rather perilous journey. I was bitten by an asp on the train while at Luxor."

Serwassy looked aghast, but quipped, "Are you telling me that you are now living proof of resurrection?"

"Well no," said Art, as he slowly followed Serwassy down the marble steps into the basement. "I'm living proof that Egyptian doctors know what they're doing, and it was nothing short of a miracle that there was one only a couple of compartments from my own. But enough about me; to what do I owe the pleasure of this meeting?"

It was notably cooler down in the basement, and his question seemed to drop the temperature a few more degrees as well. Serwassy did not reply until they had entered his office and closed the door. He pointed to a padded chair across from his desk urging Art to sit.

"The matter is grave, Professor West, and we are hoping for your assistance."

"Certainly, if I'm able," returned Art.

"Of course, we are prepared to offer you something in return— unparalleled access to some treasures or manuscripts, as you like."

"That's very kind, but you must tell me first how I can be of help."

"You know about the recent theft of the amulets?"

"Yes. But only as much as the newspapers and a friend from Israel could tell me over the phone."

Serwassy wiped his brow with a handkerchief and said, "It can only have been an inside job, and naturally we do not expect you to do the professional detective work, but we would like to give you detailed photos of the amulets, and then ask, if and when they are recovered, if you would be prepared to identify them, since you know Empire period amulets rather well. We think that with your name attached to the authentication it will help the museum recover a bit of its honor. You realize we are in a crucial fundraising phase of things for the new museum, and in need of international support to finish the task. If we appear incompetent in protecting our treasures, few will want to continue investing in us."

"I get the picture," said Art. "It's an international PR nightmare you want my help with."

"Quite so; may we count on you?" asked Serwassy.

"Of course, I will do what I can. Have you the photos?"

Serwassy produced a portfolio of large black and white photos of the two major missing amulets. Art immediately turned to the pictures of the obverse side of each one, as oddly, they both had inscriptions— one the simple Roman numerals for 666, and the other a partial Latin inscription. Art could make out two words plainly: "*Caesaris ... Flavianus.*"

After a couple of minutes of thoughtful study, Art asked quietly, "Have you any theories as to why these particular two amulets came to have such inscriptions on them?"

"It is idle to speculate," said Serwassy, "as these non-Egyptian inscriptions do not fall under our area of expertise in Egyptology. Of course, we know that this second amulet seems to have been inscribed during the reign of one of the Flavian emperors in the latter third of the first century. But why!? That we have not determined."

"Why indeed?" mused Art.

"We will talk further of this matter soon. You should know that our detective already thinks he has a lead from New York in regard to the theft. We'll call you in as needed. And if you do not mind, when I introduce you at the lecture, I should like to announce that you will be helping us in the hunt to recover our amulets."

"That's fine," said Art. "If we're done for now, I need to return to the foyer and rescue my lecture notes."

As they retraced their steps, the men passed the famous statue of the sitting scribe diligently studying a manuscript and writing on papyrus. "That's me," said Art with a laugh, "only I can't do the lotus position anymore."

Serwassy returned the laugh, adding, "You may thank Allah you did not have that scribe's job to make the Pharaohs look good."

"No," said Art, "just the Cairo Museum, I hope."

Both men laughed as they turned left at the statue of Pharaoh Ramses II and headed for the lecture theater down the hall.

13

Take Me Out to the Ball Game

ISRAELI BASKETBALL FANS NURSE the same passions as their American counterparts, and with good reason. The Maccabee team had as loyal a base as the Celtics or Lakers. Since Manny had taken over the team they hadn't missed a playoff berth. Grace remembered a dig in Arad where she noticed some Israeli and Palestinian teens playing basketball nearby. She made the mistake of asking them what they thought of the Tel Aviv team. She quickly received a deluge of choice words in both Arabic and modern Hebrew. Seems that Maccabee Elite were like the team she, as a devoted Red Sox fan, loved to cheer against—the New York Yankees.

"So are you ready to scream and shout for our team?" Manny inquired as he and Grace sped along tucked comfortably into his racing-green Jaguar XJS.

"I'll leave most of the shouting to you, sweetie. You know baseball's my game, but I promise to jump in—just tell me when! We professors have to reserve our voices for influencing young minds, you know!"

"So you'll offer a simple 'Hallelujah' now and again? I'd hate to be responsible for the demise of our educational system," he teased back.

Grace really liked this man. Her intellect and position did anything but intimidate him. He had a great mind and an even better sense of humor. And she admired his restraint in opting away from the full court press in favor of a comfortable amble through what was, at least to her mother, becoming an all-out courtship. Much to Grace's dismay,

Camelia had begun not-so-subtly throwing around the "M" word. What was it about mothers and weddings?

When Manny and Grace arrived and parked under the stadium, it was already packed to the rafters full of raucous cheering, chanting, and singing fans. The arena surged with pregame excitement. Israelis, like Europeans, embraced basketball as they did soccer as an occasion to sing their loyalties. Grace privately welcomed the relative quiet of the owner's suite. She wasted no time in ordering a frozen margarita to wash down the plate she'd heaped with hummus, pita, and baba ghanoush. Manny in the meantime loaded two kosher dogs with a variety of sauces, grabbed a bottle of Maccabee Pilsner, and somehow managed to steer himself to the front of the box just in time to see the tip-off.

"Careful you don't spill that chili sauce on your Armani suit," ribbed Grace.

"No problem," he smiled, taking another big bite, before easing out of his jacket so that he could roll up his sleeves.

The Haifa team had consistently proven themselves a formidable rival and Manny expected a tight game tonight.

"You see number forty-five, Ishmael Arafat? " asked Manny. "He's our Michael Jordan—an amazing shooter and dunker." Israeli basketball, like its European counterpart, allowed more physical play, especially under the basket. This made Arafat stand out even more, as a quick, finesse player who often blew by the man guarding him. Israeli commentators often opined that Arafat could play in the NBA, though very few Israeli, much less Palestinian, players had ever had a successful tryout with such a team. Grace had a flash back to the 80s when she had been stuck in a hotel in Tiberias with a wedding party, and had had to watch the Celtics and Lakers go at it with Magic and Bird dueling it out. She was too polite to say so, but she could quickly tell that even Arafat was not yet that caliber of player, and this game was not that caliber of game. But when Arafat took off just inside the foul line and dunked over two Haifa defenders, causing a deafening roar in the arena, even Grace could appreciate his skill.

"You're right," she yelled over the choruses of "The Cat, The Cat, The Cat." "He is fun to watch."

The game progressed as anticipated. By the start of the last quarter Tel Aviv led by a mere four points, and The Cat was hampered by five fouls. On the last foul the enraged coach berated the referees so vigorously he had gotten himself ejected. With thirty seconds on the clock and the home team having the slimmest of margins, the Tel Aviv assistant coach, nicknamed Ichabod (meaning "without glory/weight," which was a deliberate irony since he was an obese man, though some-times he was just called Chabod, meaning "weight/weighty"), mopped his brow with a towel, and put Arafat back in one final time.

Maneuvering himself into a back-'em-down position near the bas-ket, Arafat dribbled until the shot clock clicked down to four seconds, then gracefully turned and lofted a feathery jump shot just over the outstretched hand of the straining defender. The ball caressed the net and Tel Aviv escaped with a three-point victory. The stadium erupted as the classic Queen song began to play: "Another one bites the dust / And another one gone, and another one gone / Another one bites the dust!"

Manny smiled at Grace and spontaneously gave her a victory kiss as servers popped and poured the champagne. "You see? You brought my boys luck by coming tonight. A few more victories like this and we'll be in the playoffs!"

"Maybe yes, maybe no, but this has been a fun evening either way, so thank you for the invitation."

"This is only the beginning, Grace! We have a lifetime of games ahead of us!" Manny enthused.

And as Grace heard herself say, "Of course," she had already began to wonder, "Is this *the* man? And is this the sort of life I want to lead from now on?" She wanted to talk with Art and other friends about all this—they knew her almost as well as she knew herself. All she knew for sure was that these events were all happening mighty fast.

On the way home in Manny's Jaguar, Grace pensively assessed her feelings when he asked, "Are you up for a nightcap at Le Jazz Hot?"

"Not tonight, Manny. Between the game and the drive I'm too worn out to be any fun. Rain check?"

"Of course," and Manny smiled.

His kiss still lingered on her lips as she put the key in her door. "How good a wife could I really be, married as I am to my job and the work that I love so much?" she wondered as she tiptoed in, hoping not to wake Camelia.

14

Hung Up on Judas's Gospel

THE RECENT DEBACLE OVER the *Gospel of Judas* appalled Art West. Some North American scholars, so eager to claim that the document demanded an instant revision of early Christian history, had taken their case to the public in a mass marketing campaign before vetting their ideas with their colleagues and fellow scholars. Not surprisingly, the translation of the document from Coptic had been badly botched, and in a tendentious manner as well. Art harbored a righteous indignation with regard to the chicanery and posturing, and thus approached the lecture he was about to give with a certain amount of reluctance. He knew that it would cause further unsought controversy that would detract from his detailed careful scholarship, so long his trademark. He tried not to get riled up as he retrieved his satchel and returned to the lecture hall.

The room was packed and, unlike in America, the media had been relegated to the back row of the auditorium. Dr. Serwassy did not relish controversy any more than Art, especially not now with the missing amulets garnering unwanted headlines. He would not have this lecture turned into a three-ring circus, but he knew his control was limited.

Though the lights had been turned up, they still left the hall full of shadows and dark crevices. The palpable buzz in the hall diminished as Dr. Serwassy walked toward the lectern and adjusted the standing mike. Looking out on the sea of faces, Art recognized the usual list of scholars from the various universities in Cairo, including the American one.

Stepping to the microphone, the curator reminded the audience, many of whom had seen Art lecture from this very stage on earlier occasions, of their speaker's accomplishments, and then announced his pending assistance in the case of the missing amulets. He added a plug for the new museum and its Gnostic wing before enjoining the crowd to welcome the American professor to the stage.

The applause was surprising, and Art blushed a bit as he walked across to the lectern. Wearing his best Carolina blue jacket with a bright red bowtie, he cut quite a colorful figure as he adjusted his reading glasses and prepared to deliver the lecture entitled, "The *Gospel of Judas*: What Hangs in the Balance." A hush quickly fell over the hall, and Art clicked his mouse for the first picture for his PowerPoint slide lecture.

Clearing his throat, Art began: "In order to understand the *Gospel of Judas*, one must have a cursory knowledge of the Coptic language, the Gnostic movement, and where the *Gospel of Judas* fits into the historical timeline. So first a few words about Coptic.

"On first glance, this fragment from the *Gospel of Judas* might seem to be in Greek. But when you consider that written Greek may in part derive from older Egyptian scripts and letters it comes as no surprise that the Copts used what they knew when they finally, formally began to write. But in the 'what goes around, comes around' world of the ancient Mediterranean, in the first centuries BC and AD when the Coptic language was finally written down, it largely used Greek characters or letters. One popular interpretation of the history of the Coptic language, which comes from the Coptic Church itself, says as follows:

> It is important to note here that the Greeks learned their writing system from the Egyptians through the frequent travelers of the ancient world, the Phoenicians. In the course of their commercial dealings with the Egyptians, the Phoenicians imported the Egyptian script and molded it into an alphabet with a far smaller number of characters, all pronounceable and all consonants. As they traveled the Mediterranean and traded with the inhabitants of the Greek Isles, they gave their version of the Egyptian writing system to the Greeks. They in turn revised its orthography and added a number of written vowels, a system that eventually became the basis for the new Egyptian script, i.e., the Coptic one.

> The pagan Egyptian priests, as a result of the invasion of the Greek language, found themselves at a disadvantage. Their source of income as well as the power of their temples depended a great deal on the making and the sales of magical amulets. Now the curses on these amulets, written in Egyptian, cannot be pronounced by those who can afford to pay for them. If they cannot use them, properly or at all, it is safe to say that they would not buy them. To avert such economic and religious disaster, they reverted to a transliteration system for these amulets. This new system used the Greek characters along with several other characters borrowed from the Demotic to denote sounds not available in Greek. The economic success of such a system made them extend its use to other applications such as horoscopes and the like. The number of borrowed Demotic characters eventually were reduced. The resultant script was highly standardized, in the common tradition of the Ancient Egyptians.

"While some of this may be debated, it is clear enough that the end of this summary is probably correct. Written Coptic in the Christian era, bearing in mind that the first-century world largely involved oral cultures where only ten percent of the population could read and write, involved the use of the Greek alphabet plus about six or seven signs from the Egyptian Demotic script, to represent sounds that were not part of the Greek language. Like any living language, Coptic developed various dialects, the two most famous being Sahidic and Boharic. Coptic flourished as a literary language from the second through the thirteenth centuries AD, and Boharic continues to be the dialect of Coptic used in the Coptic Orthodox Church to this day in churches in Cairo and Alexandria and elsewhere.

"Our concern, when it comes to the *Gospel of Judas*, involves a much earlier form of the language, but it will be noted that I pointed out that Coptic became a literary language of choice beginning in the second century AD, and particularly among some sects of Christianity, primarily Egyptian ones. There is no historical evidence whatsoever of the use of this language in the first century AD by Christians, nor is there any historical evidence of any first-century AD Christian documents in Coptic. Those who know the history of Coptic as a literary language know that it is an argument not only without historical evidence, but against the historical evidence, to suggest that the *Gospel of Judas* might go back to a first-century Coptic or even Greek document. We do not even have clear evidence that the *Gospel of Judas* was first written in Greek, though it is not impossible.

"One other point should be made based on the quotation from the Coptic Church summary of the matter. Notice what is said about magical amulets. These amulets were crucial to temple economies, and probably the origin of the Coptic language actually goes back to the adaptations of Greek by temple scribes in order to continue the amulet business. Amulets had curses on them, or words of power of various sorts, and the owner would repeat the words on the amulet to ward off various sorts of evil, and in some cases to cause it. We must now turn to a brief review of the story of Gnosticism.

"It is my judgment that Gnosticism, as an offshoot of Christianity, certainly did not exist prior to the second century AD. But it flourished as a movement from about the mid-second through mid-fourth centuries AD. For two hundred years the Christian church listened to the Gnostic ideas, read their literature, and finally decided they were not truly or sufficiently Christian to be called by that name. Thence came the banning of Gnostic texts in the fourth century AD, first apparently by Bishop Athanasius in his festal letter of AD 367, in which he told his monasteries and communities in Egypt that only the twenty-seven books we now call the NT were the proper Christian scriptures, along with the OT. At some point thereafter some monk apparently took all the Gnostic texts out of the St. Pachomius library and buried them beneath a cliff. Of course, they were discovered in 1945 and dubbed either the Nag Hammadi or Gnostic Library. But the *Gospel of Judas* was not one of those texts found at Nag Hammadi. In fact, the history of this text is quite murky.

"Here, for example, is a summary of what we know about the *Gospel of Judas* manuscript from a popular online encyclopedia. I find this summary basically accurate; rather than read this to you I have had Dr. Serwassy photocopy the summary for you, which his aides will now distribute." The document read:

> During the 1970s a leather-bound Coptic papyrus was discovered near Beni Masah, Egypt. This has been translated and appears to be a text from the 2nd century AD. describing the story of Jesus's death from the viewpoint of Judas. The conclusion of the text refers (in Coptic) to the text as "the Gospel of Judas" (*Euangelion Ioudas*). According to a 2006 translation of

the manuscript of the text, it is apparently a Gnostic account of an arrangement between Jesus and Judas, who in this telling are Gnostic enlightened beings, with Jesus asking Judas to turn him in to the Romans to help Jesus finish his appointed task from God ... The text is extant in only one manuscript, a fourth century Coptic manuscript known as the Codex Tchacos, which surfaced in the 1970s, after about sixteen centuries in the desert of Egypt. The existing manuscript was radiocarbon dated "between the third and fourth century," according to Timothy Jull, a carbon-dating expert at the University of Arizona's physics centre. Only sections of papyrus containing no text were carbon-dated. Today the manuscript is in over a thousand pieces, possibly due to poor handling and storage, with many sections missing. In some cases, there are only scattered words; in others, many lines. According to Rodolphe Kasser, the codex originally contained 31 pages, with writing on front and back; when it came to the market in 1999, only 13 pages, with writing on front and back, remained. It is speculated that individual pages had been removed and sold.

It has been speculated, on the basis of textual analysis concerning features of dialect and Greek loan words, that the current Coptic fourth century text may be a translation from an older Greek manuscript dating to approximately AD 130–180. Cited in support is the reference to a "Gospel of Judas" by the early Christian writer Irenaeus of Lyons, who, in arguing against Gnosticism, called the text a "fictitious history" (*Refutation of Gnosticism*, Bk. 1 Ch. 31). However, it is uncertain whether this text mentioned by Irenaeus is in fact the same text as the Coptic "Gospel of Judas" of the extant fourth century text, and there remains no solid evidence for an early Greek version.

. . .

Around 1980, the manuscript and most of the dealer's other artifacts were stolen by a Greek trader named Nikolas Koutoulakis, and smuggled into Geneva. Mr. Hanna, in collusion with Swiss antiquity traders, recovered the manuscript and introduced it to experts who recognized its significance. . . . The existence of the text was made public by Rodolphe Kasser at a conference of Coptic specialists in Paris, July 2004. In a statement issued March 30, 2005, a spokesman for the Maecenas Foundation announced plans for edited translations into English, French and German, once the fragile papyrus has undergone conservation by a team of specialists in Coptic history to be led by a former professor at the University of Geneva, Rodolphe Kasser, and that their work would be published in about a year. A. J. Tim Jull, director of the National Science Foundation Arizona AMS laboratory, and Gregory Hodgins, assistant research scientist, announced that a radiocarbon dating procedure had dated five samples from the papyrus manuscript from 220 to 340 in January of 2005 at the University of Arizona. This puts the Coptic manuscript in the third or fourth centuries, a century earlier than had originally been thought from analysis of the script. In January 2006, Gene A. Ware of the Papyrological Imaging Lab of Brigham Young University conducted a multi-spectral imaging process on the texts in Switzerland, and confirmed their authenticity.

Over the decades, the manuscript had been handled with less than sympathetic care: some single pages may be loose on the antiquities market (one half page turned up in Feb. 2006, in New York City). The text is now in over a thousand pieces and fragments, and is believed to be less than three-quarters complete. "After concluding the research, everything will be returned to Egypt. The work belongs there and they will be conserved in the best way," one scholar has stated.

"So much for the encyclopedia. This is the kind of information that is readily available online for anyone to find, and what it reveals is that the manuscripts pieces have a long and dubious history, but the fragments do seem to date from the third and fourth centuries AD. I would repeat again, we have no reason to think this document tells us anything about Jesus or earliest Christianity at all from this evidence. But there is more. I can tell you that the much-publicized 2006 translation is a botched one, and recently the American agency that sponsored it announced it would be redone in light of the detailed analysis of a Coptic scholar from Rice University in Texas. Shoddy scholarship, tendentious analysis, and a desire for publicity, fame, and money, have characterized the handling of this important manuscript stolen from Egypt, and it, like the celebrated amulets, should be returned to Egypt as well. Egypt should be allowed to possess and protect its own treasures and antiquities."

There was a hardy round of applause at this juncture, and Art smiled briefly as distant cameras flashed and clicked away.

"But we must say something about the content of the *Gospel of Judas* at this juncture, for it is the content most of all that rules it out as a source of information about the historical Jesus or the historical Judas or their historical relationship. Firstly, the document reflects the dualism of the Gnostics—spirit is good, matter is evil. In this gospel, Judas offers to help Jesus slip off his mortal frame and so become a more pure and spiritual being. This stands in contrast to the early Jewish theology not only of the goodness of matter and creation, but also of the plan of God to recreate matter, so to speak, by means of the resurrection of the dead. Secondly, this document, so far as I can tell, seems to present Judas not in a favorable light, but as one working with demons. In other words, we do not have a kinder, gentler portrait of Judas in this document, which is in any case not a historical portrait. Thirdly, in this context I would stress that it is important to say that this document, like the other Gnostic documents, does not represent the theology of the later Coptic Orthodox Church in any way. The Coptic Church should not be seen as the originator of these documents, which it has always deemed heretical, so far as I can tell." There was a brief interruption as two Coptic priests stood up and applauded.

"Dr. April DeConick, a Coptic scholar, was interviewed by the *New York Times* about the *Gospel of Judas*, and she was emphatic that its translation into English was critically faulty in many substantial respects, and that, based on a corrected translation, Judas is actually a demon, truly betraying Jesus, rather than following his orders. After retranslating the text, she published *The Thirteenth Apostle: What the Gospel of Judas Really Says* to assert that Judas was not a *daemon* in the Greek sense, for "the universally accepted word for 'spirit' is *pneuma*. In Gnostic literature *daemon* is always taken to mean 'demon.' As she wrote in presenting her conclusions in the *New York Times*, December 1, 2007. 'Judas is not set apart "for" the holy generation, as the . . . translation says,' DeConick asserted, 'he is separated "from" it.' A negative that was dropped from a crucial sentence, an error the sponsoring network admits, changes the import. 'Were they genuine errors or was something more deliberate going on?' DeConick asked in the op-ed page of the *Times*. I do not know the answer to this question, but I must tell you that this is the sort of thing that happens when secrecy, rather than shared evidence in the scholarly guild, is the approach one takes to a new find.

"Let me just conclude at this juncture. The *Gospel of Judas* is an important historical document for what it tells us about a sect of

Christianity known as Gnostic, and so it helps us to understand church history in the late second and on into the third and fourth centuries. It really tells us nothing about the historical Jesus or the historical Judas, as was recently emphasized by a Jewish scholar in Jerusalem, my colleague, Dr. Grace Levine. Its importance should not be denied, but it also should not be magnified out of all proportion to its significance. This document does not open a new window on Jesus, but it does remind us of the various winds of doctrine and ideas floating around in early Christianity, which, far from suppressing such documents, interacted with them, debated them, and finally decided they were of no historical merit if one was discussing Jesus and the very beginnings of the Christian movement. I quite agree with this assessment as well."

The hall rang with applause, and even some cheers, which surprised Art, but then he could not have known that the audience had a large number of Christians present, including some Coptic ones. Word of the lecture had gotten out through St. Samens Church in Cairo and over the Internet throughout Egypt, and the Christians had bravely come out in force for the occasion.

Dr. Serwassy, surprised by the response and wanting no controversy, decided not to allow questions. Instead he stepped up to the microphone and said, "Thank you Dr. West for this stimulating lecture. We are certainly grateful for your time and for your continuing help as we seek to recover our antiquities."

While Dr. Serwassy made his final remarks, Art bent to replace his lecture into his satchel, and as he moved the bag one of the overheard spotlights bounced off of something shiny in the bottom. Instinctively he reached in and grasped the two small objects before noticing an envelope full of Egyptian pounds. Abruptly, he thrust the money back to the depths of the satchel, keeping the amulets within a clenched fist. He slung the bag over his shoulder and left the stage. Dr. Serwassy caught up with him and noticed the troubled look on Art's face.

"What is it Dr. West?"

"Someone seems to have tampered with my satchel."

"Why do you say that?"

Art held out his hand, and in it were two amulets in the shape of ankhs. "Because these were not in it before I arrived at the Cairo Museum."

Serwassy's eyes grew big, and he said, "What kind of game have you been playing with us, Dr. West? You had better hand those over to me at once, and the satchel as well. We'll need to place a call to the Antiquities Police."

Art groaned, but immediately obeyed. Things had just gotten even more complicated for Art West.

15

Meanwhile Back on the Home Front

JOYCE WEST WAS A fastidious person who always did things by the book—the Good Book. Like her model, Susanna Wesley, Joyce had taught her son Art the Scriptures, and had "raised him right." Now at age seventy-eight she was retired and living in the old home place in Charlotte, N.C., fondly known as Magnolia Mansion. Surrounded by pine trees, the rather modest-sized ranch house sat behind two gigantic southern magnolias that dominated either side of the driveway off of Sharon View Road.

Mrs. West had been a widow for some time, but continued to live a very active life, doing charity work and attending her home church, Myers Park Methodist, which she had joined as a teenager. Her daily routines found her always in bed by ten reading her Upper Room devotional and saying a prayer just before turning out the light. This slight woman (only 5'1" and weighing under one hundred pounds) fretted incessantly about her son's globe-trotting, and earlier on this hot and humid June day she had a premonition that something might be wrong. But having no answers, she turned it over to the Lord and went to sleep.

Somewhere in the dark of the night, the ringing of the phone startled Joyce out of a dead sleep. Somewhat confused and groggy, she picked up the phone.

"Yes, who is calling please?" she said rather weakly.

"Howdy Momma, I'm sorry to disturb your rest, but I have managed to get myself in something of a pickle, a Cates pickle, of course (Art's family had relatives who ran the Cates pickle company)."

"How can I help son? I'm on the other side of the world!"

"Momma, you may remember that I sent you a picture copy of the crucial page of my passport. As the British would say, it's gone missing, and I need you to fax it to a certain number here in Cairo, so I can resolve a couple of problems."

"Certainly, but I don't know anything about faxing things—should I go to Kinko's?"

"Yes, they can send a fax of the photocopy you have." He began rattling off the international number.

"Just a second, don't be so hasty, pudding. I've got to grab a pen and write this down." After a minute she said, "Okay, give me the number again. And what are you not telling me, Arthur?"

Art hesitated. "Well, some authorities here think I may have been doing something illegal, and so I will have to dissuade them of that opinion, but I've come to no harm yet, and am trusting God that I can resolve the matter quickly."

The phone line began to beep. "Momma, they only gave me a limited time to call, so if you would just take care of that fax I would sure be grateful. And as always, I love you."

"Well, I love you too. If you need anything else, you don't hesitate to call," said Joyce, not hiding the worry in her voice.

Hanging up, she mused, "That boy has gotten himself into another mess, and he is so darn trusting and naïve about people that I'll bet he's in a peck of trouble."

Knowing he hadn't fooled her for a second, Art at that very minute was in the Antiquities Police lockdown unit in downtown Cairo. He looked up through the bars of his cell to see a very large, swarthy, Egyptian glaring down and showing his teeth, of which at least two were missing. Wearing his tan-colored police outfit with the traditional Egyptian hat, he cut a menacing figure.

Dr. Serwassy had escorted Art to the station, looking grim and saying nothing. Art had handed him not only £15,000 but also the two amulets. Serwassy was enough of an expert to recognize them, not as the originals, but as exquisitely executed forgeries most likely substituted by the thief. Find the source, and one might find the originals, or at least learn what happened to them. Only when Art reached the police station did he realize that his passport had disappeared.

Art looked up at the guard, named Abdullah. "I need to speak with your superior please."

"I'll bet you do, but what makes you think I will call him?"

"Because if you don't I will be forced to use my extra cell phone to call the U.S. embassy here in Cairo, and tell them you're illegally detaining me." Art had hidden the phone in his shoe once he realized this old jail cell didn't have a metal detector.

Alarmed, Abdullah shouted out, "Dr. West needs to see the commander, now!" From a distance, Art heard a muffled acknowledgment and something else in Arabic, which he could not quite make out.

Abdullah left his post long enough to open the door at the end of the very long corridor for the commander, giving Art just enough time to call the embassy, explain the situation, report that a fax of his passport would arrive in a few hours, and plead for them to do what they could to extricate him. A Mr. Sawyer, who took the call, had just come from the lecture. Understanding the gravity and urgency of the situation, he promised to try and get in contact with those who could act quickly, but at the moment no one was around who had authority to act. Nevertheless, by the time the commander arrived, Art was sitting quietly and looking quite contrite.

"So Dr. West, you requested an audience?"

"Yes, Commander, I simply wanted you to hear from me that I have done nothing wrong, and that I have notified my embassy that I am here. I did not want you to be caught by surprise when they call in the morning and provide you with a copy of my passport, so I can be released."

Commander Mushariff was a bit taken aback by this development. He had hoped to interrogate Dr. West, but that would now be impossible.

"You realize that they may not be able to help you much, especially if you are shown to be a forger. You will be tried under Egyptian law, regardless of your citizenship."

"Let us hope it does not come to that. Frankly, I would like to get to the bottom of this forgery and find out who stole my passport as much as you. Think, Commander, why would my passport go missing at precisely the time these amulets showed up in my lecture satchel? I had the passport this morning while I was on the train. You can check with the ticket taker. Unless you think I wanted to sample your hospitality here in this jail, the only logical conclusion is that someone planted those items in my satchel, while at the same time pilfering my passport."

"A plausible theory, Dr. West, but then why has Dr. Serwassy not vouched for you? He simply turned you over, and said nothing on your behalf."

"I am afraid that he is so embroiled in one controversy, that he could not face another one, especially when, this very day, he asked me to help him solve the mystery of the lost amulets. And lest you refuse to take my word on this, ask anyone who attended the lecture. Serwassy introduced me as the man who would help recover the precious artifacts. I suspect Serwassy just couldn't risk losing more face. I am sure you will understand the honor implications, not to mention the employment implications, if he had made the mistake of introducing a forger into the process of recovering the amulets!"

"Yes, I see your point. But while we wait to hear from your embassy, as your American movie star Clint Eastwood likes to say, 'Make yourself comfortable, 'cause you ain't going nowhere fast.'"

"Right," answered Art in a slow Southern way, thinking that the commander had watched one too many of the old westerns with the Man with No Name.

16

The Emperor's New Groove

GRAYSON WAS UP TO his eyeballs in dirt, using a flour sifter to examine a big bucketful of soil. Wearing his bib overalls, tie-dyed T-shirt, and with a ponytail, he did not appear to be the usual archaeologist in training. But Grayson could hardly have been more dedicated to the task at hand, especially since he had discovered evidence of the imperial cult's presence in this town. Hardly surprising, he mused, given that Herod Philip had named the town after himself and Caesar, before building the requisite shrine or temple to Caesar. But did such shrines date back to the time of Tiberius? Had Herod Philip commissioned a temple in honor of Augustus? Archaeologists working this season hoped to find out.

Grayson was lost in his own little world listening to The Doors' classic first album on his iPod when he felt something substantial clunk into his sifter. Hastily, he picked up the object and brushed it off. At first it appeared to be a part of a cross, with the bottom part broken off, but then he noticed the open oval at the top of the vertical cross piece. What could this be? Taking his little spray gun, Grayson carefully washed the object down, turning it over and over again in his hands. On the second pass he noticed some sort of writing on the back of the object, not in Greek, but apparently in Latin: "*divi filii . . . Caesaris Augustus*" it read in part.

"Wait a minute," said Grayson, his voice rising with excitement. "Wait a minute, this was the sort of thing Doc West was talking about—some sort of amulet like the famous ones stolen from the Cairo Museum." Grayson whipped his Sony Cyber-shot out of his backpack and started taking one picture after another, his pulse rising. Could this be a sign of the emperor cult here just north of the Galilean border?

Dr. Avner walked over to Grayson's table under the tent. "And what have we here?"

"I'm not sure," said Grayson, "but could this be part of some sort of imperial amulet?"

Eagerly, Dr. Avner took the fragment, and turned it over and over. Then his eyes got big. "Grayson, this in itself is a good day's work. I think we have the confirmation of the Emperor's cult here, but why is it in the form of an amulet?"

"Doc West had been wondering the same thing. Maybe it has to do with some sort of divine protection or curse? Any way you cut it, it's evidence that the Emperor got a new groove, touting himself as something more than merely human."

"So it seems," murmured Dr. Avner as he wandered back across the tel with a big grin on his face.

"Far out," said Grayson. "I can't wait to tell Doc West. This will freak him smooth."

17

A Moment of Grace

GRACE LEVINE HAD ALWAYS been an independent person, talented, self-confident, in control. The feelings she was experiencing in recent weeks, however, had caught her by surprise. On the one hand, she really liked being dated, and even courted, by Manny. On the other hand, she was not at all sure that what she was feeling could even remotely be called love—more like satisfaction or confirmation. It was nice to know she was a desirable woman and still had the "it" factor working for her. And when she thought about how marriage would change her life and lifestyle, both for the better and for the worse, she had serious doubts about what she ought to do. While she was having a great time with Manny, she did not want to string him along, or be guilty of taking advantage of him on false pretenses. She sat sipping her cup of courage at Solomon's Porch, debating whether to take her friend Sarah into her confidence. Sarah, the owner of the shop, answered the question for her.

"What's on your mind girlfriend? You look like someone chewing on a tough problem."

"Well, as you know I'm dating a very nice man and it seems to be getting serious," Grace began.

"That hardly sounds like a problem."

"Yes, well, the problem is he is a wealthy, high-powered guy and . . ."

"Again, with the non-problems. How exactly is that trouble?"

"And he is handsome and gracious ..."

"I should be so lucky to have problems like these!" exclaimed Sarah.

"But if I were to marry him, there's much I would likely give up, including a good deal of my work."

"Now we are getting to the problem," Sarah said emphatically.

"I really don't see me domesticated, even though I really like him, and I can't imagine giving up my epigraphical work. And despite my mother's constant prodding, I think the ship has sailed on me having children, and I'm not sure I want to anyway."

"And have you discussed any of these matters with the man in question yet?"

"No, I'm discussing them with you first, sweetie. Call this a trial run."

Sarah paused for a few minutes, looking pensive, scratched her head, pushed her sandy brown hair back from her brow, and after a deep breath said, "Well here's my two shekels worth. I don't think you can decide this matter without actually having a conversation with him. I realize that sounds risky, but maybe you'll find his expectations are not as you had anticipated. With his resources, I guarantee you won't be washing floors! Maybe you'll find out he's not thinking that far into the future yet anyway. Either way, you'll at least know the lay of the land."

"Yeah, you're right about the risk. I'll either spoil things or look silly if I'm taking this far more seriously than he is."

"Or, you'll find out where you stand. You've got to make a decision and stop stewing."

"Thanks Sarah, I think. I was kind of hoping to let things slide for a while longer and see what happens, but you're right that if its eating at me this much, I need to say something sooner rather than later."

Grace had not noticed her cell phone blinking its silent ring, but did see that she'd gotten a message. "Oh, I just had a call. I'd better check this. It's Art's number." As Grace listened to the urgent message her face went from anxious to grave. "Oh no!" she exclaimed.

'What is it!?" cried Sarah as she poured Grace another cup.

"Art's in a rat hole of a jail cell in Cairo. They think he's dealing in black market objects!"

"You've just got too many complicated men in your life, Grace. This sounds like a soap opera!"

"Thanks, sweetie, that's such a comfort!" Grace swallowed some fresh coffee, gathered up her things, headed down Ben Yehuda Street, and made some plans. She would call Harry Scholer, Art's Washington lawyer. This wouldn't be the first time Harry had rescued Art from foreign jails!

18

Gaza Stripped

THE BORDER BETWEEN GAZA and Israel had long since been shut down, with no traffic allowed in either direction. Recently the shelling had started up again, as it regularly did in June, this time with Hamas firing rockets into a new Israeli settlement. Having found a way around the border checkpoint, Hamas regularly slipped people into the region—sometimes, as Ishmael had discovered, by camel. The trek through the desert made him feel a bit like Lawrence of Arabia, one of his favorite historical figures, even if Lawrence was a Westerner.

Ishmael had been monitoring the situation in Cairo. While the snake episode had not gone as planned, he took some pleasure picturing Art West in a Cairo jail. But something more needed to be done—something dramatic—since planting the forged amulets probably would not give authorities enough to ban the Westerner from working in the region. Hoping to up the ante, he'd called for a meeting with his Hamas superior, nicknamed Muktar, and with El Tigre himself.

The small, partially bombed-out flat in Gaza looked an unlikely spot for a summit meeting, but such was the caution of Hamas officials who lived constantly on watch, if not on the run. The town, which had once had a flourishing city life, now looked more like a refugee camp on the desert's edge—its residents mostly cut off from their fellow countrymen in Bethlehem and points north. The split between the Fatah and Hamas parties had only deepened over time, and the more things went wrong, the more Palestinians supported the radical approaches of Hamas. Recently, however tensions had heightened between Hamas and the Egyptians with the influx of Palestinian refugees into Egypt from Gaza.

Ishmael was bitter, even with his own family, despite the fact that he had been deeply loved, and supported in his education and basketball career. He was especially angry with his brother Issah, who frankly was just too much like his namesake, Jesus, for Ishmael to stomach. Issah totally opposed guerilla tactics to help the Palestinian people. The last thing Hamas wanted was famous Christian role models in the news. Palestinian Christians were an eyesore for Hamas. If Christians weren't the enemy per se, they were nonetheless in the way of an all-out struggle with the Jews for control of the Holy Land. Consequently Ishmael had become fixated on eliminating—or at least publicly disgracing—Art West ever since the Lazarus debacle.

Ishmael sat on a stool at a small wooden table in the derelict kitchen with Muktar and El Tigre. Despite the late hour, the sounds and smells of the night assaulted their senses. The spices from the shish kebab being cooked just down the street by a vendor mingled awkwardly with the smell of diesel fuel and the fetid odor of raw sewage. Somewhere an inconsolable baby wailed amid the distant staccato of errant gunfire. Survival was hard in a place like this, especially in the summer months when the desert heat was intense and tempers were on edge.

Muktar took his small cup of Turkish coffee, swilled it, and then opened the discussion.

"I believe we all agree that something must be done about West, should he emerge from the Cairo jail." The other two men nodded.

"I have a suggestion that might well bring him right back to Palestine and back within our grasp."

"Go on," urged Ishmael.

"How about a kidnapping of one of his high-profile friends? Then we offer an exchange for West? You know he'd at least consider it."

"Who did you have in mind?" asked Ishmael.

"Grace Levine, of course," leered Muktar. "They are both close friends and close colleagues."

"This could actually work," said El Tigre, "and I have the funds here to make it a quick, slick and silent operation. Of course, I'm more inclined to execute both of them, but that would only bring more Israeli wrath upon our heads. So, I think we must settle for West alone."

"I agree," said Muktar, "though it is a pity. We might have killed two birds, or in this case vultures, with one stone."

"Then we agree to lure West back into the area with a kidnapping?"

"Yes," the other two men said.

"Ishmael, I already have someone tailing Grace Levine, but you will need to arrange for the getaway car, a black Mercedes please, with Israeli plates."

"Consider it done," said Ishmael in quiet tones.

"In order to grease the wheels, we need to make it easy for West to get out of jail in Cairo," El Tigre continued, counting out bills. "Muktar, make sure the commander is appropriately rewarded for his cooperation."

Muktar nodded his assent. "And *Ens'allah* we will soon have captured that Western bird of prey."

The plan had been set in motion.

19

D.C. Confidential

THE PHONE RANG AT the headquarters of the Biblical Artifacts
Society, interrupting what had until then been a quiet morning for
the secretary, Suzy.

"This is Dr. Grace Levine, and I need to speak to Harry Scholer as
quickly as possible. It is a matter of some urgency."

"Yes ma'am," said Suzy, "I'll put you right through."

"Shalom, Harry," said Grace, as the connection was made.

"Grace? *Alechem shalom* to you as well. How can I help?"

"Well, our good friend Art is in a pile of trouble in Cairo. Who do
you know in the embassy there?"

"Did you ever meet Mark Ebersol? He used to work for me, but
then he went into international law. I haven't spoken with him in a
while, but I could give him a call. What tar pit has Art managed to fall
into this time?"

"He's accused of forging antiquities. Sound familiar?"

"Yikes, not again! Egyptian law on that matter is very different
from Israeli law. But I'll give Mark a call as soon as we hang up."

"Thanks Harry, you're the best!" said Grace feeling relieved.

"Happy to help, Grace. Take care." Before his passion for biblical
archaeology consumed him, Harry had enjoyed a distinguished law
practice. And though he'd helped defend Art West in the Lazarus artifacts case, he did not relish trying to go to Cairo and do so again.
As a famous Jew, his clout in Egypt was slim to none compared to the

respect he had in various quarters in Israel, and his renown could make him a target. Ironically, when Grace called, Harry had been editing an article by Professor Ronald Hendel for *Biblical Artifacts* magazine that addressed "the dance between scholars and forgers."

> It can even be argued that modern historical scholarship—including Biblical scholarship—owes some of its most important practices to the pursuit of forgeries. In other words, the scholars and the forgers are codependent (to use a trendy term), not only in the commission and detection of crime, but in the very practice of historical inquiry. This is why the Renaissance scholar Anthony Grafton calls the forger "the criminal sibling" of the historical critic.
>
> The most famous moment in the rise of historical criticism in the Renaissance was Lorenzo Valla's unmasking of a forged text known as the Donation of Constantine. In this text the emperor Constantine (fourth century CE) purportedly donated a large part of his empire to the pope . . .
>
> By carefully combing the text for its diction, style and grammar, Valla was able to demonstrate that its historical provenance was not ancient Rome. He had shown how to detect when a text was written, by a grand demonstration of historical criticism. This was a major intellectual triumph, paving the way for the growth of historical criticism in the Renaissance and beyond. This was a coming-out party, in which the scholar vanquished the forger, and a famous piece of political propaganda was exposed . . .
>
> Without the forgers, the scholars would lack the challenge to ply their craft at its highest level. Even an authentic document needs the possibility of forgery as an incentive to keep the focus tight. The Dead Sea Scrolls were initially thought to be medieval texts—or even modern forgeries—but the best scholars of the time methodically proved their antiquity. They demonstrated the historical reality of this ancient trove, shedding new light on a vanished past.
>
> Is it real or not? This question keeps us sharp and keeps the tools of historical scholarship in good repair. We benefit from the presence of forgers. But we don't want them to sleep well at night. They need to know that savvy scholars—like Sam Spade with a Ph.D.—are on the case."

Looking at his watch, Harry realized he had a small window of opportunity to call Mark before the embassy closed for the day.

"U.S. Embassy, Cairo, how may I direct your call?" said the voice.

"Mark Ebersol, please. This is Harry Scholer from Washington."

"Just a minute Mr. Scholer," said the female voice.

"Mark Ebersol here. Is that you Harry? It's been ages! How've you been? To what do I owe the pleasure?"

"I've been well; but you're working late. I'll cut to the chase. I suppose you've already heard about Art West's incarceration in Cairo by the Antiquities Police?"

"The conversation here has been about nothing else in the last few hours."

"Good. What's being done to get him out?"

"We just received the fax of his passport from his mother, and we're creating a new one for him now, as we speak. I hope to get it into his hands tomorrow morning. Meanwhile, I've spoken with the commander and Art is okay. I hope they'll release him in the morning when we present his passport. But here is something odd. The commander thanked me for taking West off his hands so quickly, and said without my asking that all potential charges would be waived. What do you suppose that's all about?"

"I have no idea, especially since the Egyptians have a history of letting Westerners languish in that jail, usually leading to ridiculously delicate negotiations for their release. I can't imagine a change in protocol, unless someone has persuaded the commander to expedite matters."

"But who would do that? I checked with my Israeli counterparts, and they know nothing about it, and the U.S. government pleads ignorance entirely. Something strange is going on here."

"Well, keep your ear to the ground, and get that innocent man out of jail please."

"Will do. Nice to speak with you again, Harry."

"And you too, Mark. Appreciate your help," said Harry, and he hung up. "Something is rotten in Cairo, and I don't like it," he mused. "I had better call Art."

20

Dispatched with Dispatch

ART COULD HARDLY BELIEVE his eyes when he saw U.S. officer, Mark Ebersol, walking down the corridor holding a new passport. After the initial contact with Mr. Sawyer, Art's further attempts to contact the embassy had met first with a busy phone and then an after-hours recording. He had received a call from Grace, but this, instead of calming him down, had only upped his anxiety level, as Art tended to be a bit high strung. A gracious commander, on his best behavior, accompanied the U.S. embassy official.

"Dr. West, I am sure you will be relieved to know we are letting you go without any charges. The train authorities confirmed they scanned your passport and it has become obvious to us that someone tried to incriminate you. We managed to keep this out of the papers, and would be grateful if you would continue to assist Dr. Serwassy."

Mark Ebersol smiled and as he handed Art his new passport. "You see, diplomacy does work sometimes."

"You can collect your personal effects including your satchel at the little kiosk at the end of this hall, and you are free to go," said the commander.

Art walked into the blazing hot Cairo sun, blinking like a blind man who had just received his sight. "I cannot thank you enough, Mark, but I must say it seems to me that whole exchange went far too smoothly and quickly."

"Yes, I find it odd as well, especially since the Egyptians have not always been cooperative. It's as if they wanted to get you out of there as quickly as possible."

"Well perhaps, as the commander suggested, this happened so the museum wouldn't suffer shame over having engaged me in the amulet matter only yesterday. In any case, it's time for me to get out of Cairo. I'm heading to Turkey to do some more research there. Thank you once more for all your help."

"You are most welcome," said Mark, "but try to stay out of trouble please. And, by the way, we have a mutual friend, Harry Scholer."

"Really! Trouble seems to follow me around, and Harry has been there to help big time. I guess I owe him a call," replied Art.

The ride to the Cairo airport in the taxi was quiet. Art knew that he was leaving Egypt with his reputation in tact, and none the worse for wear. On the other hand, who was attempting to kill or frame him and why? He was just a harmless biblical scholar, though Grace kept reminding him that he was too naïve and trusting of other people. Things would be quieter in Turkey, Art kept reassuring himself.

Typically, Art only gave his luggage a cursory inspection before he arrived at the airport. This time he completely repacked his bags, accounting for and verifying every item, so he was taken completely by surprise when his bags set off the warning bells on the Turkish Air scanner.

"Oh no," moaned Art, "what now?"

The authorities searched the satchel thoroughly, emptied it out, and sent it back through the machine, but the bells sounded again. "I see something," said the security guard studying the x-ray, "There's something metal lodged in the corner of the bag."

"May we have permission to dissect this corner of your bag please?" said the inspector, looking over his glasses.

"Of course," said Art, as they quietly proceeded to a side room where they were met by a policeman and the security supervisor.

Taking a knife, the supervisor pealed away the outer layer of leather on the outside pocket of the bag, and a little blinking device, no larger than a thumbnail, fell out.

"What is this, Dr. West?" asked the policeman.

"I have no earthly idea," Art answered honestly.

The bomb squad was called and quickly identified it as a GPS tracking device.

"It appears someone wants to know where you are at all times, Dr. West. I am assuming you will not mind if we confiscate and destroy this device."

"May I make a suggestion?" said Art. "Instead of destroying it, could you trace the source of the signal? It may lead us to who has been following me around while I've been in Egypt."

"I can't promise results, but perhaps you are correct. It may indeed provide some clues."

"I suspect that someone planted it—along with some other things—at the Cairo Museum. Check the recent report. Meanwhile, am I free to catch my flight?"

"By all means. How can we reach you if necessary? Give us your cell phone number or your business card so we can keep in touch with you."

Art handed the inspector a card, then took his battered satchel and headed to his gate.

In Gaza, El Tigre became suspicious when the signal from West's bag remained constant in one locale in Cairo over the course of a twenty-four-hour period. This probably meant they had lost West's trail. Cursing under his breath, he turned to Muktar.

"There had *better* be a close connection between West and Levine, or we may have just lost our opportunity," he snarled.

"I agree," said Muktar evenly. The plan to grab Levine is already in motion, and I see no reason to stop it now. Do you?"

"No, proceed as planned."

The black Mercedes sat unobtrusively outside Tel Aviv's famous Sharon's Villa Restaurant. Grace and Manny, having just watched their basketball team pull off another home court win, had decided to celebrate over a late dinner.

After toasting the team with a '93 El Rom cabernet sauvignon, Manny looked at Grace, his eyes serious. "I know it's not the game, or the wine or the salmon, so what's troubling you, my dear?"

Grace managed to look relieved and uncomfortable at the same time. "Manny, I'm wondering where this is all going? You know I enjoy your company, and we've just had another wonderful time together, but where do you see our relationship heading?"

"Grace," he chuckled understandingly, "you are nothing if not direct, and I assure you, my intentions are honorable. I'm not sure what you expect me to say. Do I consider us a couple? Yes, I do. Do I want to see anyone else? No, I do not! Am I ready to propose? No, but I don't think you are ready for me to do so, are you?"

Grace took a deep breath and replied, "Thanks for being so candid. I must take a wait-and-see attitude about all this, if you can be patient, as you're absolutely right. I'm not sure how this—us—would change my life and career, and I don't want to be unfair to either you or my work."

"This I understand entirely. You know I'm a workaholic as well, who loves what I do. So let's leave it at this for now: We're in this together—just you and me—exclusively. We take it a day at a time, and we'll worry about the future when we get there. No pressure for either of us. Sound good?"

Grace nodded.

"Good. How about a walk before we head back to Jerusalem?"

He stood, offered her his arm and together they left the restaurant.

Wrapped in the glow of budding love, they didn't see the shadowy figures trailing them down the now quiet street. The couple offered no resistance when, simultaneously, the cudgel hit Manny over the head and the chloroformed handkerchief covered Grace's mouth and nose. The assailants left Manny lying on the cement, while they carried Grace into the waiting Mercedes without anyone noticing at all. The engine jumped into life as the black blur hastened off towards Bethlehem.

21

Stuffed in Turkey, Bound in Bethlehem

A RT FINALLY BEGAN TO relax on the domestic flight from Istanbul to Izmir, even ordering a cocktail on the flight. His good friend Levent Oral met him at the airport, and they sped away to the new Swisotel on the Aegean Sea. The weather was warm but not blazing hot like in Egypt, and the breeze off the harbor was refreshing. While on the flight Art decided to turn off the cell phone for the next week or so, and just enjoy being unavailable. His mother was in good health, his job was not making pressing demands, and friends like Grace seemed to be thriving without him. He had not talked to his other Jerusalem pal, Khalil, in a while, but that could wait. For now he was going to enjoy good Turkish food and company, a nice hotel, and try to recover his sense of sanity.

Seated at Mezza Luna, his fried calamari and glass of chardonnay already in front of him, Art looked out over the docks at the tankers that sat just beyond the little fishing boats, and the sailing vessels. The sun, already high in the sky, reflected on the water so intensely he'd kept on his sunglasses.

"So, why so pensive?" asked Levent. The tall, tan, well-educated Turk owned a tour company that Art had often worked with, and over the years the two men had become good friends.

"I'm not sure you'd believe me if I told you! From Aswan to Cairo, there seemed to be some sort of coordinated attempt on my life—almost as if someone knew my itinerary. But how could they? I only told a few friends in Jerusalem." Art paused. "Unless . . . unless I was being tailed the whole time."

"Are you actually saying someone attempted to take your life?" asked Levent gently.

"Well if they weren't, they were certainly trying to scare me to death."

Two raucous seagulls hovered above the restaurant's patio tables hoping for some scraps while a tugboat released its freighter with a deafening horn blast.

Not wanting to cause his friend any more anxiety, Levent tried to appear casual. "It is good you are here then, so you can relax, catch up on sleep, eat some great Turkish food, swim a bit, and learn how to enjoy life once more. I've even set up a few visits to sites you've somehow managed to miss."

"Thank you so much, old friend. Besides the lecture in Ephesus, how else can I repay you?"

"Art my friend, you've already helped a good deal in recruiting tour groups, so you need not worry about that."

A tall and very dark Turkish waiter with jet black hair and an immaculate white apron arrived with heaping portions of fish and vegetables.

"Who had the pecan crusted sea bass?" he asked.

"That would be me," replied Art.

"And Mr. Levent, I gather you are once more having your shrimp tempura?"

"Indeed. *Teşekkür ederim.* Thank you."

The seafood came with dolma, green peppers stuffed with rice, raisins and cinnamon.

"Levent, why would someone want to harm me? I mean I'm hardly a threat. I don't understand it really."

"Art, you are entirely wrong when you say you are no threat."

"What!?" said Art, incredulously.

"Truth is a powerful weapon and you use it well. You say the Bible is true and that history backs it up. That makes you a threat to those who believe otherwise. Many despise Christianity and all it stands for. I'm not surprised you are a target. Obviously, someone up above must be watching out for you or you wouldn't have as many escapes as

Houdini, and we both know you are not always careful about where you go and what you say."

"Say you are right about all this," Art asked between bites. "What are they capable of, if they want to eliminate me?"

"Thankfully, you're probably beyond their reach just now, but they might try to lure you out of your safe haven at some point, so beware and be wary," warned Levent.

"We have a saying: 'forewarned is forearmed,' so I will take these words to heart," promised Art.

The stench of urine and the unceasing barking of dogs assaulted Grace's senses as she came to in the basement of the bombed-out house. Blindfolded, gagged, and with her wrists and ankles painfully bound, she had no choice but to lie sideways on some sort of makeshift cot.

Jagged fragments of memory momentarily interrupted the throbbing in her head. A flashback came to her. She saw Manny falling just as everything went black. How long had she been cooped up in this hellhole? Was Manny alright? What would her mother Camelia be thinking when she did not come home? Grace began to weep.

The sound of a creaking metal door and heavy boots scuffling towards her gave rise to goose bumps on the back of her neck. She could, quite literally, smell her own fear as she began to perspire profusely.

She felt the man—his steps were too heavy for a woman, his musk too earthy—stop close to her. A deep yet chilling voice told her, "I am going to take your gag off for a few moments and if you cooperate, give you some lentil soup. If you try to scream or shout, I will simply put the gag back in your mouth and leave you hungry—it's your choice."

Grace contemplated this, and decided she needed her strength for whatever was next, so she accepted the inevitable, and opened her mouth, but no words came out. To her considerable surprise, the soup was good, and she consumed all that was offered before the gag was reinserted.

"You will be here for a while. Of course if you give us any trouble, we will chain you down. You and we will soon find out who your true friends are." And as quickly as he had come, he left Grace in silence. The dark empty shroud of despair engulfed her once more.

22

The German Connection

D R. GEBURTSTAG SELDOM WENT out at night, a habit left over from the bad old days in East Berlin. Born Vladimir Stalin, the grandson of the famous Soviet dictator, Geburtstag had redoubled his efforts to stay out of the public eye since the demise of communism, when freedom of information returned to the eastern part of Germany. He'd lived a remarkable life in many respects, even training at one time for the Orthodox priesthood. His grandmother, a devout Christian even during the Soviet era, had a major influence on him. Exceedingly bright and intellectually curious, he'd studied at length the history of early Christianity. While growing up, he'd embraced the faith wholeheartedly, but as he grew older and was required to read the Soviet propaganda, he began to have increasing doubts. By the time he became a party official assigned to East Berlin, he'd officially renounced his former faith, despite a vestige of lingering doubt about his doubts.

Like a scout attempting to stomp out a spreading campfire, Geburtstag went out of his way to deprive Christianity of whatever he could find or buy that might be of apologetic value—the golden ankh, for example. Geburtstag was right that it might well suggest that Christians had friends in high places, which did not comport with the usual propaganda that Christianity had begun as the religion of the ignorant and those deemed superstitious, of women, slaves, and minors. If Caesar's household contained patrician Christian members, it would become harder to dismiss early Christianity, or suggest it was just the product of some syncretism from previous religions.

Yet here he was, holding a solid gold ankh with a Christian inscription. He could not display it, nor wear it in public, and yet he could not risk selling it. What to do? Everything he thought he knew had once again been called into question. Perhaps Dr. Helmut Steinbauer, an ultra-liberal German theologian and one of Geburtstag's few confidants, could give him a logical explanation. What if Christianity wasn't just the opiate of the lower-class masses in the first century?

Grayson Johnson could hardly contain his excitement. He had discovered a significant artifact only two months into his archaeological internship at Caesarea Philippi, and he couldn't wait to talk to Prof. West about the ankh with the Latin imperial reference on it.

He spent his lunch break dangling his bare feet in the cool, crystal-clear stream that ran through Caesarea Philippi, wondering out loud why his mentor had not yet returned his calls. "For sure I should have heard back from the big dog by now. Where exactly can he be?"

"Well, wherever Dr. West may be, you are right here, and it's time to get back to sifting," said Claus, the German grad student in charge of the brigade of student workers. "*Machen sie schnell*"—make it quick—said Claus. Hastily, Grayson wiped off his feet and put his socks and shoes back on. Fortunately, the sifting enterprise took place under a tarp strung between trees to keep the intense sun off the workers. "Maybe I'll be blessed with another find this afternoon," said Grayson as he smiled at the blond, well-tanned German, but Claus just grunted and headed back to the work area. He hardly knew what to make of a born-again hippie Christian from the States who loved archaeology.

The gentle Aegean waters lapped close to the white sands of the Chesme shore. Art West lay on his towel, looking up at the blue sky and blazing sun through his polarized sunglasses, drinking some ice-cold Turkish tea, and chatting with his friend Levent. He bit into a chocolate ice cream delicacy called a Magnum Bar, while Levent spoke.

"The Germans love the Turkish beaches, but prefer to go further south to Bodrum, or to the south coast at Antalya. Here it is quiet, and not many non-Turkish tourists of any kind."

"Except me," piped up Art.

"Well, you are hardly a tourist after your many trips here," said Levent.

"If eating great Turkish food and ice cream makes me a local, I'm there," grinned Art.

"Well perhaps we can talk you into staying much longer," suggested Levent.

"Perhaps," replied Art, "but all the same I'm feeling guilty that I promised myself I would not turn on my cell phone for a week. I mean I'm only on day two and I'm itching to check things out."

"Man cannot live by electronic communications alone, a slight variation on a saying from Jesus," said Levent.

"Okay, I'll give it a rest, but tomorrow we are going back to Izmir. I need to see that famous emperor inscription from Priene once more."

"I like that idea, but today we'll enjoy the sand and the sea and the seafood."

"Roger, over and out," said Art, as he threw off his glasses and T-shirt and started running for the water. "Last one in gets no dolma for supper."

"We can't have that!" said Levent, who got up and scampered toward the water.

23

Manny Things Unexplained

"You idiot, I don't have time to fill in umpteen forms, and I have no idea who hit me over the head, but I do know that if you don't put out an all-points bulletin announcing the kidnapping of Dr. Grace Levine, immediately, I will not be surprised if you lose your job! I mean, do you know who I am?! I am Menachem Cohen, the owner of your favorite Tel Aviv basketball team." His splitting headache only made his infamous temper more volatile.

Standing in the police station in Tel Aviv, Manny seethed.

The officer looked annoyed but under-impressed. "Soccer's my game, and how exactly am I to know you are who you say you are, since you were found without identification on your person."

"Look me up on the Internet, you dolt! Go to my Web site and see my picture there at www.mannythingspossible.com.

The police officer replied, "We will check it out. Just sit down over there and try and calm down. I realize you have a large bump on your head, so I have asked the deputy to bring an ice pack, and maybe you can cool down."

"I'll cool down when you alert all of your colleagues that an important Israeli is in danger and has been kidnapped."

"Mr. Cohen, did you witness anyone following you this evening? Also, has Dr. Levine mentioned being stalked recently?"

"No, no, she said nothing about anything like that, and no we weren't being followed to my knowledge. If you would send someone back to the restaurant, my car is still there and that may provide some clues."

"There are so many questions unanswered here," said Officer Strauss. "Do you have known enemies?"

"Of course! I am a successful businessman, but if someone wanted to eliminate the competition they would have attacked me. As it stands, I get left with a bump on my head, and Dr. Levine disappears. Does that make sense to you? Now get out that APB, ASAP!"

The officer had disappeared into the back of the complex, and after clearing the call with his superior, Strauss alerted the missing persons bureau in Jerusalem.

"This is Officer Strauss calling from Tel Aviv to report a missing person, presumably kidnapped—Dr. Grace Levine."

There was a pause at the other end of the line and then the voice said, "This is fortuitous I suppose, as we were just about to call you. We just had an anonymous phone call claiming that Dr. Levine was in the custody of some group calling itself the 'Sons of Allah Brigade.' No details or demands were given, just an announcement."

"Great, just great" said Manny. "What about a ransom demand?"

The voice over the speakerphone replied, "No, nothing like that, which seems strange." Reality washed over Manny and his anger momentarily dissipated into despair, yet already he was thinking about what he must do next. Things had gone from bad to worse in a split second with this announcement. A group not seeking money and making no demands presented the most deadly threat of all. If they didn't want anything it meant they already had what they wanted. Manny said a prayer that there was something else, something more that these kidnappers wanted that wasn't apparent yet. He stormed out of the Tel Aviv station and headed directly to his car in order to head for Jerusalem.

24

The Priene Inscription

THE IZMIR MUSEUM, WHILE it did not have the same international reputation as the Istanbul or Ankara museums, nonetheless housed some very important artifacts, not the least of which was the Priene inscription. This piece of propaganda had become famous in NT circles for a Greek phrase reminiscent of the very first sentence of Mark's Gospel, which speaks of "the beginning of the Good News." Art stood for a very long time pondering the stone and its inscription, which read:

> It seemed good to the Greeks of Asia, in the opinion of the high priest Apollonius of Menophilus Azanitus: "Since Providence, which has ordered all things and is deeply interested in our life, has set in most perfect order by giving us Augustus, whom she filled with virtue that he might benefit humankind, sending him as a savior [sōtēr], both for us and for our descendants, that he might end war and arrange all things, and since he, Caesar, by his appearance [phanein] (excelled even our anticipations), surpassing all previous benefactors, and not even leaving to posterity any hope of surpassing what he has done, and since the birthday of the god Augustus was the beginning of the good tidings for the world that came by reason of him [ērxen de tōi kosmōi tōn di auton euangeliōn hē genethlios tou theou]," which Asia resolved in Smyrna . . .

Apparently written in 9 BC in Asia, this inscription confused some NT scholars who believed that the emperor cult did not exist as early as the time of Augustus, about whom this inscription was written. But an inscription about the good news of the birth of a god and world savior had too many buzzwords to ignore the overtones and implications. Though the deification of rulers had been a practice long known in the eastern part of the Empire, this language specifically referred to a ruler from the western end of the Empire—a Roman no less. Had the emperor cult only begun with Caligula (and thus later in the first century AD), or did its origins go back even further before the turn of the era, as this inscription seemed to suggest? The inscription was found inside a *prytaneion*, a site known for religious ceremonies, banquets, and official receptions.

Furthermore, the form of this long and verbose Greek inscription reflected Asiatic Greek style and it employed a hyperbolic sort of rhetoric usually reserved for persons believed to be deities. This made it hard to decide how serious to take the rhetoric.

Completely forgetting his friend Levent standing next to him, Art reviewed his Roman history. After Octavian won the battle of Actium, a "golden crown" was offered to whoever proposed the best way to honor the victory and honor Octavian as "our god." Some twenty years later in 9 BC, the golden diadem was finally awarded to Governor Paulus Fabius Maximus for his idea to honor Octavian's birthday not only by calling it the birthday of a god, but also by reordering the calendar so that his birthday would mark the beginning of the year! Time would be reckoned henceforth from Augustus's birthday.

The Gospel writers, on the other hand, suggested that Jesus, not the emperor, was the real "good news" about a world savior. Jesus's birth, not the emperor's, should be a calendar-changing event. Even Grayson had remembered Bishop Wright's statement that Jesus was the reality, while the emperor was just a parody.

Art reflected again on the amulets. They provided new evidence of two things: the momentum towards a full-blown emperor cult existed already during the time of Augustus (at least in Asia and other eastern parts of the Empire), and this alarmed Christians who were Roman citizens. Indeed it may have alarmed them so greatly that, thinking they were in considerable spiritual danger, they began not merely to pray for protection against this spiritual influence, but to wear amulets as reminders of that divine protection. Gentile Christians did not qualify for the same exemption from offering sacrifices in pagan temples (including sacrifices to the emperor), that was granted to Jews, suggesting that only Gentile Christians, perhaps particularly Roman ones, would have worn such amulets.

At some point the amulet inscriptions were used to ward off evil influence from particular forms of the emperor cult and even specific emperors like Nero or Domitian, who were known for persecuting Christians. But this theory does not entirely explain why one would inscribe an amulet with the divine names and titles of the emperor.

Perhaps Gentile Christians saw other Romans devotees of the emperor cult wearing these inscribed amulets seeking blessing in the wearing, then countered this move by "plundering the Egyptians," turning the spiritual purpose of the inscribed amulet on its head by wearing ankhs as a sign of protection against the spiritual side of the emperor cult. Art chuckled at the irony. The ankh looked enough like a cross to have passed for one, especially at a distance, but at the same time, no one would suspect the symbol was now used to advertise the Christian faith. Why then, would someone want to steal or even suppress these ancient religious symbols? Because someone considers them early evidence for Jesus's crucifixion and resurrection? Could it be that they couldn't handle the truth that some of these amulets seemed to symbolize? Could it be these amulets were stolen because someone didn't like the notion that people with high enough status and wealth to buy and wear ankhs, even gold ones, may have been among the earliest Christians? Who would this revelation threaten today?

Levent had let his friend and client work out his puzzle for as long as possible, but finally he said, "Art we need to be going now, if you don't mind. I must be getting back to the office here in Izmir and need to drop you at your hotel."

"Of course, of course, let me just take a couple of more pictures and then we will be off." As his Cyber-shot clicked away, something in the back of his mind nagged at him—there was something he was forgetting to do, but what was it? It'd been three days since he'd turned off his cell phone, and the silence had been a balm to his jangled nerves and shattered sense of safety and security. Why did he feel like he was engaging in displacement activity?

25

Dog's Day Afternoon

GRACE LEVINE'S THIRD DAY of captivity brought no signs of relief or, for that matter, any significant activity. Despite the unbearable stench, stuffiness, and heat she was holding up reasonably well. Some hours before, she could not say how many, nor whether it was day or night time, two women had come and stripped off her stinking sweat-soaked clothes, gently hand-bathed her, and dressed her in some sort of soft wrap with a hood. No one attempted to move her anywhere, except a female who escorted her to a toilet in some cesspit of a place. The overpowering odors made it hard to even think straight or concentrate on going to the bathroom. Grace thanked God—multiple times a day—that she'd not been beaten, or raped, or worse. Someone wanted her alive for a reason, and for that she was grateful. But why? The women had undone the cords that had bound her hands temporarily to allow her to eat, and as she sat up on her cot and drank her soup, she heard dogs howling down the street. Where was she? How long had she been here?

Unexpectedly, the door opened. She recognized the deep male voice from her first night. "Dr. Levine, I'm pleased to see you're making yourself at home here," he leered. Grace knew from his previous attempts to goad her into a retort not to let him see her fear or anger, and so she remained silent.

"Your fate depends entirely on your friends."

Her mind went first to Manny. What had become of him? She willed herself not to cry.

"News of your disappearance ran in both *Ha'aretz* and in the *Jerusalem Post*, as well as on local and international television, but strangely, we've heard nothing from your friend and colleague Dr. West. Your precious Mr. Cohen has offered a huge ransom, but we are not interested in money, and so we have not, nor do we intend to respond to such overtures. We will deal only with Dr. West, and we have released that information to the media."

"But he's not even in the country. In fact, I don't know where he is!" said Grace, spitting the words out like bad tasting wine.

"Therefore," replied the deep voice, "we will abide ourselves in patience for a little while longer. Thereafter, we may have to resort to more drastic measures."

While Grace heard every detail, she'd concentrated on the sound and tone of her captor's voice. His English was quite good, but spoken with a distinctively Palestinian accent. He was educated, spoke in measured tones, and thus far had refrained from histrionic threats. He didn't sound like a stereotypical representative of a terrorist group, or for that matter even a strident member of Hamas. But Grace wanted to remember this voice. It might be important later, very important.

The sound of retreating footsteps caused her pulse to step down a notch or two and cleared her mind. She now understood. These people wanted a straight swap. Her for Art. But why? Understanding gave way to dread. Hobson's choice; a no win situation. She could no more stop Art from agreeing to their terms than she could free herself. Tearfully, she tried to take solace in one of Art's favorite sayings: "God can make a way, where there seems to be no way." She was hoping against hope that he was right about that.

26

News Flash

DAY FOUR OF ART'S self-imposed "Operation No Cell Phone" started with an early breakfast overlooking the pool. On his way to the breakfast bar, he asked to see the Turkish *Daily News*, the only indigenous all-English newspaper in Turkey. After collecting his usual favorites at the breakfast bar (a variety of melon slices and an onion and cheese omelet), he sat down, prayed a prayer of thanks for the food, and dug in, casually leafing through the pages of the paper.

Art noticed first a brief article on the front page that an American archaeologist working in the agora in Izmir had found some early Christian graffiti, indeed, speculation in the piece suggested it was from the early second century AD. It involved some of the divine names, but also something of a palindrome. He would have to check this out later in the day.

On page three under the World News heading, a small print headline immediately caught his attention: "Prominent Bible Scholar Kidnapped." With heart pounding, he read on. "Dr. Grace Levine, noted scholar of Hebrew University was kidnapped two days ago, and her whereabouts are unknown. Authorities in Jerusalem are looking for another scholar, Dr. Art West, as a person of interest in this grave matter." Art barely felt the shards of glass hit his chest as his glass of orange juice shattered on impact with his still-full plate.

The room went silent, patrons gaping, waiters unsure of what had just happened. "Could somebody get me a towel, please?" His voice broke the silence, and as people went back to their meals, several employees scattered. Even before help came, Art stood, brushed the glass gently from his shirt, and hit speed dial for Levent.

"I need a plane ticket to Jerusalem pronto," he said breathlessly. "Grace Levine has been kidnapped. How soon can I get there?"

"I'll get back to you back in five minutes. Just stay calm," said Levent in measured tones.

Art lost all hope of calm with his first sight of the news about Grace. Unaware of the team of waiters trying to clean the juice, omelet, and glass from his person, he strode purposefully into the lobby dialing his friend at the IAA. Sammy Cohen had worked with Art and Grace on the recent Lazarus tomb matter.

Sammy immediately picked up and said, "Shalom, Cohen here."

"Sammy, Art West. I'm in Turkey and only just now heard about Grace Levine. What's happening?"

"There is little I can tell you, except that Mossad is frantically searching for Grace, as you might well imagine. There's been no ransom demand, but the authorities are looking for you!"

"That's it? That's all you know? Has anyone taken responsibility? Asked for a ransom? Are they negotiating?"

"You know as much as I do Art. I don't know how much more I can say . . ." Sammy was trying to keep his own worry from creeping into his voice. He still had strong feelings for Grace, even though she'd moved on to another Cohen.

Art interrupted, "Can you do me a favor? Call the Jerusalem authorities. Tell them I'll be on a plane today from Istanbul to Tel Aviv, and that I want to cooperate in any way needed in the hostage negotiations."

"Shall I arrange for a police car to pick you up at the airport and bring you here?"

"That would be a big help, also could you please get me a room at the Olive Branch hotel, or somewhere else close to downtown?"

"Consider it done. You'd do the same for me, I have no doubt. Travel safe."

"Great, just when I get out of the frying pan in Egypt," thought Art, "I'm back into the fire in Jerusalem."

27

Coining a Phrase

KAHLIL EL SAID HAD long run an antiquities business on the Cardo in Old Jerusalem. Known for his honesty and fairness, he'd always cooperated with the authorities when they searched for stolen or looted precious artifacts. This warm morning found him sitting on a small X-shaped stool drinking his Turkish coffee and reading some of his favorite poetry by his namesake Kahlil Gibran in his classic book *The Prophet*. He turned to the most dog-eared page in the book and read a poem entitled "On Children."

> Your children are not your children.
> They are the sons and daughters of Life's longing for itself.
> They come through you but not from you,
> And though they are with you yet they belong not to you.
>
> You may give them your love but not your thoughts,
> For they have their own thoughts.
> You may house their bodies but not their souls,
> For their souls dwell in the house of tomorrow,
> which you cannot visit, not even in your dreams.
> You may strive to be like them,
> but seek not to make them like you.
> For life goes not backward nor tarries with yesterday.
>
> You are the bows from which your children
> as living arrows are sent forth.
> The archer sees the mark upon the path of the infinite,

and He bends you with His might
that His arrows may go swift and far.

Let our bending in the archer's hand be for gladness;
For even as He loves the arrow that flies,
so He loves also the bow that is stable.

El Said considered himself a mystic, like a Turkish Sufi, and a romantic at that. This poem always made him reflect on the life of his widowed daughter Hannah, who helped him in the shop. Now almost sixty-five years of age, el Said worried about leaving her alone saddled with the burden of the shop. Yet, as Gibran said, he must allow his child to choose her own path, and thus far, she had adamantly stuck to the path he'd forged. Some twenty-seven years earlier, her husband, who had become a radical Muslim, lost his life in a guerilla action with Hamas. Hannah, like her father, wanted nothing to do with such violence, and she had eschewed men ever since. The smells of Hannah's morning baking wafted out of the small kitchen in the back of the shop.

"Smell the cinnamon! She must be baking my favorite rolls," said Kahlil to his friend Mufti who ran the fruit shop next door. "You must have one."

"But of course, it would be an honor, and let me bring a pomegranate we can split open and share," said the little wizened man of some seventy-five years, olive skinned and no taller than 5'3". This little exchange of hospitality had gone on for more than thirty years. Just at that moment, Hannah emerged in her beautiful black-laced full-length dress, and her striking red head scarf, with a small plate of cinnamon crescent rolls and more coffee.

"Ah my dear, what would I do without you?" said Kahlil.

"Well for one thing you would find it easier to lose weight, I wager," smiled Hannah as she set the plate down on a tiny little coffee table and sat down next to her father. Mufti emerged from his shop with his paring knife and a small china bowl holding a pomegranate already spliced open for consumption.

"I suppose my dear that you heard the awful news this morning that Grace has been kidnapped?"

"Yes, just horrible. I am sure it's been done by some of our Palestinian people, maybe even someone we know. This sort of thing makes all of Islam look bad. It's a terrible witness to the Prophet."

"Well you know my feelings about this as well. The only jihad I believe the Prophet wants now of us all is the inner struggle against our sins, or at least that is how I read my Koran. We have enough trouble conquering sin, never mind making trouble for ourselves by creating more enemies from among the children of Abraham."

Mufti had remained silent during this exchange as he had many others. He mostly agreed with Kahlil and Hannah on these matters, except when the Israelis had stolen Palestinian land and bulldozed homes. Then he'd thought retaliation was in order, but he'd kept such thoughts to himself, as thus far, no Israeli had done his own family any harm. In all his years, he'd learned to work with everyone and keep a low profile.

The call to prayer from the Al-Aksah mosque on the Temple Mount rang out across the Cardo even above the din of the merchants and the shoppers. Kahlil, Hannah, and Mufti took a moment and went into Kahlil's shop where the prayer mats were rolled out in the front corner, and said their prayers while kneeling in the direction of Mecca. After a little while they once again sat together on their stools enjoying breakfast and watching the press of humanity go by: the orange vendor with his cart gently bumping down the small steps in the street; the tourist group from Korea following their guide to the beginning of the Via Dolorosa; Hasidic men, dressed in black, with beards and ringlets topped by hats, heading towards the Western Wall to pray; and the cloth merchants hoping to sell their wares deeper in the Cardo. And finally there was a customer for Kahlil's shop.

"Good morning sir, I am looking for the el Said Antiquities shop. I hear Mr. el Said is the best dealer when it comes to ancient coins."

Khalil smiled his big smile and said, "That is generous of you to say so, and clearly you have come to the right place. Let us go inside, shall we?"

A combination of aromas, both ancient and modern, overwhelmed the first-time visitor upon entrance to Khalil's shop. There was the smell of leather, but also of must. There was the smell of metal, but also of coffee. There was the smell of cinnamon, but also of smoke from Khalil's water pipe.

All sorts of pots and unlit ancient lamps hung from the ceiling. Glass cabinets on the left wall overflowed with vases of various shapes and sizes, and the right wall was crowded with a variety of items, ranging from samovars to swords. But the low-countered cases that took up the majority of the shop contained its owner's most treasured commodity—the coins.

Kahlil's integrity and good reputation ensured that the Israel Antiquities Authority had always left him alone, or had done only routine inspections. They trusted him to uphold the law prohibiting precious antiquities found after 1977 from being sold to other countries or persons in other countries. He'd encountered increasing difficulty obtaining such objects, but when he did, he meticulously cleaned, cataloged, and displayed them, carefully filing their authentication papers.

The bespectacled man who had come to the shop was middle aged, wearing a white suit with a red bow tie, prompting Khalil to ask without hesitation, "And where do you teach Professor?"

The little man looked surprised but pleased to be addressed as professor. "You are most perceptive. What gave it away? I teach classics at the University of Durham in England." He extended his hand, which Khalil shook firmly. "I am Anthony Lloyd-Jones," and the diminutive man showed Kahlil his Durham faculty card.

"And I am the Khalil el Said you seek. It is nice to make your acquaintance. Now tell me, what are we interested in today?"

"I'm looking for a specific coin, a very specific coin, from the time when Nero was emperor." He brought out the picture.

"Ah, the Aureus coin," Khalil observed. "Minted at or just after the fire in Rome, somewhere between 64 and 68 when Nero's reign ended. Yes, it is inscribed as you can see with the words "*NEROCAESARAVGVSTVS*." Of course I know the coin, but you surely realize how rare it is. I have other Nero coins here that are less dear; for instance, the famous Germanicus coin." Khalil picked out a gray coin from his case and showed it to the professor. "Here it states that Nero brought peace to the world, symbolized by the closing of the doors of the temple of Janus. The inscription on the front reads, "*Nero Caesar Augustus Germanicus Imperator*"—"Nero as the commander in chief who brought the Pax Romana."

The Englishman nodded. "That is a very fine coin indeed, but I have already procured one of those, and today I am hoping to find the Aureus coin. Can you give me an idea of how much it would cost, and more to the point, do you have one?"

"I would say not less than $7,000 American. It is both rare and gold."

The professor whistled. "I guess I must write another book to pay for that one, but I really must have it for my work. So, once more, do you have such a coin?"

"Yes and no," said Khalil. "I do not keep items of such value in the shop. I do have one such coin in my safe deposit box. Would you care to make a trip to the bank?"

"The morning is yet young. And if I am satisfied with the condition of the coin, can we do business?"

"But of course," said Khalil warmly. The sale would make his day a good one.

"Shall we leave at once? Hannah, I will be at the bank for a bit, if you don't mind looking after the customers. I will return before noon."

"Certainly Father," she said with a practiced wave.

28

Plane Suppositions

A RT SPENT THE UNEVENTFUL flights from Izmir to Istanbul, and then finally to Tel Aviv distracting himself with the implications of his recent research. He ordered his favorite Turkish cherry juice and picked up where he left off in the museum with Levent.

"Let us suppose," said Art to himself, "that there were high status Christians involved in the inner circle of power that brought them in contact with the emperor and, at least as early as mid-first century, the emperor cult. Let us also suppose that like many early Christians, they did not divest themselves of all the beliefs and practices they had grown up with, but rather selectively and progressively processed out of their lives things they could recognize as anti-Christian. But it was a hard road to be both "in the world" while trying not to be "of the world." Now let us also suppose that as the emperor cult grew, especially during and after the time of Caligula, and having been given precedent by the way the emperor had been treated as a god already in Augustus's time in the East, Gentile Christians in general, and Roman citizen Christians in particular, became increasingly alarmed by what was happening in the emperor cult. How could they protect themselves from spiritual harm and from the temptations to defect, and yet continue to try and be a Christian influence in their own social circles?"

The cherry juice was delicious, and already Art had consumed the first cup, and was asking the stewardess for more when she passed down the plane aisle again. Taking a big sip, he thought, "We know for a fact that from at least the time of Julius Caesar the contacts between Rome and Egypt grew, and Rome became the dominant partner in that relationship, but not without the effect of the Egyptian culture having influence in the other direction. We know Romans who lived in Egypt began wearing Egyptian garb, and even ankhs, to indigenize themselves. We also know that part of the Roman propaganda war was to suggest that various Egyptian gods were merely Roman gods with Egyptian names. Now let's suppose then that, beginning in the time of Augustus, there were Romans in Egypt who wore ankhs and began to have them inscribed with Latin or Greek to show where their real religious loyalties lay. It may have become customary for those who participated in the emperor cult in Egypt to wear ankhs, seeking the protection and blessing of the Emperor Caligula and his successors, and more to the point the genius of the emperor (his deceased ancestor), and these ankhs would speak of this using the Latin phrase "*divi filii Augusti*"—"the divine son of Augustus."

Art paused for a moment, and then thought, "Now suppose there were some elite Roman citizens who were converted to this new eastern religion later called Christianity. Suppose they had already been wearing ankhs, only now it dawned on them what a useful and multivalent symbol this could be—emblemizing the cross. Suppose, however, they still believed in the power of the amulet, and the reality of curses. How would they protect themselves from the nefarious influence of the *daemons*, the spiritual beings that were believed to stand behind pagan gods and religion? Well, they might well have a counter Christian inscription written on the back of their ankh, to protect themselves.

"Now let us fast forward to the time of Nero, just after the horrendous Roman fire in AD 64. Nero has begun to make Christians the scapegoats for what happened. And Christians began to go underground quite literally, meeting in the catacombs. They began to use their Jewish knowledge of gematria, the use of symbolic numbers to talk about things. And there were two specific numbers used to talk about Nero—616 and 666—the former the rendering of the Latin Nero Caesar into Hebrew and into numbers, the latter the rendering of the Greek Neron Caesar in the same way. So we would know an ankh with DCLXVI on it: 1) referred to Nero, but on the basis of the Greek form of the name, and so it would come from the eastern end of the Empire; 2) would be worn by a Greek-speaking eastern Christian seeking protection from Mr. 666 and his influence and influential cult. In other words, the Christians continued wearing ankhs like some of their eastern Roman forebears, only with inscriptions that opposed the pagan ones. Once more we would have extensive evidence not only for the ankh/cross as a Christian symbol, but for the connection between Nero and the number 666, further showing how bold the Christian polemic and apologetic could be. The one who hung on the cross (symbolized by the front side of the amulet) was the real deity. The one referred to on the back side was a parody of the real God, and the cross amulet was believed to protect the Christian from negative influence. But what about the little rhyming verse found at the Philiae temple? What should be made of that?"

Art thought back to his time with Dori, the guide from Aswan who was a Christian. He remembered how she had tattooed on her inner wrist the fish symbol, indicating her faith. "It seems," said Art to himself, "that Christians under persecution and pressure have always been using interesting but common symbols to convey their faith in a coded way, but I must think more about that rhyming verse. I need to think about the legends about Nero that grew up after he died."

As the plane began its downward journey into the Tel Aviv airport, the stewardess reminded the passengers to return their seats to the upright position and to lock up their tray tables. Art mentally shifted gears, steeling himself for the ordeal that must surely lie ahead.

Ariel Schwartz, a tall and very tan Israeli with a close-cropped beard, in full-dress uniform, met Art at the gate. His presence expedited the customs procedures. Within twenty minutes, Art found himself speeding towards headquarters in an unmarked police-issue Volvo. "Professor West. I hope you will be able to help us."

"I will do what I can," said Art, but already fear had settled into the pit of his stomach. When Jesus had said, "take up your cross and follow me," he meant, "be prepared to come and die for what you love and believe in." Would this be Art's time to prove the full measure of his devotion?

"Let us go up to Zion, to the city set on a hill, for I have heard that God is with you," said Art, paraphrasing a famous phrase from the prophet Zechariah which was inscribed on a banner that hung at the Tel Aviv airport. "I'm trusting it is true," said Art to himself.

29

In a New York State of Mind

THE "AMULETS AND ANKHS from Egypt" exhibit opened with much fanfare at New York's Metropolitan Museum of Art. Celebrities mingled with patrons, trustees, and academics. Whether there for photo or business opportunities, no one could ignore the crown jewel of the collection—the Latin-inscribed ankh. Museum administrators had no doubt that this summer show would leave them with a budgetary surplus.

Installed at the very end of the hall, the case stood alone on a raised platform. Cantilevered mirrors reflected the image of the ankh, bathed in high-intensity light from four angles. The resulting stunning three-dimensional views of both the front and back of the icon reached to the eight-foot ceiling of the room.

Curator Francis Bacon watched with a wry smile as the long line of viewers began filing through the central hall. But he did not notice a rather short Middle Eastern man approaching him from the entrance hall.

"Dr. Bacon, I presume? My name is Prester al Haq, and I work for the Egyptian Antiquities Department, the police division. I need to ask you a few questions about that ankh," he said, gesturing in the direction of the display.

"Certainly," said Bacon, but his stomach was already churning, so he popped a Maalox tablet into his mouth.

"Where, exactly, and how did you obtain that object, if I may ask?"

"The museum bought it from a private dealer of long standing here in New York. I may be able to give you his name if you like, but I will tell you from the outset, that nothing illegal has transpired here between us and this dealer. He provided all the necessary bona fides for the purchase, and we bought the object on the open market in good faith."

"I am pleased to hear that, as no one would want to ruin the reputation of so well known a museum, but I must inform you that this object was in fact stolen from the Cairo Museum not more than four weeks ago. We intend to get to the bottom of this matter as expeditiously as possible. I'm sure you're aware that Egyptian law prohibits such treasures from being sold outside the country without the written permission of the Egyptian government, which is seldom granted. I can assure you, no one had permission to sell you this object, and we intend to retrieve it."

Dr. Bacon had become so uncomfortable that he began to sweat. He had enough presence of mind, though, to end the conversation. "Mr. al Haq, as I'm sure you will understand, I must speak with our lawyers before this conversation goes any further. In the meantime, if you will come with me to my office, I'll photocopy your credentials and get to the bottom of this unfortunate misunderstanding."

"Certainly. As long as this museum is cooperative, there is no reason for me or my superiors to go to the press about this matter. I am sure we can resolve this matter discretely."

"But of course," said Dr. Bacon, pressing a handkerchief to his brow. "I am assuming that Dr. Serwassy of the Cairo Museum knows of your visit here, since he is the one who helped us arrange this exhibit some time ago, an exhibit to which we added at the last minute the ankh in question?"

"He in fact dispatched me here," said al Haq.

"I will give him a call to verify your identity and commission."

"I would do nothing less were I in your position," said al Haq.

In the back of Bacon's head there was a familiar Billy Joel tune playing for some reason. He could just make out the lyrics: ". . . it comes down to reality; I'm in a New York state of mind."

30

The Way the Ball Bounces

THE MACCABEE PROFESSIONAL BASKETBALL team rolled through the regular season virtually unchallenged, guaranteeing them a high berth in the upcoming playoffs, which loomed large on the horizon. Rumors began to circulate that several NBA scouts and GMs planned to attend the first game in Tel Aviv Stadium on June 18 to see The Cat in action. His now legendary dunks over much taller defenders had led to comparisons with Michael Jordan. The *Jerusalem Post* had even printed the rumor that His Airness himself might show up. Reportedly, MJ wanted to upgrade his floundering Charlotte Bobcats, and The Cat had caught his attention.

Rumors or not, such speculation caused Ishmael to begin to examine his priorities. Should he concentrate on becoming a bigger basketball star, and use his money to help support Hamas and its causes, or should he be satisfied to play in Tel Aviv and continue working directly with Hamas? The Grace Levine situation only exacerbated the debate. If anyone discovered or revealed his involvement, he could go to prison. Goodbye career. Yet his animus towards some Jews like Grace Levine had driven him to support dramatic action for the Hamas cause. He wanted to please its leaders—through deeds, not empty words. Worst of all, he had absolutely no one to confide in about this dilemma, not even—indeed especially not—his twin brother Issah. Like his annoying namesake, Jesus, Issah despised all such machinations and violence. Ishmael decided not to think any more about it at the moment, but rather concentrate on the playoffs. Maybe Jordan really would show up and offer him a tryout.

Manny Cohen barely noticed the sold out Tel Aviv stadium packed with fans, international media, scouts, and stars, as usual. He watched the game from his box, but had yet to focus on a single play, his mind filled instead with images of Grace. He knew the minute he'd learned of her abduction that he had fallen in love with her. Despite the huge reward he offered for her safe return, nothing had happened. The feeling of impotence was new to Menachem Cohen. He hadn't gotten this far, this fast, by sitting idly by. Yet, until the authorities heard further from her kidnappers, all he could do was pray. So he tried again to lose himself in the game.

Tel Aviv jumped out to a huge early lead over the team from Tiberias and had never looked back. No one could touch The Cat, who, by the half, had posted twenty-two points, six assists, and four rebounds, not to mention three steals—a good stat line for a whole game for any normal player.

As he was walking into the tunnel as the half time buzzer sounded, The Cat looked to his right where the security guards were standing, and his eye caught a familiar smiling face, wearing a dark Hanes shirt and sport jacket. Smoking a big cigar and looking sharp, with the lights shining off his bald head, was none other than Michael Jordan himself, who had flown in from Charlotte just for the game. In a moment that seemed to last for an eternity in Ishmael's mind, Jordan came over, shook Ishmael's hand and said in his deep North Carolina voice, "Nice half, kid, we should talk," and he handed Ishmael a little calling card with "MJ" in large letters with a cell phone number below. "Call me after the game," said His Airness.

"I will, sir," gulped Ishmael. It was going to be hard to concentrate in the second half, and not try to do too much to impress Mr. Jordan.

31

First Report from Caesarea

When he had first turned on his cell phone in Izmir, Art had noticed he had several voice messages, but he was only paying attention to the ones about Grace. Now, riding in the back of a car heading toward the Judean hills up to Jerusalem, his progress had been slowed enough by the traffic heading to Tel Aviv stadium that he had had time to check the rest of the messages carefully.

"What's with all the traffic?" Art asked the driver.

"Where've you been? On the moon? It's the playoffs." The driver caught his passenger's blank look in the rear view mirror. "Professional basketball playoffs, and the Tel Aviv team is the best," he added.

"Oh, sorry, hadn't heard."

"Yeah. Tel Aviv vs. Tiberias. Word is, a bunch of NBA scouts are here, and get this, so is Michael Jordan!"

"Wow," said Art, "he's from my mother's home town of Wilmington in North Carolina. He played college ball at my alma mater, UNC, Chapel Hill."

"All we know is that he won all those championships with the Bulls. We don't get American college basketball over here."

"Yeah, well his shot won the 1982 national championship of college basketball for the Tar Heels, before he was ever a Bull."

"Once a champion, always a champion. He's here to scout The Cat"

"The Cat?"

"Tel Aviv's star shooting guard. The Cat is his nickname. His real name is Ishmael Arafat."

"With a name like that, no wonder they just call him The Cat, especially the Israeli fans."

"For sure."

Art returned to his messages and made a note to call Grayson Johnson, but first he called his mother and reassured her that he was fine and safe in Israel. Then, dialing Grayson's number, he heard the other end of the line pick up, and the sound of Led Zeppelin's "Black Dog" playing in the background.

"Hallo," said the laid-back voice. "This is Grayson, what's up?"

"Greetings Grayson! I'm sorry I didn't get back to you sooner," said Art.

"No prob, Prof. We've been digging up some cool stuff here, but I guess you've heard the bad news about Professor Levine? I've been praying for her ever since I heard."

"No such thing as too many prayers, Grayson. Tell me more about your big find at Caesarea."

"It's a find, alright, and an important one I guess, considering all the attention it's gotten. I'm the bucket boy on this one, and man I thought my heart was going to thump right out of my chest once I washed the thing down and saw it looked sort of like a cross with some Latin on the back. *"Divi filii . . . Caesaris"*—"the divine son of Caesar," is how I translated it. I remembered what you'd been teachin' me about amulets."

"Good job, Grayson. I'm very proud of you. You're right. This is huge. It shows clear evidence of someone who was part of the emperor cult in Caesarea Philippi, right on the border with Israel. My theory is that whoever wore this amulet participated in the emperor cult, and sought the genius/spirit of the emperor's ancestors for protection from harm."

"Makes sense to me, but nobody's really askin' me."

"Just consider yourself a budding young scholar, so don't be putting yourself down." At this point Art got a beep on his phone, and when he looked at the caller ID it was from Inspector David Levi. "Grayson, the police are on the other line so I've got to run."

"Sure. Catch you on the flip side," said Grayson, and hung up.

Responding to the incoming call, Art quickly learned that David Levi and his partner, Jeremiah Sharansky, were in charge of the case.

"Dr. West, let me tell you a bit about Dr. Levine's situation. She was out to dinner with Menachem Cohen in Tel Aviv where his offices and basketball team are located. They left the restaurant, he was knocked unconscious and she was kidnapped. No ransom has been demanded, but Mr. Cohen is offering a tidy sum for her return!"

"This is strange," said Art. "It doesn't sound like the work of professionals. Unfortunately, it's possible she's being used as bait to get to me." There was silence at the other end of the line and Art remembered the message Grayson had left on his cell phone pleading with him not to hand himself over to the kidnappers.

"The thought has occurred to us also. We have already discussed this scenario. While they may not like Dr. Levine, they may be more angry with you. You're a major Christian scholar who has been quite vocal here in Israel. Your views on Christianity and politics are very threatening, especially to some Palestinians. Some people think if you eliminate the messenger, you've eliminated the message. Dr. West? Can you still hear me?" asked Levi.

"Sorry, yes, I was just thinking about another warning message I just received."

Art had not noticed that the driver was now pulling into his hotel, the Olive Branch. It was 9:45 p.m. Jerusalem time, and Art would need some rest.

"We will come and collect you in the morning first thing. Think seriously tonight about the implications of becoming an exchange hostage. At this point I suspect that we will hear soon about their demands. I also suggest you have a very good meal. A uniformed guard will be posted near your room."

Tomorrow promised to be a crucial day in the life of Art West.

32

Dancing with the Stars

THE BAD RAP CAFÉ pulsed with American rap music—the only club of its kind in Tel Aviv. Usually frequented by transplanted Americans, it had become a favorite spot of the basketball players who came from the U.S. to play for Maccabee Elite. Thus, it should have come as no surprise that the legendary Michael Jordan would swing by after the game ended at 10:30. When he crossed the threshold, everything but the music stopped. He spotted Ishmael and casually made his way over to him, as if he were in his own Chicago restaurant. The hushed crowd came to life with murmurs and rumors in the making.

"What is Michael Jordan doing here?" "Signing The Cat! Starting a new team! Buying the Tel Aviv team!" came the answers.

"Whatever he's doing here, show the man some respect, and don't ask for anything," hissed the waitress Sharona on her way to Jordan's table. Star struck herself, she found it impossible to speak.

"How 'bout two beers darling," said Michael, flashing his million-dollar smile.

"Make those Maccabee drafts, please," said Ishmael.

Sharona snapped back into her usual postgame mode, trying not to roll her eyes, as if any of these players ever ordered anything else after a win!

"It looks like you've got game, but how tall are you?" asked Michael.

"I'm listed at 6'2", but honestly in my bare feet I'm about 6'1". I do, however, have a forty-three-inch standing vertical leap, hence my nickname."

"I noticed that you play pretty righteous defense for most of a game, but occasionally you get distracted in the second half."

"Yeah, well tonight I was actually thinking about talking to you after the game, and we were up by thirty."

"Understandable, but you realize the NBA is a whole 'nother level of basketball."

"I do understand that, Mr. Jordan, and I'm hoping for a try out at some point."

"That's why I am here. I do think you deserve a full look. What do you think about coming for a tryout in Charlotte in July when the season's over? If all goes well, we might get you into the supplemental draft in August. That could work. And my word of advice in any case is that you need to get yourself an agent."

"Yes sir, Mr. Jordan. Anything else?"

"Only that once you finish the season, call me again and we will work out some travel plans. Is it a deal?"

"Absolutely," said Ishmael. "I appreciate your taking the time to come see me play."

"No problem," as Jordan quaffing his beer, wiped his mouth, and headed out the door.

Rob Shriner, the Maccabee point guard, had played all of two games in the instructional league before he was deemed too short to be an NBA point guard—despite a clear ability to distribute "the rock" and hit a good three-point shot. Shriner, The Cat's main man on and off the court, had waited patiently in the next booth. MJ had hardly stepped one foot outside the restaurant before the Maccabee guard leapt over a chair and smacked The Cat on the back.

"What just happened?" Ishmael asked his buddy.

"You just got an invite to try out with an NBA team!"

"Wow—a dream come true."

"Well, no, not quite. Only a possible door opening to that happening. You gotta keep your head on straight."

"Right, whatever," said Ishmael, who was already thinking about playing at the next level. "But now, I have to go back to reality. I'm outta here. See you at practice man." Rob looked surprised that his friend didn't want to celebrate more, but he knew from experience how hard such news could be to process.

"Take it easy, Cat."

Ishmael left the café as the fans there applauded and chanted, "The Cat, The Cat, no one knows where he's at."

"If they only knew where I was going," thought Ishmael, as he got into his car and headed home to Bethlehem. A choice was looming between the dreams of childhood and the rebellion of youth.

33

The Gift and the Swap

GRACE SAT IN THE blistering morning heat, soaked in her full-length robe. So far as she could tell, there had been no progress, or even any attempt, to get her released from this hellhole. She'd continued to eat and try to keep her spirits up, but she couldn't escape the fear and the dread by the end of the day. No one had questioned her, no one had abused her, and except for that one conversation with the deep-voiced man, no one had lectured her. It seemed strange.

Meanwhile, Ishmael and Issah were both at home in Bethlehem celebrating their mother's birthday. They did not talk politics, but Issah had told his mother in Ishmael's hearing that at noon he was going to film some sort of press conference at the police station involving an American archaeologist. This naturally caught Ishmael's attention, but he did not press the matter.

"And what about you, Ishmael? What will you be doing today?"

"I have to head over to Tel Aviv for practice this afternoon, but before I go, I have two surprises for you."

Reaching into his duffle bag, Ishmael brought out a gift and gave it to his mother.

Mrs. Arafat was by now an older middle-aged woman, very diminutive, with graying hair. On this day she wore a colorful orange flower-print dress, and she still had a winsome smile despite all the troubles surrounding her and other Palestinians in Bethlehem. Slowly unwrapping the present so she could save the beautiful paper, a look of surprise and pleasure came over her face as an olivewood carving depicting the binding of Isaac emerged. Turning it around, she admired the workmanship that had managed to carve out of one piece of wood Abraham, Isaac, a pile of brush, and a lamb hiding behind the pile.

"This is just perfect, and will go nicely with my other olivewood carvings which I love. Thank you. You are a good son. May I ask, did this come from our friends at the Three Arches olivewood shop down the road?"

"Yes mother, as always, nothing gets by your close scrutiny. I had it especially made for your collection of Bible carvings."

Issah joined them with his gift, which was heavy and came in a long box.

Ruth Arafat struggled with her little paring knife to cut the twine and tape holding it together. When she opened the box she gasped: "Issah, you shouldn't have."

A complete set of Hebron glasses, the almost indestructible glassware that everyone in Israel wanted, sat in the bottom of the long box. The opaque glasses were swirled with pink and red and purple like a flag around the middle of each glass. She picked up one glass and held it to the light, admiring it.

"Well, this means I need to go back to doing more entertaining! Thank you, Issah, and thank you, Ishmael. These are both wonderful gifts that a mother is proud to receive. You are the two best sons I could ever hope to have." Both boys kissed their mother on her cheeks, and then prepared to go their separate ways.

Ishmael slipped out the back door wearing a black shirt and pants with black loafers, and headed down the alley towards the valley near Shepherd's Field. The haze was rising fast, but he could still see the mound in the distance known as the Herodium, the old fortress Herod the Great had built as a refuge, and possibly the place where he was buried. Many times Ishmael had climbed all over that mound, exploring the ballistas, the ancient equivalent of cannon balls slung by catapults at the foe. Herod was a truly paranoid man, fearful of death and of being supplanted as king. Ishmael had no doubts about the veracity of the story of the slaughtering of the innocents in Bethlehem. But this line of thinking gave him pause. Did he want to be like old King Herod? Was killing really the best way to support the cause of oppressed and wronged Palestinians? He was not sure. But a prisoner exchange was not murder, and he had resolved to do his part.

Inspector Levi himself came for Art at the Olive Branch Hotel at 9:00 that morning. Wearing a white shirt and stone-washed jeans, Art had prepared himself for a hot and difficult day. As they eased back into traffic, Levi said, "We were right. If you agree, then there will be an actual swap of prisoners, and the demands of the Palestinians are that no Israeli police be anywhere near the exchange. However, we will take the risk of having a homing device implanted in your shoe."

Art paused long and hard as the reality of the message swept through him. "My life for Grace's life," he thought. Art was breathing heavily when he answered the inspector. "Yes, I'm going to do this. But if these people *are* professionals, won't they check me for such a thing?"

"It's possible; however, this device is so tiny, they most likely won't find it, but hopefully we will find you. You're determined then to go through with this?"

"Oh yes, I'm adamant about it. I will trust myself to God, but Grace is too good a friend not to make the effort to free her, especially if it's me in particular they want."

The police station stood gleaming in the sun with its white limestone reflecting the light. Art remembered the days he had spent here under suspicion of forgery and theft during the Lazarus tomb explorations. He was glad to be on the right side of the law on this occasion. Art was not a brave person—indeed he was a sensitive man and a pacifist by conviction, more apt to withdraw from a fray than engage in one—but he'd spent the previous night in prayer. He'd especially focused on Acts 18:9: "Don't be afraid, because I am with you, speak and never stop because there are many who'll listen." This had comforted Art, and he had been able to get some sleep. "Perhaps God can work all of this together for good." Then the inspector called ahead to the station and alerted all his people.

Walking into the station, the first person Art met, for the first time, was Menachem Cohen, who shook his hand saying, "There are no words to tell you how much I am grateful for what you are doing, and you may rest assured that we will move heaven and earth to get you released after the exchange."

"Well," said Art, "only God can move heaven, and let's hope there is no earth moving to do, because that would mean I was buried already!" And then he smiled and chuckled a bit to himself.

"I like that," said Manny. "I'm impressed with a man who can tell a joke in the face of this grave situation."

"Again, let's hope it's not a grave situation, or else we will need an undertaker."

Art had always dealt with awkward or dangerous situations by making light of them. A little pun never hurt anything, especially when he was trying to keep the dread from taking over his thoughts.

"Well gentlemen, here are our instructions. You may read them for yourself."

The police had received a single sheet of paper the previous day. Cut word-by-word out of the daily English newspaper, the note read:

> AT 11 A.M. DELIVER WEST TO THE CHECK POINT TO BETHLEHEM. BLINDFOLD HIM. LEAVE HIM WITH NOTHING AND NO ONE. WE WILL NOTIFY YOU WHERE AND WHEN TO PICK UP LEVINE. ALLAH AQBAR.

The wall. It had become a source of great hatred and controversy for the Palestinians. The city of Bethlehem on the West Bank had been walled off from the surrounding Israeli settlements and territory, nearly ruining the tourist trade in Bethlehem for many months. Last Christmas, officials had prohibited the Palestinian Christians from leaving the city even to attend mass at the Church of the Holy Sepulchre in Jerusalem. Hardly anything better symbolized the divisions and animosities in the land than this wall, which had been decorated by Palestinian youth with spray-painted swastikas, slogans vilifying Israelis, and pictures of oppression and torment.

"Well, every Christian needs to make the pilgrimage to Bethlehem. I guess I'm no different," said Art.

The ride in the police van to the checkpoint did not take long, but it was probably the longest six miles of Art's life. He had no idea how this would all turn out, but if he was honest with himself, he had to admit that he did not expect this to turn out well. The van sailed through the Israeli side of the checkpoint without pause, but was stopped at the Palestinian side. A Palestinian policeman leaning into the driver's window said, "Our instructions are that Professor West needs to exit the van here, and walk through the entrance in the wall over there. He must be blindfolded, and no attempts should be made to follow him—not by foot or by car or even by helicopter. I will personally escort him through the gate, and he will then be handed over to the parties in question."

Art exited the van and Inspector Levi blindfolded him. "Go with God," he whispered in Art's ear. "We will do everything necessary to get you released. I believe they are not stupid enough to harm you and set off an international furor. But I am sure they will make it clear that you are never to return to Israel again."

Art said nothing as the Palestinian officer took his arm in a vice grip and marched him toward the entrance in the wall. Art's shoes scraped along the dusty road, and the sweat coursed down his neck. The sound of traffic had ground to a halt as both sides of the checkpoint had stopped all comers during the time of this event.

David Levi watched Art pass through the archway and disappear to the left. "Alright men, we must head back to Jerusalem now." He steered the vehicle into a U-turn and went back through the checkpoint. They had kept their end of the bargain.

Just after breakfast someone moved Grace into the back of a bread truck from a famous Palestinian bakery that had shops in both Jerusalem and Bethlehem. Hands and feet bound, and with a bag over her head in addition to the gag, she could hear a walkie-talkie squawking. A message came across in Arabic saying, "We have the package. Time to deliver. Wait for a bundle to take with you." Some fifteen minutes later the driver took a small package through his window, cranked up the engine and turned the truck towards Jericho, another Palestinian city.

Not knowing what to expect, and preparing himself for almost anything, Art had not considered that he might be stripped naked and reclothed with a whole new set of apparel, including new shoes. Yet that is exactly what happened when he found himself in some kind of house near the Bethlehem gate. By nature a modest man, embarrassment and shame came over him as he stripped down to nothing but the blindfold. Yet no one did him any violence, and he discovered the new clothes fit reasonably well, even the new shoes. Once dressed, someone silently handcuffed his hands in front of his body before leading him to the back seat of a waiting car. Middle Eastern music blared from the radio as Art bumped along with what he'd determined were three others. He knew a few Arabic phrases and guessed he was in for a long ride.

The bakery truck hurtled down the highway from Bethlehem to Jericho slowing for nothing, stopping not at all. When it reached the tributary of the Jordan near Jericho, the driver slowed long enough to throw the small package into the river. Meanwhile, back at the Jerusalem police headquarters, Levi's partner, Jeremiah Sharansky, informed the assembled group that it appeared the kidnappers had taken Art down to Jericho.

The bread truck, however, turned around in Jericho, headed back up the winding road to Jerusalem and stopped at a now derelict but once famous place called the Good Samaritan Inn. Formerly a tourist hotel, it had been abandoned during the last wave of the Intifadah and now was frequented only by goats and the occasional visiting Bedouin goatherd. Someone unceremoniously heaved Grace out of the van and carted her off into the back of the building. In what used to be the lobby of the small hotel, she was dropped on a small moth-eaten sofa. The retreating footsteps and the screech of tires told her she was now alone—alone but free. The odor of goat droppings had never smelled so sweet. Now began the waiting.

At precisely noon, a young Palestinian boy handed an envelope to the first officer he saw, before running off in the general direction of the city of David. The alert officer, seeing the cut-out letters, wasted no time in delivering the message to Levi who then announced to all present:

> FIND THE GOOD SAMARITAN,
> AND YOU WILL FIND THAT SHE IS INN.

"Great, now we've got a riddle to decipher," he moaned. "Looks like they misspelled the word 'in,' or did they?"

Issah, who arrived early hoping to film the upcoming planned press conference, offered, "Maybe it's a reference to the old Good Samaritan Inn on the Jericho-to-Jerusalem highway? It's abandoned these days."

Before anyone could comment, Inspector Sharansky said, "West is moving again, but I don't like the look of this. According to the GPS, he's floating down the Jordan!"

Officer Levi shouted, "Sharansky, how about you take two men and follow the signal. I'll take a team and check out our cameraman's suggestion on the Jericho highway."

"Might I have permission to film this, since it was my suggestion?" asked Issah politely.

"I don't see why not, but let's move. Time is of the essence."

"You're not going anywhere without me!" said Manny.

34

The Miracles of St. Sama'an's

OF ALL THE COPTIC Churches in Egypt, Art's personal favorite was the "Church on the Garbage Dump" in Cairo. The story involves an old legend about how the huge rock cliff, out of which the church was carved, was moved by a miracle to its present location through the auspices of St. Sama'an, a tenth-century Coptic saint. But its modern history is equally remarkable and better documented.

Stuck in the back of Art's Bible, which was now sitting in his room at the Olive Branch hotel, was a dog-eared, ten-year-old article he had copied from a Web site because it brought him great comfort.

CAIRO'S GARBAGE DUMP PRIEST HAS CAVE CATHEDRAL

By Dan Wooding
FATHER SAMA'AN has possibly the most unusual parish in the world. It is located on Muqattam Mountain, home to 30,000 garbage collectors, or zabbaleen, in Cairo. But this extraordinary man has brought a wonderful beauty to the ashes of this teeming area of narrow dirt lanes. His incredible 'Cave Cathedral' is the largest church in the Middle East. It seats 20,000 and would do justice to the Hollywood Bowl with its modern sound system, and

closed-circuit television. It is spectacular, as a huge overhanging rock covers most of the amphitheatre. The church is affiliated with the Coptic Orthodox Church, which has about six million adherents in Egypt, or 13.5 percent of the total population.

As word has spread through the Middle East about the Muqattam Cave Cathedral, it has drawn together evangelicals, Orthodox, and Catholics. Its pulpit has attracted not only the Coptic Orthodox pope, but also western evangelicals.

Clad in Orthodox garb and sporting a beard, Sama'an met with me and a few friends recently before the regular Thursday service, which was attended by thousands of believers from Cairo. They left the village's pungent odors and crowded into the cavern for a night of vibrant singing with the help of a praise choir.

Before the service began, I witnessed Father Sama'an pray for a sick young woman in his office. It was an extraordinary sight, and one I had not expected to see from an Orthodox priest. It was almost like a scene from The Exorcist, as he stomped on the floor and commanded spirits to leave her.

After it was over, he went to the service, and I noted that while his sermon started quietly, the voice of the humble priest slowly turned into thunder. Although it is an Orthodox church, the message sounds like Billy Graham's.

Many in the congregation had spent the day collecting and sorting through a mountain of garbage. Cairo's 14 million people daily produce an estimated 7,000 tons of garbage, but municipal and private trucks collect less than 50 percent of the cities refuse. During the past 35 years, thousands of Christians, fleeing poverty in rural Upper Egypt, have congregated into villages within Cairo's garbage dumps, collecting trash and recycling metal, plastic, paper and bones. Although the villages are disease-prone and poverty-stricken, an incredible Christian community has emerged as believers have developed schools, health clinics and churches.

Through an interpreter, Sama'an explained how his ministry began. "It started because of one Egyptian garbage collector," he said. "Through him, I became a changed man and eventually a worker for the Lord.

"I was living in Cairo, and was a counselor in one of the big companies. I had lost one of my precious watches. It was very expensive and I was very sad. One day, I received a knock at my door. A man in a long dirty dress, carrying a bag, asked me if I had lost something. I asked him how he knew that I lost something. I was afraid of him.

"The garbage man told me he had asked at all of the apartments in the building and everyone had denied that they lost something. 'So, sir, please tell me what you lost.' I told him I lost a watch.

"He took it out and said, 'Is this the one you lost?' I was shocked. I told him to please come in and asked him his name and where he lived. I also asked him, 'Why didn't you take the watch for yourself?'

"He replied, 'My Christ told me to be honest until death.'

"'You are a Christian?' I asked him and he said he was. I didn't know Christ at the time, but I told him that I saw Christ in him. This watch was very expensive, it cost about $11,000.

"I told the garbage collector, 'Because of what you have done and your great example, I will worship the Christ you are worshipping.'"

So began the Christian life of one Farahat, who eventually became an Orthodox priest and took the name Father Sama'an, after an eleventh century saint. He began visiting the Muqattam area and was confronted with a terrible state of affairs there, with drunkenness, sickness and violence. So he began to emphasize the need for repentance.

"Only if our spiritual life with God is improved, God will provide for our well-being," he told Christianity Today. Egyptian physicians began providing free medical assistance, and Sama'an continued to preach a message of repentance. "People have to give their lives to Christ," he asserts.

Father Sama'an said the first thing he asked God for was "his plan for this place and towards these people." He continued, "On Sunday, at six in the morning, I came here to the top of the mountain to a cave to pray. I started to pray for three weeks. After the third week, on March 15, 1974, in the middle of the day, I asked the Lord, 'Why am I here, what is your plan for these people? The people here are very hard and difficult. They live being drunk all of the time. Just lead me, Lord.'

"While I was praying," he said, "a big storm of wind blew papers from the garbage all over, millions of papers, and one paper fell right in front of me, and I was bowing, praying, and I picked it up. It was a page from the Holy Bible--very strange. Of millions of pieces of paper, why this one? It was from Acts 18:9: "Don't be afraid, because I am with you, speak and never stop because there are many who'll listen."

He said, "At that point I started to work here for four years in homes and on the streets, in open areas here in this area, then meetings in homes, and then in bigger churches, then in this church. And four years after, the Lord chose me to be a priest.

"It's not our work, or by our strength, but by His power says the Lord our host. And all this work is the work of the Lord. The secret is the Holy Spirit. There are hundreds of workers with me."

He explained that beside the "big" meetings, they have other meetings at the cave church, like the Monday morning meeting in the smaller chapel which is also carved out of stone; it has huge stone carvings depicting stories from the life of Christ on its walls.

"This is attended by 700 women," he said. "There are prayer meetings, young men's meetings, and family meetings."

I asked Father Sama'an what he thought the poor could teach us. "Simplicity," he began. "What is great is a man who comes to Jesus Christ. What is old is gone and the new is now completely changed—new heart, new mind. This is what happens when one comes to Jesus Christ, and this appears in his natural and practical life after coming to Christ."

He added, "The Lord wants to use the simplest things—with five loaves he will feed thousands. This is our God. Believe through his word and he does miracles. Amen."

When I said goodbye to this extraordinary cleric that night, he hugged me; and the bearded priest whispered, "Please pray for me." Maybe we could all do that!

Whenever Art got depressed, or had struggles, he would reread this story and remember that his life had been greatly blessed. He had had occasion to visit the Church on the Garbage Dump only last year, and it had been a wonderful experience. He saw all the crutches and wheel chairs of people who believed that Christ had healed them. He admired all the beautiful carved pictures from the Bible that artists and sculptors from around the world had come to contribute to this church. Whenever he wondered if miracles still happened, he would pull out this article and these pictures and remember that God could still do great things.

Riding in the back of the car now, his thoughts turned once more to that article, and the comforting words, "Don't be afraid for I am with you." "Perhaps," thought Art, "God can work all of this together for good. If he can turn a garbage dump into a saving church, he can certainly rescue me."

The car sped on through the afternoon heading continually south. The driver had been instructed to take the long way around to Gaza, and enter by the Egyptian side after dark. The dirt roads were pot-holed and exceedingly bumpy once the car got off the Jericho highway. Good thing the air conditioning still worked in the old Mercedes, as they were well and truly riding through the Judean desert.

Ishmael had done some hard thinking as he made his way through the alley behind his mother's house. He had to get serious about basketball. As much as he hated some Jews, he loved his mother more, and wanted to provide better for her. A career in the NBA would make that possible! Even before his Hamas colleagues had taken possession of Art West, Ishmael had made a decision. He had helped capture and exchange Levine for West, but this would be the end of his participation in this operation. Satisfied with himself, he never gave the small Palestinian boy in his shadow a second thought.

35

"I Looked over Jordan, and What Did I See?"

JEREMIAH SHARANSKY'S TEAM MOVE quite quickly as the beeping signal continued to head rapidly south. Two small ATVs were on hand in case they had to go off road. Now the signal was beyond Jericho and heading south by southwest towards the Dead Sea. As Sharansky told his team to take the Masada highway, he couldn't shake the feeling that West was already dead, and floating down the Jordan.

David Levi's team, which included a medic, had pulled up at the abandoned Good Samaritan Inn, and Issah hopped out and began filming instantly. The officers, guns cocked, came up to the front of the building fully prepared for a confrontation, but they were met with nothing more than a handful of disinterested scraggly looking goats. Levi decided to take the direct approach—"Dr. Levine, are you in there!?"

A muffled whimper came in reply. Manny started toward the building but the inspector held him back. "I can't let you go in there until we've cleared the place, Mr. Cohen. There could be traps—explosive traps." He held up a hand to stop Manny from starting another tirade. "It's too dangerous."

"But I served..." protested Manny.

"Then you'll understand this is a direct order."

Levi had him there. Manny reluctantly stepped back.

The Israeli officers carefully entered the building scanning for any possible trip wires. Proceeding ever so cautiously, they scanned the demolished lobby looking for clues until Levi caught sight of a form on a dilapidated couch. He approached the couch slowly, again making sure it wasn't a trap, and saw a disheveled form lying there looking pathetic. Kneeling down, he gently removed the canvas bag on the now weeping figure. He untied the gag and blindfold, and began working on the ropes around her hands.

"Thank you," she croaked. "Where's Art?"

"We don't know, Dr. Levine, but we are thankful you are still alive. Did they physically harm you?"

"No, they even fed me, but it was hard to eat, in all the heat and stress."

"Well, you are safe now. I am Inspector David Levi, and these are my deputies, and you may actually recognize the cameraman, Issah. You've worked with him before. I won't let him film you personally without your permission of course. He will document the crime scene, however."

"Where's Manny?"

"He is waiting outside in the car. I told him to stay there until we returned. Can you walk?"

"Yes, I think so," said Grace, trying out her legs.

Slowly walking out the front door of the Good Samaritan Inn, Grace actually quipped, "So you're the Good Samaritan? Who knew he was a Jew after all?" Their laughter was cut short by the arrival of Manny Cohen running toward Grace unable to wait until she reached the car. He swept her up into his arms. While she couldn't keep the tears from streaming down her cheeks, she didn't have the strength to return his advances or answer any of the questions he fired at her between kisses.

Inspector Levi's cell phone beeped. "Yes?"

"Hi, it's Jeremiah. We found West's clothes floating down the Jordan, and recovered them, but there is no sign of him."

"Were the clothes simply floating down the river one by one, or were they bundled together?"

"They were all bundled together in a laundry bag."

"So apparently they swapped clothes. Smart!! However, a body dumped separately would move slower than the parcel of clothes. So we should continue to search the banks and notify local authorities."

"I agree," said Sharansky and signed off.

As Inspector Levi got back into the front of the car, Grace immediately wanted to know the status of her friend Art.

"We've not found him, dead or alive, but we did find his clothes bundled into one package and floating down the Jordan. Apparently his captors expected us to put a tracer on him."

"Apparently," said Grace, "And now the even harder task begins."

"Right," said Levi, who had hoped to enjoy this rescue for a moment. But there was still work to be done.

36

Long Time Gone

THE ROUNDABOUT JOURNEY TO Gaza City seemed like it took forever, and Art, to keep his mind off the present, decided to work a bit more on the puzzle of the inscription in the Philae temple. "Back from the Styx" seemed the key phrase. It seemingly referred to the legend of Nero *redivivus*—the story in which Nero had, or would, come back from the dead. Art hoped he wasn't heading for a journey down that river in the opposite direction.

He knew for a fact that the rhetoric of Nero returning from the dead and wreaking havoc on the Empire was part of Roman, Jewish, and Christian folklore. Nero was indeed, and wanted to be, worshipped as a god in the imperial cult, particularly in the eastern provinces of the Empire during his own lifetime. But the Nero legend about his *parousia*, or "return," developed later. One form of the story predicted that Nero would return from the east with the dreaded Parthian cavalry and archers who had defeated the Romans in battle in the past. Nero had concluded a peace treaty with the Parthians who, in turn, worshipped him as the God Mithras, the one who comes back from the dead. These stories arose because Nero was privately executed and never given a public funeral or burial. Tacitus, the Roman historian at the end of the first century, even suggested that Nero had not died at all, but instead remained in hiding waiting for the opportune moment to return. This, however, was not true.

Various imposters, first in AD 69 and then much later in 80, had posed as Nero, and the later one, Terrentius Maximus, actually managed to get a Parthian pretender to the throne to support him. But by far the most important of the imposters arose in about 88 or 89 during the reign of Domitian and had won the support of the Parthian King Pacorus II. Roman historian Suetonius supported the counter-rhetoric suggesting that Domitian himself was the second Nero or Nero come back from the dead. Interestingly, the Jewish version of these ideas, found in Revelation, involved even more apocalyptic rhetoric.

A Sibylline Oracle suggested that Nero would return and wreak havoc on Rome itself, and in Sibylline Oracle 5 Nero becomes the archenemy and eschatological adversary of God's people. Comparing the stories in the oracle with Revelation 13 and 17, Art concluded that John of Patmos saw Mr. 666 as having had a mortal wound, but as someone different than the book of the Sibylline oracles suggested. Back from the dead, and far from attacking Rome, in Revelation Mr. 666 restores and enhances the beast's power. If indeed John wrote his Revelation during the reign of Domitian, it would be hard for that audience not to equate Domitian with Nero, precisely because of his persecution of Christians, particularly in the very region to which the seven letters were written by John.

But like all such apocalyptic images, they intentionally draw on universal symbols. Many evil rulers could sit for the portrait painted in 2 Thessalonians 2 or Revelation 13–17. Art found it interesting that the Christian document the *Ascension of Isaiah* also associated Nero with the antichrist figure, and that the Sibylline Oracle indicated that the name Jesus in Greek gematria added up to 888. What did all this mean for deciphering the graffito from Philae Temple? Art suspected it was a Christian graffito, probably referring to Domitian, though it could have referred to later persecuting emperors as well, like Trajan, or much later, Diocletian.

The car finally slowed to a rolling stop, and Art heard the driver's window drop followed by a rapid conversation in Arabic ending with "*Salam alechum*" and the usual response. The car then moved on slowly. He could hear children playing nearby, and the sound of the call to prayer—undoubtedly a Muslim town, but where?

His torso jerked forward as the car came to an abrupt halt. A voice outside the car gave an order, and Art was yanked from the back seat of the car and hurried along to some enclosed place. Laughter and applause greeted his arrival before an unforgettable voice, in bad English learned from Western movies, spoke.

"You are welcome to the hell and your worst nightmare, Professor West." And just as Art thought "only Jesus can save me now," someone hit him hard on the head, and the lights really did go out.

37

Saving Grace

GRACE SAT IN HER kitchen slowly sipping her mother's broth, trying to regain a sense of reality. She certainly was more shaken than she at first admitted to herself. But now that she was safe, there was just sheer exhaustion. When the voice that had spoken to her when she was bound and gagged in Bethlehem wasn't haunting her, she slept curled up tightly in the fetal position. Camelia knew that she could nurse her daughter back to health, back to real shalom—a real sense of peace. But she was fighting on two fronts. She knew that Grace needed to heal quietly, but she also knew that her daughter feared for the fate of her good friend Art.

When Grace awoke, Camelia suggested, "How about we go for a little walk down to the park and back? Maybe sit on a bench for a while and watch the children play?"

"Whatever you say," murmured Grace listlessly. Camelia's head snapped around to look at Grace. Acquiescence had never been a part of her daughter's makeup. They always enjoyed lively conversations, even heated debates and arguments. They enjoyed butting heads—the immovable object meeting the irresistible force. In the days since she was rescued, Grace had shown no interest in going to work, had returned few of Manny's calls, and had neglect to charge her cell phone.

Once again the phone rang in the kitchen, and Camelia picked it up. It was Grace's friend Hannah el Said. Camelia handed Grace the phone.

"Hello, old friend," said Hannah.

"Hi, Hannah, thank you for calling," said Grace in a monotone.

"Grace, I was wondering if I could persuade you to come over to the shop. Father and I want to see you, and I know we are all worrying about Art. I thought perhaps we could have lunch and say a few prayers for his release." At last the penny dropped for Grace. This was what she could do for Art! With newfound enthusiasm and a spark in her voice she agreed. "Of course, of course I will come. It's the least I could do."

Camelia was surprised but pleased to hear the change in her daughter's voice. "Mother, if you don't mind, I am going over to the el Said's just for a while. We're going to pray for Art. I promise to walk with you later."

"Sure, honey, that's fine," said Camelia.

Grace put on her sneakers, grabbed her purse and keys, and hopped into her red Mazda.

"Who knew that the road to recovery would be for Grace to go to an interfaith prayer meeting for a member of yet a third religion?" muttered Camelia. "Life is strange, and then you die." Camelia reckoned she was never going to figure out her daughter even after almost a half a century of trying.

38

Have a Little Talk with Jesus

NOT A CONFRONTATIONAL PERSON, either by nature or by faith, Issah had a dilemma. He knew that his brother was somehow involved with Hamas, and though he had no proof, he suspected Hamas had something to do with the recent kidnapping of Grace Levine. And now that his fellow Christian's life was in danger, a man he had worked with on several shoots, he knew he had to do something, or at least try. But what? His brother was still at ball practice in Tel Aviv and would not be home before dinner. Maybe by then Issah would think of a plan.

The daily press briefing on the search for Art West had few attendees this morning. After five days there was not much new to say, but Issah, who was filming for CBS, simply left the camera rolling just in case.

"Naturally we do not negotiate with terrorists," Inspector Levi confirmed, "but short of that we are doing all we can to find and rescue Dr. West. We still have not been approached by the kidnappers, and we still do not know who exactly they are or what they want. They've made no ransom demands. Nor do we—or Interpol—know whether Dr. West is still in the country. Anyone with any leads should please contact us. Finally, Mr. Menachem Cohen has confirmed that because no one claimed the ransom he offered for Dr. Grace Levine he is prepared to increase it by 50 percent if Art West is safely returned. That is, he is offering $1.5 million!"

It was dusk by the time Ishmael returned home, and Issah decided to wait until after dinner to talk to his brother. They sat down with their mother for shwarma (lamb cooked on a spit) with sour cream in a pita wrap, with fresh tomatoes and lettuce as well. Ishmael ate three and still had room for baklava and some Turkish coffee.

After they had all savored the meal, and it was beginning to settle in their stomachs, and after they took their dishes into the kitchen, Issah turned to Ishmael. "Let's go out and have a smoke, Brother."

"Alright," said Ishmael. In truth these two brothers did love and respect one another. In Palestinian homes the fraternal kinship bond was often the strongest of all ties, save for the relationship with one's mother.

They walked down the alley in comfortable silence, crossed the street, and went to sit on the park bench where they had so often watched the sun go down over the Herodium.

"So I hear that you actually met Michael Jordan," said Issah.

"Yes I did," said Ishmael proudly, "And he is interested in giving me a full tryout with his American team next month."

"Then it will be all the more important that you tie up some loose ends here before you go," said Issah.

"What lose ends?" said Ishmael, not yet on his guard.

"Ish, I've known for a long time about your involvement off and on with Hamas, and I even understand it. When Jamaal was killed right before your eyes, you were only twelve. I know what a fire that lit in your heart. But it's time to let it go."

"Funny you should bring that up tonight. Normally I'd start one of our usual arguments, but this time I think you're right. I've made up my mind that if I want to pursue basketball, and maybe provide some real security for our family, especially Mom, I need to leave that behind."

"Good," said Issah relieved. "No, great! That's smart, and I'm glad to hear it. And if that's the case, I need to ask you a harder question." He paused to look at the Herodium, before steeling himself to look his twin directly in the eye. "Did Hamas, and you, have something to do with the kidnapping of Grace Levine?"

There was a long awkward silence, during which Issah saw tears quietly rolling down the cheeks of his brother.

"Yes," he said quietly, "but how did you know?"

"Well, you know how nosy the little boys are in this neighborhood. One of them followed you to that abandoned house a few blocks away, and told me what he saw." Ishmael couldn't believe he had been so careless.

"But now we have a further problem," Issah continued. "Do you know, or can you find out where Dr. Art West is?"

"Well, not precisely, but I do know he's in Gaza City somewhere."

"And do you have access to wherever that is?"

"Probably. Why? I don't like where this conversation is going."

"What don't you understand, Ishmael? You could be charged with aiding and abetting a kidnapping, and even being accessory to a murder if West dies! The Israelis are hardly likely to show you any mercy—not just because the case involves a prominent professor, but what about you? National basketball star, but secret Hamas leader? How do you think that's going to play out? Do you really think you have no blood on your hands if West dies?"

Again Ishmael sat for a moment in silence, thinking. He really did not want to totally screw up his chance at playing professional basketball—for Michael Jordan no less. "So, what are you suggesting I do, and who exactly besides you knows about all this?"

"As far as I can tell, I'm the only one who suspects anything, so I suggest we do something about this."

"We?"

"Yes, you and me. Here's what I have in mind. Tomorrow through whatever channels you've got, you find out where exactly West is. I mean precisely. Then on Friday, you and I are going for a little ride to that location, by whatever circuitous route necessary. No police, no Mosad, no Hamas friends, just you and me.

"My idea is this. We're identical twins. Let's use that to our advantage! Your Hamas cronies have never paid any real attention to me, right? So I wear your Tel Aviv warm-ups and pretend to be you. We'll go out there with you pretending to be me—some crazy cameraman—who will threaten to kill me, disguised as The Cat, unless they release West. We both know Hamas desperately needs the money and support you've been giving them, and is counting on more as you become more famous and wealthy. They won't shoot the goose that lays their golden egg! And I doubt they hate West more than they need you."

"And what happens then?"

"You, still pretending to be me, take West out to the car, and drive off. Fast! Either I stay behind with them, or I jump in the car and we all three escape."

"You don't know them! If they even for one second think they're being conned, they'll kill you!"

"That's a chance I am prepared to take for both you and for Dr. West. Anyway, you're the future of this family, I'm not. But listen, I'm not done. I tell them to give you a fifteen-minute head start, and then they give chase. Only, you're going to throw them a major curve ball when you take West over the back roads past the Gaza checkpoint into Egypt. If all goes well I'll tell them to drop me in Bethlehem, when we lose your supposed trail."

"That's crazy, but it might just work, and it might just save West's life. Their plan was to sweat him for all the info they could get in a week, then shoot him execution style with major publicity and film sent to Al Jazeera. El Tigre himself is coming to do the interrogation."

"Well, that means we've got exactly one chance before things go too far." Issah looked deep into the eyes of his twin. "I am my brother's keeper, and I don't want you to go to jail just because you've been trying to get revenge for losing Jamaal all those years ago. Despite all our differences I do love you. And I love our mother, and you know that seeing you disgraced would break her heart. Maybe the Great One will honor this effort to save a life. But the only way this works is if they believe I am you for long enough for them to hesitate before shooting me, long enough for you to get West out of there."

"*Encha Allah*"—as God wills—said Ishmael.

"As the Lord desires," said Issah.

39

Gaza Stripped . . . Again

SAND. IT WAS EVERYWHERE. All over the floor, in the bathroom, on the cot where Art tried to sleep. It was in his clothes, in his mouth, in his hair, in his ears. The first couple of days in captivity had been bearable. Lots of questions to which Art had no answers. Lots of bad English and preaching about America as the Great Satan. Art knew the side of America his tormentors did not know, and so he tried to explain. He argued that a nation should not be judged on its worst behavior, but on the basis of its best, if its best is a regular feature of what that nation is trying to do and be. The Hamas leaders were unimpressed. Art still did not completely understand why they wanted him in exchange for Grace. To lecture him? Feed him bad food? He'd know soon enough.

El Tigre, a man personally responsible for tormenting and torturing Western hostages, arrived on the third morning. Art could sense immediately the shift in his captors' demeanor. They were not merely respectful of the man, they were deferential. Who wouldn't be to a man who had the ear of Osama bin Laden himself? Before the sun had even cleared the horizon, Art found himself forced into a chair, hands tied behind his back, blinded by the glaring lights of a videocam. No more political lectures. He could tell playtime was over.

"So, Mr. West," began El Tigre, refused to call the man Doctor, "no doubt you are wondering why you are here. What is it that your people call us—'infidels?' Well we will see just how faithful you are to your God, and your God to you. You will recant your faith in Christ. We will publicly shame you and your faith on film, which we will release to the media and the internet—to Al Jazeera, to CNN, to everyone. We will publicly humiliate your faith, just as you Americans try to humiliate Islam in your country. If you choose not to cooperate we will break first your fingers, then your toes, then your arms. You get the picture. So Mr. West, are you ready to make a movie?"

"I don't really know who you are, or why you do this, but there *is* a God, and he will deal with you in due course." El Tigre answered with a deep laugh. "I also don't know," Art freely admitted, "what my level of pain tolerance is, but I can tell you that this will be an exercise in futility for you. If you are going to kill me anyway, then you had best get on with it. I will not be recanting my faith in Jesus Christ. Not now, not later, not ever."

"I figured you would make a nice speech like that, and now we have it all on film. Let's see what the pain leads you to say next," sneered El Tigre. "Omar, untie Mr. West's hands and stand him up. See that table behind him? Yes, that one. Why don't you take his right little finger—and lay it out. Yes, just like that. Now Omar, I want you to take the hammer and smash that finger. Yes, I said smash it."

Art's whole body tensed as he felt his hand being held upside down behind him pinned to the small metal table. He could hear the sound of the rise of the hammer, and then its swift fall, and then all he could hear and feel next was his own bellow as the pain coursed through his whole frame. He was then dragged to the shower, and thrown in, and hosed down, having been stripped of all his clothes except his underwear. His clothes were put back on him, and one little rag was used to tie up his finger, and then he was dragged back to the chair and forced to sit down again.

El Tigre nonchalantly lit a cigarette as if he'd just finished having a satisfying round of sex. After smoking the cigarette down to the filter, he placed the ember against Art's neck. As Art flinched, the Moroccan growled in his ear. "If you do not soon cooperate, Mr. West, you will regret it, I assure you."

El Tigre returned to his seat and looked again at Art. "I ask you once more, Mr. West. Will you renounce your faith in Jesus Christ so we can let you go? Will you not just once say something like 'Jesus is not God's divine Son'? It is only words. You don't even have to mean it. Why not spare yourself more agony?"

Art responded with just an incoherent moan.

"Omar, it seems our guest has chosen the taser. Zap him," El Tigre ordered.

As instructed, Omar turned the device on Art's right arm. The electrical shock ran right through Art's body, throwing him to the floor, which was the last thing he remembered before he passed out from the pain.

"It is a pity," said El Tigre, "but we may have to kill the man without getting all that we want from him. Throw him in his little cell and lock him up. I want him to suffer for a good while and think about what is happening to him. I have found that if we wait, say, twenty-four hours, his whole attitude may change, because now he has experienced a taste of what is coming his way. Continue to give him water, but do not feed him for the rest of today. We want his head and stomach to hurt as well before we question him again tomorrow morning. And we will use more severe methods tomorrow, as needed, while still keeping him alive. You see, killing him is too easy. The real revenge will come when he begins to feel his pain, and recants his cherished beliefs. Then we will have made his faith and his God appear small. Then we will have humiliated him and will have it on tape to show the world."

40

Law and Order in the Big Apple

CURATOR BACON HAD HAD better days. The grand opening of his amulets and ankhs exhibit had gone exceedingly well. The one-day take from ticket sales for the opening was over $300,000, exceeding even the most robust expectations. At this rate, he had no doubt that the exhibit would quickly sell out, assuring the funds for further such extravaganzas. There was just one little problem—the Egyptian man sitting in his office yet again this morning.

The museum's lawyers had suggested that the best way to handle the matter without shutting down the exhibit was to actually give Mr. al Haq the name of the seller. Let the Egyptian harangue and haggle with the dealer. This suited the curator just fine.

Sitting now in his office across from him in the plush burgundy lounge chair, Mr. al Haq had taken the liberty of lighting up one of his Egyptian cigarettes.

"If you don't mind, Mr. al Haq, smoking is forbidden here," Bacon said, hiding his annoyance, not to mention his allergies to cigarette smoke. "But I do have some good news for you. Our lawyers have given me permission to reveal the name of the dealer who sold us the artifact. His name is Mr. Amstutz, as you can now see from his card." Bacon handed the card to al Haq, who then rose to leave.

"You will find him on the lower east side of Manhattan. I hope he can give you what you need. If not, don't hesitate to contact me." Bacon desperately hoped never to see this persistent little man again.

"You may count on it," said the small swarthy man, who had still not put out his cigarette. "I have watched your show *Law and Order* many times, and I know justice can be done even in New York. Let us hope I do not have to call on Mr. Sam the prosecutor to get the right outcome," al Haq grinned, revealing a broken front tooth, covered partly in gold.

Bacon somehow knew, as he ushered al Haq to the door, that the man would not return to Egypt empty handed.

41

Go into Your Closet and Pray

JERUSALEM HAD WITNESSED A lot of prayer meetings over the last two thousand years in a lot of interesting and odd places involving all sorts of people, but a prayer meeting consisting of one Jew and two Muslims on behalf of one Christian had to be one of the most unusual prayer meetings ever in the city of Zion. The Western Wall was famous for all the paper prayers stuffed into nooks and crannies, and Grace planned to walk through the Cardo to the Wall and say a few extra prayers for Art while there. There was still no word or any sign of him at all. Grace had with her a copy of a poem about prayer Art had once sent her, and she intended to stick it in the Wall when she got there.

CRACKS IN THE WALL

Cracks in the wall,
There by design,
  Prayers on plain paper
One of them mine
  Rabbis are chanting,
Torah held high,
  Sunlight is fading,
In the blue sky.
  Guards are watching,
Passing the time,
  Nodding acquaintance
With the Sublime.

Herod's temple,
All that remains
Limestone platform,
Withstands the strain,
Mosque's gold dome
Shines in the light,
Whose God is honored
By what's in sight?
Prayers of the righteous
Meant to be heard,
But the papers are silent,
Say not a word

"We want Messiah"
Yeshiva boy cries,
The irony is thick,
And darkens the skies
Christians with kipas
Stand by the shrine,
Praying to Jesus,
As someone divine.
The wailing wall,
Heard Jesus' lament
That he would have gathered,
If Zion'd repent.

Cracks in the wall,
Filled up with our prayers,
Perhaps it is this,
Which keeps God right there
Perhaps when Messiah
Comes (once again),
Perhaps then the Spirit
Will descend through the air,
Perhaps then true monotheists
Will kneel at God's feet,
Be filled with his Spirit,
The Father's Son greet.

True children of Abram
Meet at the wall
And confess Trinity,

The One for us all.
Is this a dream—we three could be one?
Just as God is,
Whose plan is not done.
"Something there is
That doesn't like a wall"
But this one unites
The One with us all.

The poem revealed how much Art respected the other monotheistic religions even when he didn't agree with their theology. He believed God loved everyone and wanted everyone to love God with all their hearts. He believed that the best way to witness for Jesus to Muslims and Jews was simply to be as Christlike as he could, loving everyone. It was this very characteristic which had made so many people both love and hate Art. And in the case of the little group gathered in the antiquities shop, it was all love.

The smell of antiquity hung over the room. Hannah had simply set out three small stools for them to sit on together in the middle of the show room and put up the closed sign. The three friends sat down, and after a cup of tea, bowed their heads and began to pray.

Kahlil began. "Almighty God who is all-seeing and all-knowing, we commend to you now our dear friend Art West who is in peril. We ask that you put a hedge of protection around him, keeping him from mortal harm. We ask that you might intervene before tragedy happens, and we leave the matter in your hands." Together they responded, "Amen."

Hannah went next. "God you are great, and we trust that you, who care about justice as well as mercy, can do all things. You know even now where Professor West is, for nothing is hidden from your all-seeing eyes. We ask that your will be done in this matter, most especially that you rescue the innocent man, Professor West, who does not deserve to have his life taken now."

They sat in silence for a few moments until Grace began to pray the only way she knew and felt comfortable—in Hebrew. Specifically, she prayed from memory the whole of Psalm 18. For her friends she translated a part of it. "I call to the Lord who is worthy of praise, and I have been saved from my enemies. The cords of death entangled me, the torments of destruction overwhelmed me, the cords of the grave coiled around me, the snares of death confronted me. In my distress I called to the Lord, I cried to my God for help. From his temple he heard my voice, my cry came before him, and into his ears . . . He parted the heavens and came down . . ." She had recited the psalm for herself during her recent captivity, and suddenly the horror of those days came once more into her mind and overwhelmed her. She began to weep uncontrollably. Hannah wrapped her arms around Grace, and Kahlil offered words of comfort, but it took a good while for them to calm her. "Someone must save our friend. Let us hope that Art is right when he says that God can make a way when there seems to be no way."

Afterwards, Hannah accompanied Grace down the Cardo through the covered passageways to the Temple Mount. She promised to wait for Grace as she went into the women's area on the right side of the Wall and prayed. The brilliant blue sky did nothing to dissipate the heat or the reflection of the sun off of Herod's limestone retaining wall. Grace worked her way through the throng of women that always came on Friday mornings to pray, to the Wall itself, where she recited Psalm 18 once more, and carefully inserted a rolled up scroll of Art's poem into the Wall, high enough and secure enough so that it would not readily fall out. Feeling a little weak and claustrophobic amidst the pressing crowd, she extricated herself and met up with Hannah.

"I have a nice little surprise for you. I have reserved a little table for us at your favorite pizza place near the old Jewish quarter."

"*Shokrun*," said Grace in Arabic. "I could really use some solid food about now." Little could they imagine what was transpiring at that very moment in Gaza.

42

Playoff Fever

THURSDAY NIGHT TEL AVIV swarmed with Maccabee and Jaguar fans for the IBA playoffs. The Eilat team posed a serious threat; they were big, they were powerful, they were deep, they could defend, and man could they shoot. Ishmael knew how much his team was counting on him to help them win this championship, but it was hard to keep his head in the game knowing the task that awaited him the following morning. Issah had really shocked him with his confrontation, but he realized his brother was right. If he did not want to live in the shadows the rest of his life, running from the Law, he had better try and make amends in the Art West matter, and then turn his back on his past with Hamas. The NBA certainly did not want a player with a major criminal record.

The packed stadium resounded with chants of "The Cat, The Cat," which seemed to distract the players. The first quarter proved sloppy for both teams. Nonetheless, the Eilat Jaguars were living up to their name, prowling up and down the court, setting hard picks, and making the Maccabee team pay for its defensive lapses. By the end of the first quarter, with Tel Aviv behind by five, Ishmael and Rob Shriner sat down on the bench to talk a little strategy.

"They've clearly watched a lot of film," said Rob the point guard. "So how about if we cross them up a bit by first posting you up down on the low block, and then next time down the floor having you run around a couple of picks to free you up for a shot."

"Sounds like a good plan," said Ishmael, and the other players agreed. The coach sat back and let them talk at this point, picking his moment as to when to intercede.

Manny was sitting in his luxury box, yelling at no one in particular because his team was losing. "Come on, we can play better than that. This is for all the marbles! Our boys need to get it together."

About half way through the second quarter the tide turned in Tel Aviv's favor when Eilat's 6'11" center, Doran, got into foul trouble with his third. This opened up the lane for Ishmael, and he wasted no time taking advantage, scoring ten quick points towards the end of the quarter so that Tel Aviv inched in front by three points by halftime. Their coach, Johnny Cousey from the States, was much happier with the effort in the second quarter, and on the way down the tunnel to the locker he said to Ishmael, "At the beginning of the third quarter, I want you to go down into the paint and make a statement dunk that will get the crowd going nuts. That will help us start the second half off strong."

"Will do coach," said Ishmael. With his forty-three-inch vertical leap, this would not be difficult to do.

The second half went far better for Tel Aviv, although Eilat made a game of it down the stretch, scoring thirteen straight points early in the fourth quarter. Ishmael came through in the clutch, making several highlight shots and dunks, and after the game Manny came to him and said, "Nice work kid, glad you guys have the day off tomorrow before you play again on Saturday. GET SOME REST!"

But there would be no rest for Ishmael on Friday. Rather it would be a day of reckoning.

43

Geburtstag's Birthday

Though mainly a recluse, Vladimir Stahlin (aka Geburtstag) was a vain man. He had decided to celebrate his sixty-fifth birthday with a lavish meal at one of Berlin's finest restaurants—Alt Luxemburg in Charlottenburg. The restaurant specialized in traditional German dishes served in fresh and innovated ways. Geburtstag had his butler call not only to make a reservation, but to make sure the restaurant knew that it was his birthday. He enjoyed their famous dessert presentation complete with singing frauleins and a picture for their "birthday wall." Donning his best suit, Geburtstag allowed himself one more indulgence—he would wear the golden ankh just this once. No one would have any idea what it was or its provenance or special character. He felt safe in the town that he had lived in for so very long.

The limousine pulled around precisely at 7:30. Not only was a glass of champagne already chilled and ready for Herr Geburtstag, but so was a beautiful blond woman dressed in a revealing black and white dress waiting for the man she chose to call "Fritz." The color TV played on mute, while the sounds of Sade singing "No Ordinary Love" filled the cabin. When Geburtstag went out on the town, however rarely, he went out in style.

During the thirty-minute ride to Alt Luxemburg, Fritz and Gigi polished off the first bottle of *Krug*. Trees and flowers in full bloom flashed by as they sped along. The driver slowed the vehicle slowly to a stop and opened the back door before Geburtstag realized they had arrived. The champagne had unexpectedly left him a bit fuzzy.

Gigi pulled her white mink wrap around her shoulders and helped her date out of the limo. He quite amiably was prepared to be led by this beautiful woman most anywhere. She'd accompanied Geburtstag before and knew him to be a generous tipper, so she went out of her way to please him.

Though Geburtstag's tastes were normally rather plebian and traditionally German (he loved Wienerschnitzel, for example), on his birthday he liked to experiment a bit. This year he'd resolved to try the rolled saddle of rabbit in coffee sauce. He would insist on the four-course meal—Gigi thankfully was not one of those salad-eating sticks of a woman—and no doubt their "after-play" would rival any dish Chef Wannemacher could offer. Fritz settled back in his Victorian wing chair, holding the hand of Gigi, and for the first time she noticed his jewelry.

"Mein Liebchen, what is this new cross, or whatever it is, you are wearing? It is stunning," remarked the ever inquisitive Gigi.

"If you must know it is an ankh, not a cross, an ancient Egyptian piece of jewelry. Actually it's called an amulet, believed to ward off evil, and attract the good, and obviously my dear it is working tonight, because here you are, and you look mighty good."

Gigi blushed and replied, "It is nice of you to say so." There was something in her that was at least a little bit attracted to older men with power and wit.

The opening course involved a dark rich beet soup, like Russian borsch, and the salad was mounded with romaine lettuce and a scrumptious house dressing. Both Fritz and Gigi were having a great time, and to cap it off they had ordered a bottle of the finest Riesling in the restaurant. This restaurant was wise enough not to serve enormous portions, and so when the rabbit came, both were still hungry. The rabbit proved to be succulent, the sauce slightly piquant, and the roasted potatoes a good match.

After the dinner plates had been cleared away, there was a brief pause to allow things to settle. And then in came a rolling cart, escorted by four fetching women, and when the hood was opened "cherries jubilee" met their eyes. The girls began to sing the old Deutsch version of "Happy Birthday," the waiter set the cherries aflame, and Gigi offered a toast. Just then a photographer arrived and took a picture of Geburtstag and his Fraulein for the birthday wall. Fritz, ever on his guard, asked where the picture would be displayed, and the waiter assured him it would hang in the entrance way and they would send a copy to his flat. Satisfied with that, he asked no more questions. What the waiter failed to tell him was that the picture would also go up on the restaurant Web site that very day.

Nothing could spoil the mood created by good food, good drink, a celebratory occasion, and a beautiful companion. No sooner had they gotten into the limo than Fritz's hands were all over Gigi. A smart girl, she knew that this man of sixty-five years—like a swimmer who had not practiced for a long time—would soon wear himself out without getting beyond the first lap, so she just snuggled down and waited for sleep to overtake her date. Sure enough, before the car even arrived at the house, he'd fallen asleep on her ample bosom. All was well that ended well without any muss and fuss.

Interpol had been diligently scanning the Net for evidence of the whereabouts of the Egyptian amulets. They were satisfied that they had found the first one in New York, but had yet to have even a hit on the second. Horst Jaeger, director of Interpol's Electronic Surveillance Division, had taken a personal interest in the matter. As he did each morning, he entered the words "golden ankh" into Google, and clicked on a series of images. This morning, he was pleasantly surprised to find something new. A man, looking slightly inebriated next to some blond bombshell, was clearly wearing a golden ankh! Checking the source of the picture led Horst to the Alt Luxemburg Web site. He wasted no time phoning the restaurant, and asking for Frau Wannemacher, wife of the famed chef and hostess for the restaurant.

"Hallo?" said Frau Wannemacher, who was answering as the restaurant was about to close.

"Is this Frau Wannemacher"

"Ja, you have her."

"This is Horst Jaeger of Interpol, and I have a question for you, but I must ask you to be discrete."

"I assure you I am the soul of discretion," said Wannemacher.

"Good," said Jaeger. "There is a picture recently posted on your Web site of an older man wearing a golden ankh. I am sure you must have seen him recently."

"He celebrated his birthday with us just last evening. You'd like his name?"

"That is correct."

"Well, it's not a state secret. It's Herr Fritz Geburtstag, a local man.

"Thank you, and I trust you will mention this conversation to no one."

"You can rely on me," said Frau Wannamacher, hanging up and hoping she'd not just gotten one of her patrons into hot water.

44

Issah Intervenes

THE ROUNDABOUT RIDE TO Gaza City through the desert at dawn in an old Mercedes was both beautiful and bumpy. The brothers planned to arrive early, catching the Palestinians before the events of the day transpired, and they had no idea that they'd be a full hour ahead of El Tigre. Some higher authority seemed to be orchestrating the events of the day. Ishmael had called ahead to make sure his Hamas friends knew he was coming and, more importantly, to confirm the locale. Ishmael had moved far enough up the chain in Hamas and had been directly involved in the Levine and West matter, so this information was not kept from him. Omar suspected nothing out of the ordinary. He was actually pleased that Ishmael wanted to witness an "interrogation" and took this as a sign of his toughening up and becoming more involved.

After the game, Issah and Ishmael had poured over every step of their plan, making doubly sure they looked as identical as was humanly possible. When they had finished trying on each other's clothes, trimming each other's hair and beard, and double-checking everything in the mirror, they were convinced that even their mother Ruth would have trouble telling them apart. This should instantly confuse anyone. Issah even had on Ishmael's signature Nikes.

They arrived early enough that traffic was not yet heavy, and Ishmael had no trouble finding the bunker on the east edge of town close to the road they often used to enter the city. Pulling behind the building, Ishmael drove in front of the two cars parked there, and quietly slipped out of the car. No one was stirring yet on the back side of the building, and, as planned, Issah slipped out, raised the hood of the two old cars, disconnected the battery wires on both, and slowing closed the hoods. Then, coming around the house side of their car, Ishmael grabbed Issah by the shirt, headed over to the back door of the bunker and kicked it in. To look convincing, Issah had scratched up his face a bit to make himself look as if he had been roughed up.

Startled, Omar and one other looked up only to think they were seeing double. The man with the gun appeared to be Ishmael, but then the man to whose head the gun was pointed, also appeared to be Ishmael.

Ishmael then said in a loud voice: "I am Issah, twin brother of Ishmael, and no friend of Hamas. I gather that my scum of a brother here has helped you kidnap Professor West. I also gather that you have him here. Hear me when I tell you that if you do not release Professor West into my custody immediately, not only will Ishmael your money man die, so will you, and quickly." At this point he pulled back the trigger on the gun. The Hamas operatives could not stifle their gasps.

Issah then said, "My brother is a traitor to our cause and struggle, but believe me he's not joking about shooting me, or you."

As a demonstration, Ishmael suddenly pointed the gun up to the concrete ceiling and fired off the one bullet. The nearly deafening sound was followed by the crackling of concrete hitting the floor.

Omar, staring hard at Issah, said, "Why not just leave Ishmael with us and take West? He is after all one of us."

"No," said the real Ishmael, "there is no time for games or negotiations now. You can see I am serious about what I intend to do to Ishmael, so get West out of whatever cell he is in AND DO IT NOW!"

Hurrying, Omar unlocked the cell, and dragged Art out by his hair. He was hardly conscious, much less alert.

"Here is your great man," laughed Omar. "We have already almost ruined him. Go ahead. Take this piece of trash out of here."

Pointing his gun at Issah, Ishmael said, "Pick up this man, Mr. Great Athlete, and bring him to the car." Issah went over, put his arm gently under the shoulder and armpit of Art, and began walking out the door of the building. Ishmael slowly backed towards the door.

"Do not try and follow us," said Ishmael. "You will regret it if you do." Omar, now standing in the doorway, spit in the general direction of Ishmael, and made an obscene gesture.

Leaping into their car, with Art carefully laid on the back seat, Ishmael slowly backed the car out from behind the house keeping his window down and the gun pointed at Omar. Reaching the narrow street he accelerated into gear, not noticing the small black car coming down the alleyway, beside the road. El Tigre, sensing trouble, quickly pulled around to the back of the house. Omar shouted something to him, and then he was off in a flash after the twins.

45

The Old Via Maris

FOR THOUSANDS OF YEARS pilgrims and travelers traversed the old "sea road" that led down the coast of Gaza and into the Egyptian territory. The Philistines and sea peoples had patrolled these roads in King David's time, and the Philistines had even made Gaza one of their capital cities. The Holy Family had likely come this way down into Egypt, as had the patriarchs Abraham, Isaac, and even Moses before them. This was the main and quickest way to get to the Egyptian border. Alexander had doubtless come this way, as had Pompey and Julius Caesar and Marc Antony and Augustus too.

The old Mercedes with its huge V-8 engine was making good time, but Ishmael had decided to put one more wrinkle into the plan, just in case he was being followed. This old Mercedes was a junker, which he had bought for next to nothing the previous week. Ishmael's plan was to lead astray whoever might be trailing him. They had made arrangements to ditch the old car and pick up a new one at Khan Yunus before the Rafa checkpoint that took one into Egypt. Ishmael had paid a friend to take the Mercedes on a little "holiday" into Egypt, to the resort town of Naha Diqla, just south of Rafa. If anyone was still trailing that car, they would come to a dead end in Naha Diqla if not in Khan Yunus. Meanwhile, Ishmael planned to double back heading north through the desert and on to Bethlehem along the way they'd come that morning.

El Tigre was no man's fool, but he could be tricked. He reckoned as he saw the old Mercedes speed off south that the Arafat boys were heading for Egypt. He figured he was about a mile behind them. Catchable. But he couldn't yet see them.

With tires screeching at the turn off at Khan Yunis, Ishmael whipped the old Mercedes into a lower gear and headed straight for the town square. The car dealer was waiting for him. "*Salam Aleichum.*" Ishmael nodded and asked for the bathroom, racing toward it, razor kit in hand. Quickly shaving off his slight beard, he put on a kafia and headed back to the car. Issah had given some water to Art who was still not fully conscious but able to drink, and handed the keys to the old Mercedes over to Mohammed, an old friend from school.

"*Shokrun*, for helping me with this," and he handed the young man a roll of money. Jumping into the white car, Ishmael followed the Mercedes to the intersection of the main road, until it eased into the southbound lane. As he waited to merge, Issah attended to Art, taking a wet compress and wiping his wounds and forehead. "He has a broken hand," he observed.

About to reply, Ishmael instead stiffened as he saw El Tigre's small black car whizz past, in pursuit of the Mercedes. Ishmael had warned Mohammad of this possibility, and hoped he'd keep the pedal to the metal. Allowing another minute to pass, Ishmael took the left turn and headed back to civilization.

Things had turned out better than he could have hoped thus far, but they needed to get Art West to a hospital. They'd agreed Issah would take the car on to the hospital, dropping Ishmael off in Jerusalem at Rob Shreiner's pad. The two basketball players then would return to Tel Aviv, where hopefully he could somehow get his head back to basketball. But how could he? His twin now looked more like him than he did himself. As the Issah look-alike who had liberated West, Ishmael had become a marked man, but when would his former friends see through the ruse?

46

The Tiger vs. the Cat

EL TIGRE DID NOT like to lose. Indeed, he found losing totally unacceptable. Like The Cat, he was a fierce competitor, only in a much more dangerous game. When El Tigre found the Mercedes abandoned in Naha Diqla, he'd thoroughly searched the village, and had to admit he'd been had. Without question or hesitation, he blamed the brother he thought was Issah, the one who had apparently been willing to kill Ishmael.

Omar had detailed the West rescue to El Tigre, who found his rage tempered by curiosity. How had that mild-mannered Christian cameraman come up with a scheme like that? This particular escapade appeared to be the handiwork of a veteran plotter, but who helped him? He could understand how Issah might desperately want his fellow Christian freed, but he couldn't believe that Issah had acted alone. Despite tales of sibling rivalry, especially two brothers of different religions, it never occurred to El Tigre that perhaps the twins had plotted this *together*. As long as the cameraman stayed in the country, he'd deal with him soon enough.

Meanwhile, The Cat was being ribbed by Rob during the whole ride between Jerusalem and Tel Aviv. "Man, you look so young! You look like you've never shaved," kidded Rob. "Whose gonna believe you're an NBA prospect when you look like 'The Kitten' instead of The Cat?"

"Alright, alright, say what you will now, but the beard will come back. I was just tired of all the sweating and itching. Right now, we need to get our act together. I'm guessing Eilat will kick our butts tomorrow if we don't."

"Yeah, that could happen, so we have to defend our home court advantage," replied Rob. Rob was actually a very likeable guy, though he did like to pull pranks from time to time. He grew weary of players who took themselves too seriously, when in fact they were playing a game, a basketball game. Sometimes people, especially embattled people, need to have something to cheer about, and sports gave them such hope in small doses.

"So how do we take the Jags tonight?" asked The Cat.

"I'd say get them into foul trouble again. We need to be aggressive. You noticed how the refs called a zillion fouls whenever someone drove the ball into the lane. So I say that in tomorrow's game, I'll do a lot of driving the lane and then kicking out the ball, mainly to you. If they don't try and stop me, I'll just keep going all the way to the hoop. If they do, and they foul, no big deal. We all know I'm the best free throw shooter in the league. If we get a couple of their starting five in foul trouble, like Daron, we should be good. But the one person who definitely, positively, absolutely can't afford to get in foul trouble is you. Just do your perimeter thing, and only go to the hoop when you can see a lane and dunk it. Capisce?"

"Yeah, as usual you are making good sense, which is why you are the point guard and captain on this team." They continued strategizing the whole way to Tel Aviv, knowing as they did, how to maximize each other's game.

"So, tell me again, why exactly you shaved off the beard that made you look so sexy?" asked Rob.

"It's a long story. But hey, I'm the Cat, so since I have nine lives, there's no rush in telling it." Ishmael flashed his million-dollar smile and they both had a good laugh.

47

The Journey to Sinai

WHEN ISSAH PULLED INTO the drop off circuit at Jerusalem's Sinai hospital, a wave of weariness and nausea unexpectedly came over him. He wasn't used to plotting and planning. He was used to filming such scenarios, not being the main actor in them. He'd been running on caffeine and adrenalin, and his body had begun to rebel. Hopping out of the car, and picking up a groggy, nearly comatose Art West, he walked quickly into the lobby. As a Palestinian, Issah knew he had to deliver West to the doctors with some dispatch and get out of there, not least because he'd be mistaken almost certainly for his brother, and then be mobbed.

In a loud voice to no one in particular, he shouted, "This man needs a doctor immediately!" As he gently set his charge down in a chair near the check-in counter, Art looked up and said with faint recognition, "Who are you?"

"My name is Issah." Then as quickly as he'd come, he vanished through the throng of patients, families, nurses and attendants.

"Hey, aren't you The Cat!?" yelled a bystander as Issah zipped towards the entrance.

Nurse Leibowitz stood over Art, assessing his situation and calling for a gurney. "We need to get this man some treatment immediately. Orderly, wheel this man into Emergency stat!"

Miriam Leibowitz was a large, experienced, no-nonsense nurse, and she'd heard it all. After asking Art West his name, which Art slowly told her, she then asked, "And who was that man who seems to have saved you just in time?"

"That was Jesus," smiled Art, "his name was Jesus. I was saved by Jesus, or Issah, as he's called in Arabic."

"Right!" said Nurse Leibowitz, "and I'm the Virgin Mary. Well sweetheart, it's clear to me that you need more than physical treatment, but first things first. We need to attend to that broken hand, your burn, and your general shock before Mr. West goes south!"

48

Amstutz's Antiquities

JOHANNES AMSTUTZ WAS A tough customer. He had to be to deal with the sorts of people he had to deal with and still make a reasonable profit. But when Prester al Haq came into his shop he had a premonition that he'd met his match. Flashing his gold-tooth grin, Mr. al Haq sat down without invitation in the plush chair directly in front of Amstutz's desk. Filled with antiquities stuffed into cases, hanging from the ceiling, crammed into the corners, sitting on the stairs up to the second level, cluttering up every inch of space on counter after counter, some pieces of which had not been dusted or moved in a half century, the shop resembled an indoor flea market.

"Mr. Amstutz, I presume?" said al Haq.

"You presume correctly. How can I help you?" said Johannes.

"I have been directed here by the esteemed curator of the Metropolitan Museum of Art, who tells me you sold him a particular object not long ago—an Egyptian ankh. Have I jogged your memory?"

"Yes, what if I did? It was all completely legal. I will have to check my files, but if memory serves, I bought the object from a dealer who provided the bona fides for it."

"That is very interesting, but as we all know, such documents can be, and sadly regularly are, forged. Unfortunately, I'm here to tell you that this item was stolen from the Cairo Museum. Perhaps you heard of this theft some time back?"

"Well, no," said Mr. Amstutz, "I live in and by a much more ancient past, so no, I tend not to read the papers. They're just depressing anyway." In fact, Mr. Amstutz did not even have a computer. He still typed on an old typewriter, and wrote out his bills by hand, with some help from a long-suffering secretary.

"I see. Well unfortunately, ignorance is neither bliss nor does it exonerate a person when they break the law," said Prester. "So to begin with, you must tell me who sold this object to you, and you must show me the bona fides."

Amstutz sighed deeply, and got up out of his chair and turned around and began rummaging through a gray filing cabinet directly behind his desk. After about five minutes of diligent searching, he found the papers he wanted.

"Here, you can see the bona fides, signed at the bottom by the dealer."

Looking carefully over the document, which had a very impressive stamped seal at the bottom and a guarantee statement saying that this object had been bought at auction from an Egyptian dealer in Luxor, there was at the bottom the following:

FELINE INDUSTRIES
PURRVEYORS OF PRECIOUS PRODUCTS
MSSR. GARRARD LE CHAT, OWNER

And there was an undecipherable signature and date.

Mr. al Haq didn't know whether to laugh or swear. "Did it never occur to you that this document was a fraud, Mr. Amstutz? I mean really, is there such a person as Monsieur le Chat?"

"Come, come, Mr. al Haq. There are many odd names in this world, including yours. I am a busy man who does dozens of deals every day, and when my accountant looks at bona fides and declares them genuine, I accept them. I am not a document expert, my expertise lies in making deals for antiquities. If I have made a mistake, then I am sorry for that, but the object has already been sold, and if you wish to retrieve it, then I suggest you must go back to Mr. Bacon. I have dealt in good faith."

"Mr. Amstutz, as you well know, after being so long in the business, the law is more interested in your behavior than your intentions. If you have bought and sold a stolen piece of antiquity that belongs to the

Egyptian government, then this matter cannot be resolved by a mere passing of the buck, though trust me some bucks will be passed before this is all over. You will be called to stand trial in Cairo, unless we can get this object back. Unlike American law, Egyptian law focuses on the instigator of the crime at the point of sale. That would be you. So I ask you now, if you value your freedom and don't wish to make not only a costly trip to Egypt, but one which will require that you 'retire' there permanently, who exactly sold you this object? Would it be perhaps a man who calls himself El Tigre?"

Despite his long experience and comfort in making shady deals, Johannes Amstutz in his old age had lost some of his courage, and his ability to fight off accusations and charges, false or otherwise. He could see in Mr. al Haq a person much like a bulldog who, when he had once fastened himself on your pant leg, would never let go.

Johannes replied meekly, "Now that you mention it, I believe that is what the gentleman called himself. An odd name don't you think?"

"Not nearly as odd as an experienced antiquities dealer accepting a bona fides as obviously fake as that one!" sneered Mr. al Haq.

"I will indeed return to Mr. Bacon, since possession of the object is what we want, and not merely compensation for loss. But you may be assured that I will be getting back to you, and I will expect your full cooperation as, among other things, we intend to track down El Tigre, run him to ground, and see that the rest of his nine lives are spent in the comfort and convenience of an Egyptian hard labor camp and jail!"

And when Mr. al Haq banged his fist down on the desk in front of him as he arose to leave, Amstutz nearly jumped out of his chair. His secretary, discretely listening in on the intercom, sat back and smiled a knowing smile. The old con artist had finally met his match.

49

"Every Breath You Take, Every Move You Make"

A FTER LEAVING THE HOSPITAL, Issah went straight to the Jerusalem police to report that Art West had been found and was now at Sinai Hospital. He gave as few details as possible, explaining to Inspector Levi the need for discretion, even silence. Levi did not entirely accept or like the idea, but for now he was glad to have one less high-profile case. He knew that Issah, now oddly looking like his brother, had omitted a great deal, but Levi knew the cameraman as a reliable and honest man who kept his sources confidential. Several phone calls ensued to confirm Issah's story. Dr. West was indeed recovering from his ordeal. Officers were dispatched to guard his room. As for Issah, he decided to stay at the station, camera at hand, for the news conference, which would likely be held by mid-afternoon.

Levi's next calls were to Art's mother in North Carolina, then to Grace and Manny in that order. When the phone rang at the Levine flat, Grace's mother, always first to grab the phone, picked it up. "Shalom, Levine residence."

"This is Inspector Levi, may I please speak with Dr. Levine?"

"Yes, but may I ask what this is regarding?"

"Certainly, ma'am, Art West has been found, but is in Sinai Hospital."

Camelia dropped the phone on the desk and went running to the stairway to awaken her daughter who was taking a nap upstairs.

"Grace, come quick! They have found Art, and he's still alive!"

When Grace heard the words she had been praying to hear now for days, she jumped off the bed and raced downstairs to the phone. "*Shalom alechem*, this is Grace Levine."

"*Alechem shalom*, this is Inspector Levi at the police station. I wanted you to know that Professor West has indeed been found alive. He is currently being treated at Sinai Hospital. His condition is listed as satisfactory, although he is in the intensive care ward. Since he has no relative here, I will request permission for you to visit. Just a word of caution. He seems to have been rather badly . . . ," Levi hesitated, "abused." Grace refused to let her mind start exploring the implications of that term.

"Thank you so very, very much." Grace hung up beaming. Her mother hadn't seen her this animated in weeks. After her own phone calls to Art's mother, Manny, Sammy Cohen, Sarah, and Grayson Johnson, she jumped into the car and headed for Sinai.

The hastily called news conference drew the usual cast of characters from the local papers and television crews. Issah had just enough time to run home and change, but now he focused his lens on the podium, where, with usual punctuality, inspectors Levi and Sharansky appeared.

"We will hope to have more to tell you in due course, but we can report that Professor Arthur West of the United States has been found, and is being treated. We ask that you respect his privacy. We know that the same group that kidnapped Dr. Grace Levine also kidnapped Dr. West. As you know, the group calls itself Sons of Allah Brigade. No demands were made or ransom paid for Dr. West's return. He was delivered by an unknown man to the hospital this morning. Because this is an ongoing police investigation, we will say more when we know it." Levi stepped back and Inspector Sharansky told the small crowd that they would not be taking questions at the present time.

Issah wrapped up his filming and shut down his camera, and as he looked over the crowd he saw mostly familiar faces, with one odd addition. A wiry man in black, with a black moustache and a black beret, had just turned to go. Though Issah had never seen him before, the man in black re-imprinted Issah's image in his own mind, vowing to watch every move Issah made until an opportune time, for now he knew that it was Issah, disguised as Ishmael and still very much resembling him, who was surely the mastermind behind the rescue of Art West. Ishmael would not have initiated such a rescue.

50

Grayson's Gesture

Though he was one of the last to hear that Art West had both been kidnapped and then found alive, Grayson was, in some ways, the one who reacted most strongly. Art West had long been his hero and mentor, and were it not for his help, Grayson would not be digging at Caesarea Philippi at all. When Grayson got the news, he went straight to his dig supervisor, then asked for—and received—permission to take a few days off to go see "Doc West." He stuffed his backpack, complete with digital camera to show Doc West what he had found thus far, and hit the road.

With traffic the trip from Caesarea Philippi to Jerusalem would take at least three hours, maybe even more. He didn't care. He'd missed Doc West during these months of digging. Few on the team were familiar with the NT, at least in terms of its theological substance and importance. There was so much to discuss.

Along the way he listened to his favorite praise musician, Chris Tomlin, and said some prayers for Art West. He had a sense that West had been through the ringer, and he rightly worried that he'd suffered both physical and psychological damage. Grayson was pretty realistic about what could happen to someone who had been taken by terrorists and tortured.

The sun was going down over the Mediterranean as Grayson began the climb up the winding road into the Judean Hills and Jerusalem and wondered, "Why does it have to be so hard for God's creatures in this land to get along? It's a small country; it shouldn't be so difficult."

Sinai Hospital sat on a promontory overlooking the northwestern side of Jerusalem. By the time Grayson arrived it was dusk, nearly dark. Munching on his Halvah bar as he entered, he went to the visitor's lounge where he found two people he knew well—Hannah el Said and Grace Levine. "So, how's the doc doin'?" asked Grayson.

Grace stood up and gave Grayson a hug. "How good of you to come, and on such short notice! They have managed to put a cast on his right hand, but his little finger was smashed by a hammer. It's not ever going to be back to normal. Thank goodness he's left-handed! There are multiple burns on his neck and body, but nothing that won't heal. The doctors are concerned that Art experienced some sort of electric shock while wet. They're not sure of the details yet, but it seems to have messed with his nervous system. He's awake and coherent for the most part, but his brain is processing things very slowly. He's pretty beaten up—one eye is shut. His kidneys are bruised. They're allowing us to visit in five minute sessions, and you get the next one, at 8:30."

Grayson smiled at both women and said, "Y'all are the best. Doc's blessed to have friends like you."

"And Art is blessed to have students like you," said Grace. "Mine should be so invested in archaeology and the Bible."

Grayson feared he'd breakdown and cry when he saw his mentor, but he resolved to keep it simple. No questions. He would just tell Doc how glad he was to see him, show him his pictures, have a little prayer, and then leave. How much more could he squeeze into five good minutes?

Despite all his mental preparation, when Grayson came through door 207 he couldn't stop the tears. The battered man lying in the bed hardly resembled the exuberant Art West.

"Grayson, thanks for coming. You didn't have to. I'll survive," whispered Art.

Wiping his eyes, Grayson said, "Man, nothing would have kept me from coming. I was so worried. But let's talk about something for sure positive. I brought my pictures from the dig to show you." Extracting the camera from his pack, he hit a few buttons, cuing the slide show for his professor's one good eye.

"Yes, that's certainly an ankh, and sure enough there's the inscription you mentioned." Grayson saw it as a good thing that Art still remembered the ankh and its inscription.

"This one seems to have an inscription like the one in New York. It's more likely to be non-Christian, don't you think?" asked Art.

"Yeah, the one that ended up in the Met said, '*Caesaris..Flavianis . . .*' and this one says '*divi filii... Caesaris*,'" said Grayson. "Dr. Avner was way impressed with this find, and surprised too. Dude hadn't considered the possibility of an emperor cult presence in Caesarea. But I have a question. Suppose this belonged to someone just visiting Caesarea Philippi, who like, lost it or something? But the other inscription we found about the augury makes it more likely to be indigenous to the site—right?"

"I think so," said Art in a weak voice.

"Well, I'd better let you get some rest, but could I say a prayer with you?"

"I was hoping you would," said Art.

"Lord Jesus, you are the Miracle Healer, and there's a lot that needs to be done for Doc West to be right, so I'm askin' that you drop down some of that healin' balm you have, the very balm of Gilead, and we will give you the praise and glory. Amen."

"Amen," said Art.

Nurse Leibowitz had been about to intervene and get the guest out of the room until she realized the young man was praying.

"No worries, I was just leavin'," said Grayson. The nurse nodded and said, "Try to stick to the five minute rule next time. Dr. West needs his IV changed."

As he rode back down the elevator, it was hard to know how to feel about this situation. Would Doc West ever fully regain his health? Grayson resolved to redouble his prayers and petitions.

51

The Midas Touch

Not everything Kahlil touched turned to gold, but he certainly knew how to handle and sell gold coins. Professor Anthony Lloyd-Jones of Durham University was keen to buy the singular example Kahlil had in his lock box, but there'd been a glitch when he and the good professor had gone to the bank. Kahlil had forgotten that he needed to call ahead. Banks in the Middle East keep odd hours, and often take half-day bank holidays especially in the summer. By the time they'd arrived, the bank was closing. They made a second appointment for the next week.

Kahlil decided to have a morning cup of coffee at Solomon's Porch, and Professor Lloyd-Jones had agreed to meet him "for a spot of tea" before they walked down the hill to the bank. In Jerusalem one was always walking up or down a hill. Like Rome and Istanbul, it was said that the city was built on seven hills, but most of the time it felt like there were a lot more.

Kahlil arrived first, whistling a Middle Eastern tune.

"Well, if it isn't Omar Sharif himself," quipped Sarah.

"We live in hope, we live in hope, nice to see you once more Sarah," replied Kahlil.

"And you. What brings you to my side of town, besides the great coffee?" asked Sarah.

"I'm meeting a customer here before making a trip to the bank," replied Kahlil.

"Oh, say no more, say no more, I'll not pry. Wasn't that just awful what happened to Professor West?"

"Indeed, and I plan to go see him after this transaction. Have you any late word on his condition?"

"I talked with Grace last night, and all she would say is that it's slow going, slow progress. His nervous system seems pretty messed up I guess. All we can do is pray for a speedy recovery. What will you have this morning?"

"I'm feeling a bit adventuresome this morning so I'll go with a white chocolate mocha, please, grande size."

Professor Lloyd-Jones sauntered into the shop.

"Ah, your timing is excellent, please give this good lady your order, it's on me," said Kahlil.

"Oh I wouldn't think of imposing," said the proper British gentleman.

"Not at all, not at all, and this is my town, so if I manage to come to your fair city, you can return the hospitality," replied Kahlil.

"Well, if you insist, I'll have a small pot of Earl Grey please, with some cream."

"Coming right up, but I can tell you now, you are the first and only customer today who wants cream in his tea!"

"Force of habit, force of habit," replied the professor.

When they had settled into a booth up on the second floor with a nice view of the shops and traffic below, the professor said, "Spent some time in Scythopolis the last week, and the more I study the city, the more convinced I am that the Romans had more than a marginal presence in the region."

Kahlil, who loved to hear about the history behind the antiquities, motioned for him to continue.

"I know some believe that the Syrian-based legions that patrolled this region were mostly local conscripts and auxiliaries, but I don't agree. I can't help but think there was a significant Roman presence in the Holy Land, not just during the Jewish War in the 60s, but even well before then."

"Do you know anything about the excavations going on up north in Caesarea Philippi?" asked Kahlil.

"No, I do not, but I would certainly be interested. Anytime a city got a makeover and a Roman name, naturally, Roman influence increased!"

"I heard that they found a Roman priestly inscription up there, and an ankh with some sort of Latin inscription. You have not heard about this?" asked Kahlil. "It was in the local paper last week, a brief piece."

"No, however that is quite exciting, but the bit about the ankh is strange. Why the combination of Roman and Egyptian?"

"Honestly, I don't know," said Kahlil, "but I trust that my friend Art West can some day figure it out."

"You mean the gentleman who was in the hostage swap? I hear he's in a bad way."

"He's in hospital recovering here in Jerusalem, and I plan to see him later today, once we are through with our business."

"Please send him my best for his recovery. I met him once at a classics conference in Durham—nice chap. And tell him that I am here all summer and would love to have a meal and a chat sometime, when he has recovered and is feeling better."

"I certainly will," promised Kahlil.

The men finished their respective coffee and tea and headed down to the Jerusalem International Bank. "*Boker tov*, Mr. Chansky," said Kahlil, addressing his personal banker.

"Good morning to you as well, Mr. el Said. Are you ready to do some business?"

"Indeed, and may I introduce you to Professor Lloyd-Jones of Durham University in England."

"A pleasure, sir," replied the suave and sophisticated tall banker. He looked every inch the executive banker with his three-piece suit, tie, and matching pocket silk. "Follow me," he added.

Having unlocked the vault and watched as Kahlil carried his personal box to a table in the antechamber, Mr. Chanksy discreetly left the men to their business.

Kahlil produced the beautiful coin in mint condition.

"This is indeed the gold Aureus coin, minted during the last and most troubled years of Nero's reign, after the fire of AD 64. Tell me once more the asking price?"

"I have checked with other dealers, for as you know, the price fluctuates just like any precious commodity. I believe I told you $7,000 when last we met, and other dealers this week told me it should be at least $7,500, but I don't want to be unfair, since I have already quoted you a price. Can we agree on $7,000 then?"

"Yes, and I am prepared using my Barclay card here to do the transfer into your account."

"In addition, I have for you the bona fides, notarized, you will see, and dated to 1975, which means you may indeed take this out of the country. As you know, you must show this form at customs, but there should be no problem."

"Excellent," said the professor. "Let's call it a deal." And he extended his hand to Kahlil.

The walk up to the hospital proved both long and challenging, but Kahlil knew he needed the exercise, and he would take a taxi back to the shop. When he arrived at Sinai there was an ambulance idling right in front of the entranceway. Two orderlies were standing by, chatting about something. Kahlil, who was still perspiring a bit from the climb, came up to them and, being curious, asked, "What's happened?"

"Oh, it's a bloody mess," one said. "And really a tragedy. Issah Arafat was a great friend to all."

"Issah Arafat the cameraman and brother of the famous basketball player?"

"Yes, that Issah. He was found gunned down in an alley in Bethlehem this morning with a note in Arabic attached. It read, 'You want to live like Issah, now you must die like you believe he did—too soon.' It was on the morning news late edition just a little while ago. We watched in the lobby here."

"Is he dead then?" said an incredulous Kahlil, who had long known this gentle man.

"Oh yes, quite dead, sadly. Almost too many gunshot wounds to count. He was rushed here on the call from his mother who found him. There will be many at his funeral."

Kahlil walked into the lobby toward the elevator in a daze, debating whether he should tell Art about this or not. When he entered room

207, Art immediately brightened up and said, "Kahlil, old friend, what a great joy to see you. But something is deeply troubling you, you cannot hide it, I see it in your sad face."

"First, let me tell you how glad I am to see you safely on the mend! I hesitate to tell you about what is bothering me, as you are just recovering from your trauma."

"Well, as you say, I am on the mend, at least according to Nurse Leibowitz, and if she thinks so, it must be so. Tell me, what is the bad news?"

"A friend has been gunned down. Truly a tragedy. He was a good man."

"Who?" said Art, afraid to say more. "Who?"

"Issah Arafat, I am afraid."

Shock, panic, and grief came over Art's face as the tears began to flow.

"I should not have told you, I really shouldn't have," said Kahlil, now regretting his words.

"Issah died for me, Kahlil! He died for me!" said Art choking back the tears. "He is the one who rescued me, he and his brother. Issah was one of the most Christlike persons I have ever met. We've worked together." Kahlil found himself wrapping his large arms around Art as he sat there in the hospital bed.

Kahlil, prompted by an old memory from his Gospel studies at the British school in Jerusalem, quietly recited a familiar verse: "'Greater love hath no man than he lay down his life for his friends.' Ordinarily I'd be glad for the Bible's words to come true, but this fulfillment comes with a heavy price. We have all lost a friend. God have mercy on us all," whispered Kahlil.

52

Bad News Travels Fast

THE LIGHT ON THE cell phone was blinking insistently when Ishmael came off the court from practice. Flipping open the phone, he played the message, a message he never wanted to hear: "Come at once Ishmael, come at once," his mother urged, "Issah's been shot many times. I fear he is dead, we're in the ambulance heading to Sinai hospital." Ishmael fell to the floor of the gym and began wailing loudly. Rob came over and knelt down beside Ishmael, saying quietly, "What is it, man? What is it?"

"They've shot my brother! Can you take me to Sinai Hospital? Now?"

"Of course, of course. It'll be alright. It will."

The cell phone rang while Grace was in the middle of a conversation with one of her doctoral students at Hebrew University. It was her first day back in the office and she had a pile of things to do, but when she saw the call was from Kahlil el Said, she figured she had best take it. He never called unless it was important.

"Grace, we need you here at the hospital as soon as you can make it," said Kahlil urgently. "Art has taken a turn for the worse, and it's all my fault. I told him that Issah Arafat had just been shot and killed. I had no idea Issah rescued him from his captors. Now he's inconsolable. I think the doctor is giving him a strong sedative."

"I'm coming! Don't let them knock him out before I get there," stressed Grace.

"I'll do my best," said Kahlil as he hung up.

Ruth Arafat sat in the emergency surgery waiting room weeping. Her husband had been dead for some years. The boys were all she had left, and now she had lost one of them. She called Ishmael, and then her priest from the Church of the Nativity who was already sitting with her trying to comfort her, and praying.

"Father Abbas, why would God let a gentle Christian man like my Issah be brutally murdered like that? Why? He was too young to die."

"I don't know why child, but remember that Jesus himself, the one for whom you named your son, died violently and much too soon, though God used his death for good. In this world we have trouble, lots of trouble, especially for us here in the Holy Land, but we must trust that a God who is the source of life can overcome the world with its disease, decay, and death."

"What will I do without my Issah? He was my comfort. Must we begin planning the funeral even now?"

"This can wait until tomorrow. One day's trouble is enough for now. I assume Ishmael will be here soon and he can help," said Father Abbas.

Kahlil had also called Hannah to come. She quickly closed up the store and hurried to her small car, parked just outside the Damascus Gate. Though both widowed, and already acquainted, custom did not deem it appropriate for Kahlil to approach Mrs. Arafat. Hannah would be the one to offer the family condolences and whatever help necessary.

Grace and Hannah arrived almost simultaneously. Hannah informed Grace of her need to offer family condolences and help to Ruth Arafat, while Grace explained she'd been dispatched to try and console Art. They agreed to compare notes later.

When Grace rushed into Art's room, Nurse Leibowitz was standing by the bed looking none too pleased that Kahlil insisted she wait to give Art the sedative. Grace looked right at her and said, "Hang in there a minute, and we will all get out of your hair."

"Art, it's me, Grace."

Art rolled over in bed, his face red and swollen.

"Now listen my friend, you cannot help Issah by making yourself so upset that your healing is set back. What was it that Paul said about not grieving as one who had no hope? I know you believe that Issah is even now with his namesake, for 'to be absent from the body is to be present with the Lord,' says your Scriptures. So you need to keep the main eternal verities about Issah in mind, and I am sure he did not rescue you in order for you to make yourself more ill—capisce? Issah was a good man. So tell me you have heard me, and then you should lead us all in a word of prayer, in thanksgiving for the life of Issah. Isn't this what you would do when you were at your best?"

It took a minute or two for Art to stop crying and gather himself. "Of course, you're right, Grace, as usual." There was a pregnant pause, and then looking at both Kahlil and Grace and even Nurse Leibowitz he said, "Could we all join hands just for a moment?"

In a very weary voice Art said, "Heavenly Father, Grace has spoken truth into this situation and I agree with what she has said. And so we do now give thanks for the man who was a good Christian, and who indeed gave his life so that another could have life again. Help me Father to honor that sacrifice, not with guilty feelings for things I cannot change, but with a resolve not merely to get well, but to be as good an example and witness for your only begotten Son, as Issah was. We give thanks for his life, which was not in vain, and served you well. Give me the strength and courage to be as brave a witness as he was, remembering the words from the Scriptures, 'Blessed are those who die in the Lord . . .' Amen."

A long silence followed, before Grace and Kahlil said, "Amen." Nurse Leibowitz understandably did not immediately jump in with her clipped orders, but simply said, "It's time now for the sedative, and unless you all want one, I suggest you leave the room."

Amid hugs and kisses, Grace and Kahlil exited as Art was saying, "Thanks so much for being here for me . . ."

53

Ankh-Xiety on the Strasse

MR. GEBURTSTAG COULD NOT know his luck was about to change. Horst Jaeger had dispatched his very top German agent to confront "Mr. Birthday" (which is what Gerburtstag means) about the golden ankh he had worn on his birthday. The unexpected doorbell ring at 9:30 in the morning had Claus scrambling to pull his morning coat into order before striding to the door.

"Yes," said Claus, "have you an appointment with Herr Geburtstag?"

"I don't need one," and abruptly showing his Interpol police badge, Heinz Beckenwald added, "You must let me in now, and I must see your employer immediately!"

The man had such an air of authority that Claus did not feel he could refuse.

"Let me see if Herr Geburtstag can receive you."

"Oh he'll receive me, or I'll receive him at the station," said Beckenwald.

After some ten minutes, Claus returned, looking quite flustered. "Herr Geburtstag will see you now," he said, ushering the agent into the study crammed with books and antiquities. The subject of the investigation sat quietly in his tall maroon chair, smoking a cigarette.

"How can I be of service, Herr Beckenwald?" asked Geburtstag.

Producing a picture from out of his small satchel, Beckenwald handed the picture to Geburtstag and asked directly, "This is you, *ja?*"

"Why yes it is. This must be the picture taken at my birthday party. And your interest in it is . . . ?"

"We notice you are wearing a gold ankh there, which I assume you have in your possession?"

Geburtstag hesitated a bit. "And what if I do? I purchased the object quite legally."

"Whether you did or not, this is a stolen and priceless art object which belongs to the government of Egypt, and I am here to collect it from you."

"But how could you possibly know that this particular ankh is the one in question?"

"That is none of your concern. You will show it to me now."

Geburtstag was backpedaling as fast as he could, because he realized that if Interpol kept snooping around, sooner or later it would become clear that he was indeed the grandson of the famous Stalin, and this would bring him all sorts of unwanted attention. He stood and went to his safe. Turning the dial twice to the right and once to the left, it opened quite readily and Geburtstag handed the officer a small black velvet box. "It's in there."

Beckenwald, holding his picture of the two images, front and back, of the ankh, compared what he found in the little box to the two images and said emphatically, "*Natürlich*, you will cooperate with me when I tell you, Herr Stalin, that this is indeed the stolen ankh."

Geburtstag's pulse began to race when he realized he'd been unmasked and stripped of his secret identity. "But of course," he replied hastily. "I had no idea this was a stolen art object. It should be returned to its rightful owner."

"*Richtig*," said Beckenwald sarcastically, "of course you are completely caught by surprise to discover such a mistake! But be of good cheer, as long as you hand this over to me now without objections or legal actions, I can assure you that we will not be troubling you again soon."

"I value my privacy highly," sniffed Geburtstag.

As Beckenwald rose to leave he added, "If we discover that there are other purloined objects in your possession, then it will not go as easily for you next time—*verstehen Sie*?"

"Yes, Herr Beckenwald, I understand quite well," said Geburtstag, whose pulse rate had risen to an unacceptable level. "Excuse me for not seeing you out. I seem to be a bit short of breath."

"Understandable," said Beckenwald. "Oh, did I fail to mention that there will be one follow up visit? You may expect an agent of the German tax office to knock on your door before long to do an audit."

"Thank you for the warning, err, advance notice," replied the out of sorts Geburtstag.

And, as he left, Beckenwald recited an old limerick to himself. "He returned from the ride with the lady inside, and the smile on the face of the tiger."

54

Short-handed Manny

GRACE'S ORDEAL HAD KNOCKED all of the playboy bon vivant nonsense right out of Manny. He realized he was in love, and he wanted to get serious. Grace, on the other hand, had decided she needed to put the relationship on the back burner for a while.

"I'm just not ready to make a serious commitment," she said over pizza at her favorite place on the edge of the Jewish quarter in Jerusalem. "Sitting in that hole, not knowing what was coming next, made me realize that there are so many things I still want to do, professionally, academically, and yes, personally. But I sill need some time. You know how much I love being with you and I don't want that to stop. But if you can't be content just to date me right now, then I'm afraid I'll have to stop seeing you."

"Grace, I've laid my cards on the table. I love you. I want to marry you. And I realize our feelings must be mutual. That said, I'll try to give you the space you need, though you have to know it won't be easy," cautioned Manny. Having had so much success in his business life, he was not used to coming up short in his personal life.

"Thank you, Manny. I knew you'd understand. They say 'good things come to those who wait,' so let's wait and see what comes, okay?" asked Grace.

"Okay, as long as we are not waiting indefinitely," stressed Manny with a forced smile. The approaching waiter gave them a welcome chance to change the subject, as they assured their server that all was well, and yes, they'd like some more tea.

"So what will your team do without Ishmael, at least for the next two home games?" asked Grace.

"It's a horrible predicament," said Manny. "He must be with his mother, and there will be the funeral. We understand that of course. But Ishamel's like our Kobe Bryant—we're a strong team, but not a deep team. There's no way to replace him. Coach Cousey thinks the best way out is a strong defense until he returns. We just don't have the steam for 'run and gun.'" Grace looked at him blankly, so he added, "Without Ishmael, we don't have anyone to take the ball to the basket and score so quickly—or often."

As a former player himself, Manny had always maintained a hands-on approach to the team, while still giving his coaches all the authority they needed. Knowing his team, he worried more about how their feelings for Ishmael and his family would affect their game. They'd had a lot of success very quickly and the team had become very close. Menachem Cohen knew the team well and what its chemistry was like, and he fretted a lot when things didn't go well.

"I hope it works out Manny. I wish I could be there tonight, but I just can't. I'll be there for Monday's game though, with bells on." She smiled her famous big smile, and Manny realized he would wait for her as long as she needed.

"I'll hold you to that!" said Manny. He understood that she needed to miss the game tonight because of West, and though he had yet to figure out their exact relationship, he knew better than to pry.

55

A Mother's Work Is Never Done

THE CLOSE-KNIT CHRISTIAN COMMUNITY of Bethlehem rallied around Ruth Arafat. Her church women's league took over providing meals for the family, and Hosni, the local funeral director, streamlined the arrangements for them.

Ruth had not anticipated the depths of Ishmael's anguish. She assured him that his brother had gone straight to heaven.

"You must not blame yourself, for whatever it is that you and Issah were doing, it was for a cause that honored God—yes?"

"Yes, I believe it was, *Ummi*," said Ishmael, using for the first time in years his childhood name for her.

"Then, you must be strong now for Issah, and for me. You're the only man left in the family, and I *need* you. I expect you to come with me to church in the morning. I will want to lean on your strong arm the whole day. We will deal with Monday when it comes. All things have already been taken care of by Hosni who has seen to the arrangements. We must be there no later than 3:00 tomorrow to receive our guests." Her voice softened. "And Ishmael, I know how hard it must be for you to miss your games this weekend."

He looked startled at the mention of basketball, but quickly recovered. His brother was dead. The playoffs, and even his NBA chances, had long since left the front of his mind. "Rob told me they'll be wearing black arm bands tonight in honor of Issah. Coach Cousey promised to be first in line tomorrow at Hosni's and I know you've already seen the flowers Mr. Cohen sent. I'm really more worried about what I'm supposed to wear tomorrow?"

"You will wear a proper suit, please. I have picked out a nice gray one with a black tie that suits you. Go into your room and see what you think. I laid it out on your bed."

"One more thing, Mother," asked Ishmael, again sounding a bit like a child. "Do I have to speak tomorrow or Monday?"

"There will be occasion to say something at the funeral if you like. As for tomorrow we will simply be receiving people and thanking them for their prayers and support."

Ishmael was thinking, what could he possibly say?—Issah was dead, and it was all his fault. Ishmael's mother interrupted his reverie. "In about a half hour, you and I must go over to the funeral home, and see how they have prepared Issah's body. We must tell them if we are comfortable with the way he looks and what clothes they have put on him. I have given them several outfits to choose from."

Ishmael had not counted on this responsibility, but he gritted his teeth, and simply said, "Of course." He didn't trust himself to say more. He was determined to do all he could to be supportive, and cause no more trouble.

Issah had been a married man and his wife had chosen to live in one of the few Jerusalem neighborhoods that were integrated with Palestinian and Jewish families. His children attended schools with Jews, though there had been some taunting and cruelty from time to time. Both Issah and his wife, Rachel, had felt strongly about being brave and trying their best to work for change in Israel, showing that Jews and Palestinians could get along with one another. While there were no silver linings in a brutal killing, Issah's mother was without question relieved that Issah had surely not been shot by a Jew. That would have only made things worse. As she went back into the kitchen Rachel was there cleaning the stove.

"Thank you dear; that is very good of you," said Ruth.

"It is the least I could do," replied Rachel. "For I know a mother's work is never done." Rachel was a vivacious and beautiful woman of about thirty-five with deep brown eyes, olive skin, and an infectious smile. She always wore brightly colored dresses and scarves, and she had often been a help and a comfort to Ruth, sharing as they did the same Christian faith. Somehow, Rachel seemed to be the one who was doing the best under these horrible circumstances.

"How is it possible that you seem so calm?" asked Ruth.

"I'm trying to stay calm for the children. I was so blessed to be married to your son for eight years, and I keep telling myself life is a gift, not a right. But I have shed many tears late into the night. In the daytime it is better; best to keep busy. 'I can endure all things in Him who strengthens me'—isn't that what the Scripture says?"

"Ah, this is why I worry about Ishmael who does not know the Savior. We must pray for him now, as he blames himself for what has happened. How could he have anything to do with Issah's killing?! I do not understand it. Why would he feel guilty?"

Rachel pondered for a moment how much to tell Ruth of what Issah had confided to her before he made that fateful trip to rescue Art West. She decided to simply say, "Well it does not matter now. What is done is done. We must just comfort him in his loss, and try and point him in the right direction, not dwelling on the past."

And so these two women began to make their peace with the loss of a son and a husband in different ways, with different understandings, but in it all sharing the same faith and Lord.

56

Johannes's Bark

JOHANNES AMSTUTZ HAD SURVIVED World War II, immigrated to New York, set up a thriving antiquities trade in a cutthroat industry, and waded through countless frauds, cheats, con artists, and thieves. But the ever persistent Mr. el Haq, with that sickening gold tooth grin and regular visits, had indeed rattled the usually unflappable Amstutz. As the sun rose over the skyscrapers and his own palatial loft apartment on the upper west side of Central Park, he remembered his meeting with Curator Bacon first thing today. He would have to hurry to make the 8:00 appointment. No time for his usual scrambled eggs and bacon fixed by his maid. No time to grind and brew his own specialty coffee. No, today he would take a taxi, a rarity for the frugal Amstutz.

The ride over to the museum did not take long, despite some early morning traffic. Amstutz had recently spoken with his lawyer, who advised him to be cordial but non-committal. Above all he was not to sign any documents without his lawyer present to scrutinize every line. This was only a preliminary meeting. The lawyers would weigh in later.

The sun was already shining brightly on the museum steps, and it seemed Johannes was the very first non-employee to enter the building. The security guard, alerted to his arrival, opened the door immediately. Wearing his best dark suit and a blue-and-black stripped tie, he looked every inch the New York businessman.

While he was not greeted by Bacon in any cordial way, the curator did recognize his presence with a nod, as he ushered Amstutz into his opulent office. "Good morning Mr. Amstutz, good of you to be punctual," said Mr. Bacon in a matter of fact tone of voice.

"Good morning, Mr. Bacon. Thank you for meeting me so early. We've done business for many years, and I'm happy to accommodate your hectic schedule."

"As I'm sure you're aware, you and I must resolve this ankh dilemma, and more particularly, we must get the ever present Mr. el Haq off our backs. It's become increasingly clear that you sold us stolen merchandise." Handing over some forms and pictures that had been faxed from the Cairo Museum, Bacon added, "And it appears inevitable that there will be a lawsuit involving us both as co-conspirators to defraud the Egyptian government of its rightful property."

"And what are you proposing?" asked Amstutz. "As I read the New York law, if I believe I acted in good faith, and have the bona fides, I'm not liable."

"Ah, but apparently in this case *international* law will supersede the jurisdiction of state and federal laws. The Egyptians have decided to press this particular case. So we could be extradited to Cairo for a trial. And from what I gather from our sources, the U.S. government will not protect us in this matter."

"What? But we are U.S. citizens!" barked Amstutz.

"Yes, but there is this little matter of extradition treaties between the U.S. and Egypt. Perhaps you will remember the Camp David accords between the U.S., Israel, and Egypt? In those agreements the U.S. became partner with Egypt in various matters, including matters of international law. I am afraid we are out of luck when it comes to claiming no jurisdiction."

Amstutz was dumbfounded. He thought that his lawyers could protect him as usual. These matters were usually settled privately. Apparently he was very much mistaken this time. "How then are you suggesting we make this go away?"

"First, you will have to sign a document saying you made a mistake in purchasing and selling this item. Not terribly painful, and the good news is that it carries no further legal ramifications. Then, you will have to refund our money. Our insurance will not cover this situation. Thirdly, we will return the ankh to the Egyptians once the current special exhibition runs its course. On this point, the Egyptians have been generous. We will recoup our expenses for setting up the exhibit itself. Finally, I will give you my word that the museum at least will not prosecute you for this matter. In the future, you may be sure we will more thoroughly investigate any purchases made from you! Our legal department has prepared a document detailing this arrangement. This is the only way for you to avoid a legal quagmire—not merely at the hands of the Egyptian government, but from us as well." Bacon firmly placed the document in front of Mr. Amstutz.

"We'll just see about all this!" Amstutz huffed and bluffed. "Naturally my own lawyers will closely examine the fine print on this document before I sign anything. We'll get back to you before long."

"Make sure it's within the week." Bacon stressed.

Mr. Amstutz, though furious and fuming, knew he had neither the clout nor the cash to argue. If he was to salvage his business and freedom, he would cooperate. But maybe, just maybe, his lawyer would have a bright idea to save his profits. Hope springs eternal.

57

Funeral for Jesu

ISHMAEL BARELY NOTICED, MUCH less cared that his basketball team narrowly lost game two of the playoff series. He didn't care about their heroic defensive fight or Eilat's buzzer-beater shot to win the game. He cared even less about the respect his fellow Palestinian Muslims, supporters of Hamas, and others still maintained for him. He didn't even much care about his basketball future, or his current freedom. Issah was dead because of him. Rescuing West had been dangerous, but they would never have been in that situation if he had not participated in the kidnapping of Dr. Levine in the first place. A person without hope is the most pitiable, and yet the most dangerous sort of person on earth. Ishmael had no hope of ever seeing his brother again, no hope of apologizing, no hope of ever receiving forgiveness, no hope of reconciliation.

Happy memories came flooding back to him: the day he first beat Issah in a game of basketball, and Issah, rather than sulking had congratulated him; the day Issah got married to Rachel, and had asked Ishmael to be his best man even though Ishmael was not a Christian; the day Issah won a journalism award and gave credit to his brother for encouraging him in the direction of being a cameraman; the day Issah came to him as the sun went down in front of the Herodium and offered a way to start making things right in regard to Grave Levine and Art West. All these memories led to all these tears he now shed. There would be no more times like that with Issah. He was not at all like that slogan seen on some bumper stickers: "Now that I've given up hope, I'm feeling a lot better."

The day began simply enough with a breakfast, which neither he nor his mother ate. Rachel had fixed it all and they all sat down together—Ruth, Rachel, the children, and Ishmael. But only Rachel and her brood ate. Hosni sent a car to ferry them first to St. Catherine's Catholic Church, and then to the Mount of Olives, where Issah had asked to be buried.

As they drove through the streets, people stopped, hands folded in prayer. If they were Muslim, they bowed in the direction of the cortège as it went by. The day promising to be very hot indeed, but for now the clouds over Bethlehem matched Ishmael's mood.

Ishmael had no idea that Issah had so many friends! Manger Square was teeming with a crowd of mourners waiting to enter St. Catherine's church next to the Church of the Nativity. CBS, one of Issah's employers, had sent a film crew, and colleagues from all over Middle East were arriving. By 9:00 St. Catherine's and the Franciscan monastery grounds overflowed with friends, colleagues, teammates, and community. The family arrived moments behind the hearse carrying Issah's closed casket. Ishmael wondered why people tried to make dead people look as though they were alive but just sleeping. "What's the point?" he asked himself. "He's dead and gone."

The procession was made into the church from the cloister courtyard with its lively fountain and gorgeous flowers. The priest, Father Abbas, had arranged everything carefully, and there was a specific order of entrance for the family and then the more distant relatives, and then a few friends. But when Ishmael got inside, he could hardly believe his eyes—there were no seats unfilled, and indeed, there were many people standing in the right and left aisles up against the walls. The procession involved some quiet organ music, and the family was preceded by two handsome Palestinian acolytes who would go ahead and light the candles on the altar. Ishmael flashed back to a much earlier day when both he and his brother had been acolytes in this very church, before he had become a Muslim.

The pallbearers had placed the casket in the exact center under the dome of the central tower. After several instrumental hymns in minor keys, Father Abbas made his way up to the pulpit. "We are here today to celebrate the life of our greatly beloved brother Issah Arafat, who was taken from us entirely too soon through a cowardly act of human violence."

These words shot like an arrow through Ishmael. As a member of Hamas he believed that violence against an enemy constituted bravery, perhaps even warranting a special place in paradise—but never was it seen as an act of cowardice. Now, listening to the priest presiding over his brother's funeral, he wondered, how much courage does it take to gun down an unarmed man? None. The man in the pulpit spoke the truth.

Father Abbas continued. "As you all know, Issah was a faithful Christian throughout his life. He was baptized here in Bethlehem, made his first communion here in St. Catherine's, and became an acolyte. It has been said that you become what you admire. Gentle and kind like his namesake our Lord, Issah admired no one more than Jesus Christ, and sought to be his faithful servant. The good news is that already he will have met his Lord face to face and heard the words, 'Well done good and faithful servant. Inherit the kingdom.' But that is not all. For the Christian, life does not end at death, not even in heaven. Heaven in our Christian tradition is but the antechamber of eternity. For when our Lord Jesus Christ returns, he will raise those who have died in him, and together they will live in the cathedral of new and eternal life here on this earth. Therefore, on this day we do not grieve Brother Issah as a lost soul. He may no longer be among us, but we know right where to find him—in the arms of the Lord. Many of us can't help but feel lost. We have lost the comfort, the companionship, the courage, the wise counsel of our brother Issah, but only for a time. For there will be one day a great family reunion for those who are in Christ and participate in the resurrection of the redeemed."

"What does Father Abbas mean by the resurrection of the redeemed?" pondered Ishmael through a cloud of tears. "Does he mean one must be a Christian to participate in that resurrection? And how did redemption in Christ make one amongst the righteous?" Too many unanswered questions crowded into Ishmael's mind, and he resolved to pursue this further, privately, with Father Abbas.

"Some people say life is too short," urged Father Abbas, "but for the Christian this is not so, because it is everlasting, beginning in this life when one has faith in Christ, and continuing on into eternity. This is why in our burial ritual which is yet to come, you will hear the words that the beloved is buried 'in sure and certain hope of the resurrection.' Now this hope is not just wishful thinking. It is hope based on the historical fact that Jesus rose from the dead those many centuries ago, making our Lord's history a preview of the believer's destiny. As 1 Corinthians 15 says, resurrection will happen for those in Christ when he returns." Father Abbas continued on for a while and closed his homily by expressing the family's gratitude for the community's prayers and food, and a desire that any gifts in Issah's memory go to the church orphanage fund.

Ishmael, taking his turn to stand up and speak to the congregation, had barely managed to simply give thanks for the life and example of his brother, and say how greatly he would miss him, before tears prevented him from saying more. Grace Levine came forward wearing a black dress with white collar and a black hat. She told a handful of stories about Issah and their work together. Miguel Sancho, a CBS director, extolled his colleague's professionalism. Finally, one of Issah's Jewish neighbors from Jerusalem spoke about how he admired Issah's commitment to peace and living together in harmony. But the last person to speak was unexpected.

A side door opened, and those in front who could see beyond the casket let out an audible gasp, for there in a wheel chair, looking thin and rather pale, sat Art West, who had insisted on coming and giving a tribute to Issah. Positioned in front of the lectern, he took the microphone and began by apologizing that he could not address them in Arabic.

"Nurse Leibowitz of Sinai Hospital has placed me on a very short leash." The remark cut the tension in the room. "So I will be very brief. Issah Arafat was not only my friend with whom I worked on occasion, but he was my Christian brother. And never was this clearer to me than the day he came to rescue me from my captors. There are no words big enough to thank him—to express my gratitude to his mother and family—for giving me back my life. It was he who planned and executed my rescue, and for this generous self-sacrificial act, he himself was executed. I have long believed that Jesus saves, but Issah was the living embodiment of this fact, the living witness who put flesh on the bones of that belief once more for me. There is a Bible verse I wish to leave with you that is apropos, a word of Jesus—'greater love hath no man than he lay down his life for his friends.'"

Art choked up. "I know that I am greatly loved because of Issah's singular act on my behalf, and all of you many people here are testimony to how greatly Issah was loved, and we are all, all in his debt, and privileged to be called his friends. And I know were he here today he would have me say, that we must forgive whoever did this to him, for it is only forgiveness that breaks the cycle of human violence and retribution."

Father Abbas could see that there were hardly any dry eyes in the cathedral, and nodded to the choir to begin one of Ruth's favorite hymns, "For All the Saints Who from Their Labors Rest." He pronounced the benediction and added, "For those of you who are joining us for the graveside service we have been assured by the checkpoint guards on both sides that we will not be troubled as we proceed to Silwan and the Mount of Olives."

The ride to the Mount of Olives was uneventful, and as the cortège arrived the bells of the churches of Jerusalem rang out for Issah. It was windy atop the mount, but it could not detract from the magnificent view of the Old City or the glowing Dome of the Rock.

Ishmael thought about the controversy over the foundation stone that sat beneath that dome. According to Mulsim tradition the famous Foundation Stone was the very rock from which Mohammed ascended into heaven accompanied by the angel Gabriel. Once there, he consulted with Moses to receive the sacred prayers, which Muslims recite to this day. According to ultra-Orthodox Jewish tradition the Foundation Stone was the rock of Mount Moriah where Abraham offered his son Isaac in sacrifice to God, and also the spot where Jacob wrestled with the angel. And then there was the Christian tradition that affirmed that it was on this very stone that Queen Helena, the mother of Constantine, had constructed the Chapel of St. Cyrus and St. John which, later became the church of Hagia Sophia, or Holy Wisdom. Three religions, three irreconcilable traditions. No wonder no one could remember a time of peace.

Just below the retaining wall in front of the Seven Arches Hotel stood an Orthodox rabbi with the key to the Jewish cemetery atop this part of the Mount of Olives. Because of his great service on various occasions to the Jewish communities both in Jersalem and elsewhere, Issah had been declared one of the thirty-six *tzaddikim*—a tradition that affirms that each generation hosts thirty-six righteous men whose presence justifies the world's existence. As such, Issah's family had been given special permission to bury him in the cemetery with Orthodox Jews. Issah longed to be buried here because he believed the Jewish tradition that when Messiah came he would appear first on the Mount of Olives. Those buried here would be among the first resurrected to greet the Messiah. Neither Ruth nor Ishmael could think of a place Issah would have rather been interred.

The group assembled near the very end of the top row of graves. Issah would rest among famous Orthodox rabbis, who had many stones laid on the top of their graves, stones of remembrance left by their family members and disciples. The graveside service was brief, but before the casket was placed in the stone encasement box, which had his name on it in three languages (Arabic, Hebrew, and English—Issah, Yeshua, Jesus), Ruth asked Hosni to open just the top of the casket so she could kiss her son goodbye. Holding Ishmael's shaking hand, Ruth leaned over and kissed the forehead of Issah and said, "I will see you at home my son. I will see you at home."

So moved by this gesture, Ishmael crumbled to his knees holding on to the hem of the dress of his mother and he said, "God forgive me, Ummi, forgive me for I knew not what I was doing." Summoning up all her strength, Ruth raised Ishmael up from his knees, gave him a kiss on the cheek, and whispered, "You are forgiven, for whatever it is you think you have done. I know how much you loved him and you did not mean Issah any harm at all. Let it go son, let it go."

Grace, Manny, and several other friends stood nearby as the family filed out of the graveyard. Art's medical team had not allowed him to come, so Grace said an extra prayer on his behalf. She looked around at the stones of remembrance stacked on the tombs around her. These stones would be left unturned, but the Israeli police intended to leave no stone unturned to find Issah's killer. Issah's tale was far from over.

58

Tracking the Tiger, Recovering the Cat

INTERPOL HAD TRACKED EL Tigre for many many years, but no one had been able to stop his ever-changing brand of terrorism. He had the uncanny knack of disappearing, leaving only his vicious smile behind, like the Cheshire cat in *Alice in Wonderland*. He operated all over the world, and yet no one had been able to catch him on a plane or at an airport. He was a master of disguise, adept even at disguising his fingerprints. He was equal parts jewel thief, terrorist plotter, hired assassin, hostage taker, and heartbreaker. It would seem he would have used up his nine lives long before the Art West matter arose.

Growing up in the French region of Morocco, El Tigre had developed enough knowledge of both Middle Eastern and Western cultures to manipulate each to his own advantage. He knew well the Western propensity for being curious, and he knew how to use that against men such as Amstutz and Geburtstag. He knew also that for many Middle Easterners issues of honor and shame far outweighed those of life and death. A true Middle Easterner would rather die with dignity than live in shame. El Tigre fell into that category, but struggled with the implications of suicide, considering it a shameful way to die.

He remained elusive in more than one way; his motivations were unclear. Neither money nor fame seemed to stir him, but his genuine hatred for Western culture (especially in its American form) could easily occupy him for the rest of his life. He might not get the chance. Something remarkable happened when Interpol recovered the golden ankh from Herr Geburtstag. On the reverse side, they discovered a partial thumb and index finger print, *which did not belong to Geburtstag.*

The Cat was napping at home. He'd slept, undisturbed, well into Tuesday morning. He'd turned off all the phones, and even disconnected his radio and television. So he was blissfully unaware of his team's disastrous road show. Eilat clobbered Maccabee Tel Aviv 127–89. The visitors never got closer than nine points. The mighty Maccabee team had been humbled, and there was not a speck of arrogance, posturing, or preening left in them. Worst of all, they had to play in Eilat again for Game 4 scheduled for Wednesday night. The question up and down the country among sports fans was, would The Cat be available to play, and even if he was, would he be back to anything like his normal form?

But when Ishmael awoke, he felt refreshed. The oppressive guilt and heaviness, while not entirely gone, nonetheless had lifted enough for him to have a thought for his beleaguered teammates.

"Mother, where have you put my cell phone?" shouted Ishmael in the general direction of the front room of the house.

"It's here in the empty fruit bowl on the hall table. I can tell you it's been buzzing and buzzing for hours."

"Yeah, I'm sure. If you don't mind I'll return at least one or two of these calls. I'm not going anywhere today, but I was wondering, will you need me tomorrow? I'm thinking about driving down to Eilat. Maybe lend some moral support to my team. Speaking of which, do you know what happened in the game last night?"

"Let's just say you don't really want to know. The paper is on the kitchen table though, with every detail in black and white."

Picking up the local edition of the *Jerusalem Post,* Ishmael read about the dismantling of his once proud team. Now they were 2–1 down in the playoffs, and because of the 2-3-2 format they might not have another home game. Losing two more on the road was a distinct possibility.

Ruth Arafat was a mature and wise Christian woman who took it as a very good sign that her son was thinking again about basketball. He needed to get his mind off the past, and this interest of his was a hopeful sign.

"Ishmael, I'll be just fine. You should certainly go ahead and rejoin your team tomorrow. If I need you, I'll call. Tomorrow I was going to be with Rachel and the grandchildren for most of the day anyway. Perhaps I will just stay the night with them."

"Sounds good, but are you sure?"

"I am very sure. I'll watch the game like I always do, and hope to see you out there scoring."

The phone call came through to Manny Cohen while he was sitting in his deck chair at the resort hotel in Eilat arguing with his broker about an investment. When he noticed the number belonged to Ishmael, he put his broker on hold and switched to the other call. "Ishmael, I am surprised to hear from you. How are your mother and your family?" Manny understood and accepted that at a time like this Ishmael must put family first.

"She's doing remarkably well, and I wanted you to know she's given me her blessing to rejoin the team tomorrow. I thought I'd drive down in the morning, and see what Coach Cousey wants to do with me for tomorrow's game. I realize I'll be a little rusty, but it's only been a week, so I think I am pretty much good to go."

Manny paused and then said, "Everyone will be thrilled to see you, me included."

The drive to Eilat was a long one, but Ishmael decided not to check into the team hotel first. Instead he went straight to the practice facility near the stadium. "Man you are a sight for sore eyes," greeted Rob, as Ishmael ambled into the locker room. "Without The Cat, we obviously suffered a cat-astrophe! Welcome back, man," and everyone chuckled at the lame attempt at humor.

"Thanks, and thanks for all your support over the last few days. I'm here, and I mean to play at least some tonight, depending on what Coach Cousey wants," reassured The Cat.

"What I want is about thirty points, ten boards, five steals, two blocks, and good defense, all before half time—are you game?" listed his Coach, coming up to pat him on the back.

"I may not be *that* game, but I still remember how to play," he said with some feeling. At that moment he noticed the black armbands all the players were wearing in Issah's honor, and he felt the warm tears begin to roll down his cheeks.

"I'll do it for Issah. He would have wanted me to play the game I love so much."

"For Issah," shouted all his teammates, and closed ranks. They seemed whole. They seemed like a real band of brothers once more.

59

Deciphering Apocalyptic Amulets and Ankhs

A RT HAD REACHED THE point where he was sick and tired of sitting in bed in the hospital and even more tired of hospital food and protocols. He was itching to get back to work. His doctors had put him on a walking program to prevent his muscles from atrophying, and he was now doing a fine job of motoring up and down the halls. His tiny flat near the old City of David was looking better and better all the time. Kahlil el Said sat watching Art, back in bed, stew in his juices.

"I mean honestly, I've been here for over a week, and you'd think I was some sort of invalid," complained Art.

"They're just being cautious. You've had a very bad shock to your system, and just because they found no major nerve damage doesn't mean you're healthy," cautioned Art's antiquities chum.

"I suppose I don't have a right to gripe. Let's talk amulets and ankhs for a bit, shall we?"

"I thought you'd never ask," smiled Kahlil.

"Here's what I think I know thus far. Ankhs were one form that amulets took, and as such they were believed to work like charms or talismans. The particular ankhs I'm interested in are Egyptian, but they have Latin inscriptions, and in one case a Latin number—666. They must have been worn by Romans—high status Romans—but would that include Christian Romans as well as pagan ones? I'm inclined to think so. We do know with reasonable certainty that the gematria number for Nero was 666, just as 888 was the number for Christ. And while there's debate about whether their assigned numerical value was based on Hebrew, Greek, or even Latin letters, the references are *not* much in dispute. The graffito I found on the Philae Temple suggests an association with the resurrected Nero myth, and this in turn suggests a reference to Domitian. But who would have dared put such an inscription on a pagan temple back then—some foolhardy Christian? The graffito and the 666 ankh also suggest that literate, high–status Christians were involved with or in some way connected to the emperor cult. But why would they still be involved if they were Christians?"

"I have an answer to that last question," interrupted Kahlil, "for cover, maybe! Remember the stories of how many Jews appeared to practice Catholicism during the Inquisition and even much later than then, while actually practicing their real religion in secret?"

"Yes! That makes good sense of the mindset of a person in a minority and indeed illicit religion. The ankh makes me think that 666 in the book of Revelation must refer to Nero and, more particularly, any later Nero-back-from-the-dead figures like Domitian. The reference in Revelation to someone who suffered a mortal wound but then lived seems clear enough, and the collateral evidence from *Ascension of Isaiah* supports this theory. This suggests that Revelation was written in the 90s. We need to keep in mind that it had meaning for those first-century Christians, and was not meant to be merely a prophecy about the distant future. Furthermore, nothing in these prophecies of the New Testament suggests that Israel will be redeemed or restored before Jesus returns, which means nothing should impede persons of good will negotiating peace in this land, peace that helps preserve the lives of Palestinians, Jews, and Christians.

"Amen to that," interrupted Kahlil. "Isn't it interesting how interpretation of prophecies, or misinterpretation of prophecies, still affects our politics today?"

"Yes, indeed. Hey, I just thought of something I hadn't ever considered before," said Art, sitting up sharply. "Grayson may be right. Whoever upholds the apocalyptic truth about Jesus will be in the line of fire for those who would want either a Palestinian military solution or an Israeli military solution to our problems here. Then too, the whole historical approach to 666 and apocalyptic prophecy will be most bitterly attacked by Christians who uphold a Zionist theology, who insist that Armageddon is on the horizon, and the Rapture just around the corner. In other words, the approach I'm taking to Revelation will displease many Muslims, Jews, and Christians, while pleasing others in the same groups."

Art stopped to catch his breath. His thoughts were moving in several directions at once as he connected the dots not only between the ankhs and Christianity in general, but between the ankhs and the apocalyptic thinking that led to their being inscribed by Christians with things like 666. Gulping down two cups of water from the bedside pitcher, he continued.

"But there's more. Going back to the Book of Revelation, on the one hand John wants Christians to entirely leave justice, including vengeance, in the hands of God, but, on the other hand, the book warns that Christians should literally be prepared to suffer, and if need be even die, for their faith. Look at Issah. He was prepared to sacrifice his life for others, for love, for the truth. And the Book of Revelation simply reaffirms what I'm saying. It's not about struggles of human armies versus human armies. Only Christ is worthy to unseal the seals of judgment or to come in person and judge the nations of the world. We're not worthy or wise enough to do that."

"It is this very theology of love and non-violence and following Jesus which paradoxically produces the most violent response, because if it's true that there are no 'military solutions' to the human dilemma, even here, perhaps especially here in the Holy Land, then those who have staked their lives on plotting, planning, bombs, subterfuge, lies, secret ops, and the like have lived and died in vain, and no one wants to be told that. No one wants to be told that 'those who live by the sword will die by the sword' accomplished nothing good. I now understand why these views are so threatening to persons like terrorists. It implies they're striving against the wind and eventually will be blown away like chaff. It implies that they are not only *not* doing God's will, they're opposing it."

"If the Scriptures are true, and I believe they are, then we must believe that those who wait on the Lord and the intervention of his Son are doing the right thing and will renew their strength. The way of suffering and the way of the cross are the ways of truth, until Christ returns to sort things out for one and all. Until then, Christians should live by the example of suffering love, the example of Issah. I now understand why

I have been a human punching bag for those who are not prepared to wait on the intervention of the Prince of Peace to bring peace."

Kahlil was silent throughout all of this witnessing, and was not sure how he felt about some of it. As a Sufi Muslim, he absolutely agreed that things should be left in the hands of God, and that the real struggle was not against flesh and blood but against sin, powers, and principalities. He could certainly see how those entities and their human agents called terrorists would be entirely opposed to such a message, such a truth. He could also see how militaristic Jews and Christians would not like this message of non-violence either, or at best would view it as an opiate for the people.

"Well, that's enough theologizing for one day," said Art. "How about we order out for some of that Old Quarter pizza, and not tell Nurse Leibowitz?"

"Now that's the most dangerous and subversive thing you've said today," quipped Kahlil, and they both had a good laugh.

60

Grace Notes

THE EMERGENCE OF ART West from the hospital on two feet and smiling was seen as a major accomplishment by the staff at Sinai Hospital. True, he would need to return for neurological checkups and rehab for his hand, but on the whole he'd been deemed fit enough to release to the free world. Grace had volunteered for the privilege of collecting him, and was looking forward to taking him to brunch so they could catch up.

When they arrived at Solomon's Porch the place was packed. Heading up the stairway, Grace and Art waved to Sarah as she mopped her brow and filled yet another order. The increase in summer business had allowed her to hire some help. A young raven-haired Israeli girl with "eretz Israel" tattooed in Hebrew on her right arm ushered them to their table and asked for their drink orders.

"Coffee of the day with cream for me," said Grace.

"Not me, I'm celebrating," said Art. "Bring me a caramel macchiato with whip cream. I'm livin' large today."

Grace smiled, relieved to see Art out of the hospital, and beginning to act like his old self. "So mister, what's all this stuff about ankhs and amulets? Isn't that a bit tangential for a New Testament scholar?"

"Not when were talking about first-century ankhs and amulets, especially when they have inscriptions involving the emperor and the imperial cults. But Grace, my rule this morning is no amulets before omelets. Tell me about you, and what's happening with your man of the world. When's the wedding?" Art laughed.

"Well, that's something I wanted us to talk about," said Grace a bit awkwardly. "I'm not sure where the relationship is going. I guess I'm mainly concerned that getting serious with Manny will totally change my life, that I won't be able to do my research, that I won't have time for schmoozing and working with my friends. I might even have to move to Tel Aviv, God forbid."

"Oh yes," said Art rolling his eyes. "It would be tough living in a mansion, cruising the Mediterranean, or at least sipping a martini at the country club. I could barely tolerate that myself."

"But seriously, don't you think it would make it difficult for me to work at Hebrew University and for us to do some of the joint projects we've talked about?"

"Grace, I think you can do ten hard things before breakfast. And besides, with the new rail line from Tel Aviv to Jerusalem, who says you need to do anything but read on the way to work anyway? More to the point, what does your heart tell you about you and Manny? I can't see you doing the marriage of convenience thing. True, it would get your mom off your back, but would you be happy? Would you feel fulfilled? Do you feel it's something God would bless in your life?"

"I honestly can't answer all those questions yet, but I will say this, just talking has allayed some of my fears. Manny would never insist I stop my work or give up my friends, but I guess I just don't grasp yet how much time and effort would be consumed by marriage."

"Listen Grace, I think now is the perfect time to think about settling down with someone who makes you happy, who loves you. And, not that it matters all that much, but you have my blessing."

"It does matter and I do appreciate your blessing. I don't want to mess up our professional relationship or our friendship."

"Never! After all the things we've gone through together. Besides my mom, there's no one I'd rather exchange myself as a hostage for than you. You're my best friend, and that will never change."

Grace smiled and sighed. She been afraid that Art might feel she was abandoning him. "You know I feel the same way about you, Art West. Now getting back to the original topic, what in the world would I do with my mother who is so set in her ways here in Jerusalem?"

"We both know your mother is a pretty resourceful woman, to say the least. You don't think she'd agree to move to the beach if she had her own flat not far from ya'll? I mean, c'mon, doesn't Camelia love the beach?"

"You make it sound so easy," said Grace.

"Well, as my granny used to say in her good ol' North Carolina made-up vocabulary, 'Why do you have to complexify things so much?'" replied Art. "It doesn't have to be that difficult, does it?"

"I suppose not, but enough about me. I want to hear about amulets, so it's time to order omelets, isn't it?"

"I thought you'd never ask," said Art. "I'm completely starving."

When the raven-haired girl whizzed by, Art flagged her down and Grace ordered. "For me," she said, "I want a sesame bagel, double toasted with low-fat lox spread on the side and some more coffee, please. I've got to watch my girlish figure, especially if I am going to contemplate becoming a bride!"

"You go girl," said Art. "As for me, I want the sharp cheddar cheese omelet with onions and mushrooms, and that turkey bacon y'all serve. And some fresh orange juice, and a side bowl of cantaloupe, and if I think of anything else I'll holler."

"You're not from around here, are you?" smiled the waitress.

"No, I'm from that other promised land—North Carolina," beamed Art. "Should I sing you the Carolina fight song?"

"Please don't!" laughed Grace. She was so glad to see Art back to being his usual irrepressible self. "Now let's get down to cases. What's the story on these amulets or ankhs or whatever."

Art started to make sense of all the pieces. "The story is that the emperor cult was strong, even in Israel and Egypt. The story is that there *were* high-status Christians who got entangled in the emperor cult mess. The story is that they got so entangled they felt they needed to wear talismans to ward off the influence of the evil spirit of the emperor. The story is that the 'cross' as a Christian religious symbol may have begun as an ankh that looked a bit like a cross, only with an inscription on the back to protect the wearer from Mr. 666 and his cult. The story is that this was going on throughout at least the latter half of the first century. It looks like Domitian was indeed the Mr. 666 that John of Patmos was talking about, or at least he was the first one to truly sit for the portrait of the Christian-hating latter-day Nero figure, the persecutor of the church.

"The story is that John of Patmos, far from endorsing some kind of militaristic response to evil, was telling Christians in any and all situations three things. First, that vengeance is God's; leave justice in God's hands. Second, be prepared to suffer and bear your cross. This is the natural reaction of evil to a gospel of non-violence and love and peace. Finally, and perhaps most interestingly, he was warning that no generation of Christian, right up to the return of Christ, should think they were exempt from such suffering and persecution, not even my generation of Christians. There is no escapist theology in apocalyptic literature in the New Testament.

"You see, Grace, many Christians in North America and else-where, especially in the Orient, have bought the myth of the Rapture theology. They have assumed that suffering is neither required nor inevitable; indeed they have assumed the opposite. They think if they are good Christians they will avoid suffering and become healthy, wealthy, and wise. That escapist idea is very different from the message of Jesus about cross-bearing, rather than just cross-wearing. And here's another interesting bit: If I'm right about the ankh being the first cross, the Christians were not wearing it to protect themselves from any physical suffering. They were wearing it for spiritual protection from the 'pollutions of idols,' because at least the high-status Christians still had to have contact with the imperial cult and its activities. They tried to stay out of pagan temples and avoid pagan meals, as Paul and John and James had warned them. But they were not entirely successful in doing so, not least because some of them were part of Caesar's household and even part of the praetorian guard, as the book of Philippians informs us. So, they did the next best thing. They wore a talisman, an ankh, to ask God to ward off spiritual harm from the emperor and his growing cult."

"Wow," said Grace. "And what's the evidence for all this?"

"Well, there are the two ankhs of recent fame. There is the graffito found in Philae Temple in Aswan. Now you have to say, if there was a Christian graffito even in Philae critiquing Domitian as the man back from the Styx, the supposed god-walking-on-the-earth, then this reaction of Christians must have been pretty widespread. I gather from Grayson that the emperor cult had even crept as close to the Holy Land as Caesarea Philippi. We ought to take a ride up there and see what's happening at that dig. While we're at it, we need to see Scythopolis as well. I gather from Kahlil, who was telling me this in the hospital last night, that there is a classics scholar from my old stomping grounds, Durham University, named Lloyd-Jones who has been working on the coins of Nero and the emperor cult in Nero's day. He would be interesting to meet. He seems to think there is evidence even at Scythopolis of the emperor cult."

Grace had long since finished her bagel and was sipping her coffee when this last revelation hit her between the eyes and prompted an instant response. "No way! Right under our noses and next to Beth Shean?" exclaimed Grace.

"Yes way!" said Art. "And we should check it out!"

"You're on. When shall we go?" asked Grace.

"How about tomorrow? My calendar is pretty free about now."

"All right then," said Grace, and she called for the check. She was not letting Art pay for this. He had already paid enough, almost with his life, to get Grace rescued. "I just had an idea," said Grace. "Maybe I could get Manny to sponsor your archaeological work."

"I desperately need a patron. Of course you might have to marry the man first, before he'd get that generous," teased Art.

"Who knows? Maybe I'll kill two birds with one stone."

"Or at least make two men happy in two different ways with one act," replied Art.

And as they left the café Sarah smiled appreciatively at the relief and even joy on Grace's face.

61

Hoop Dreams

SET ON THE RED Sea at the Gulf of Eilat, Israel's southernmost city is an "artificial" city. Israel wanted to have a port city on the Red Sea, so it built one. Some fifty-five thousand people live in Eilat, along with an abundance of tourists who consider Eilat a resort. Created after the 1947 U.N. Partition Plan and built up from nothing, the city became a thriving community, despite its great distance from almost all of the rest of Israel.

Ishmael believed that the strategy Rob had proposed for Game 2 could certainly work in Game 4. It had to work. If Tel Aviv lost Game 4, then Game 5 became an elimination game for Tel Aviv. He wanted to get the series back to their home court where they had a fighting chance.

As the team warmed up for their short practice, Manny Cohen sauntered onto the court. "We've got a lot of work to do down here men, but I have every faith in you to bring this series back to Tel Aviv. Just relax . . . then pummel Eilat!" The team shouted their assent and went back to warm ups. They'd long ago grown used to their owner popping in on practice. Manny paused before leaving. "Ishmael, a word please?"

They walked out of earshot. "I've learned that Interpol is tracking down El Tigre, and that there may be attempts at reprisals against you for whatever involvement you may have had in the Art West matter. Apparently there's a rumor that you were in on the plan with your brother to get West rescued. I honestly don't want to know the particulars, so I am not asking. I am telling you this, however: you're my most valuable player and team asset, so I've doubled team security. The other players don't need to know why. I'll just say rowdy fans have us a little concerned, if anyone asks. You'll have someone with you the whole time you're here. We're too close to both Egypt and Jordan to take any chances."

"Thanks Mr. Cohen," said Ishmael. "I really appreciate the concern." But this led to a new concern planted in the mind of Ishmael. If Omar or one of his other contacts in Hamas thought he'd been in on the ruse to get Art West freed, it could mean trouble for his family. And if El Tigre was taken prisoner, he could be called as a witness. Things were getting complicated.

At precisely 8:10 on Wednesday night the teams took the court and the Maccabees found their fans concentrated mostly on the right side of the arena and behind the goal at the right end of the court. Eilat could smell blood, and Ishmael planned to thwart their plans to move in for the kill.

In the first quarter Ishmael tried to put everything out of his mind and concentrate on the game, but, being a player who mainly relied on instinct and athleticism, he found himself being too deliberate, outsmarting himself some of the time. Once he worked up a sweat and established a game rhythm, he successfully removed anything not game related from his mind. By the middle of the second quarter he was back to his old form. His jump shot was falling, his "turn around fadeaway" was falling, and he'd already gotten two Eilat starters into foul trouble. The score as the horn sounded at the end of the first half: Tel Aviv 49, Eilat 46.

In the locker room, Rob corralled a more confident team, "Okay, we've punched them in the mouth in the first half, but they are by no means discouraged. If anything they're just mad they didn't play better. So we've got to match their intensity in the second half, one play at a time. We need to do a better job screening for Ishmael. Rasmussen, when we get back out there, I want you to set a monster pick to free up Ishmael for a dunk—if Coach agrees."

"Good idea, Shriner," said Coach Cousey. "We'll run with it. Remember, their big star—the German guy Heltmann—has three fouls. If we keep pressuring him, we'll have him in deep trouble by the end of the third quarter. This means we need to feed the post some so he'll have to guard Ishmael and whoever else is backing him down. Be aggressive, drive the lane, and go get 'em. We can do this!"

The Tel Aviv team that charged the court after the halftime speeches believed they could do it. The Cat had a magnificent, unstoppable third quarter. His best play ever may have been when he jumped from just inside the foul line, changed hands in midair and threw down a thunderous dunk over Heltmann. Helpless to stop him, the Eliat center turned it into a three-point play for Ishmael by fouling him. Mission accomplished. The fifth foul for the huge German meant he'd be riding the bench for most of the fourth quarter. From then on, Tel Aviv put its foot on the gas and sped away to a 115–96 victory, completely demoralizing the frenzied home crowd.

The Maccabee players were tired—a good tired, the weariness of winners—but they hardly had time to celebrate. It was off to bed and then morning practice at 9:00. They were tied with Eilat, and now the series was a best of three games. They needed to go all out to win the pivotal Game 5.

62

Grabbing a Tiger by the Tail

A LIFE ON THE run is difficult: always hiding, always watching, always careful, always piling one lie on top of the previous one. Horst Jaeger was an older Interpol agent who enjoyed the vintage American TV series *The Fugitive*. He liked the Harrison Ford movie version of the story as well. When he contemplated the life of El Tigre over the past twenty years, it both astounded and exhausted him. He had been on everyone's most wanted list for twenty years. But he'd finally, finally made a vital mistake.

In carrying the golden ankh into Germany, he had taken it out of its case and put it around his own neck, touching it with several of his fingers and one thumb. Usually so meticulous, he never thought to wear gloves this time, perhaps because of the many cocktails enjoyed during the plane ride to Germany. Now that Interpol had both the ankh and the prints, Jaeger hoped they'd soon catch "the Fugitive."

The forensic lab work shocked more than one person at Interpol. They knew El Tigre as a Moroccan, never suspecting that he came from a wealthy French family with only business connections to Morocco. El Tigre, they'd just discovered, was in fact Jean Jacque d'Villiers, a child of a wealthy vintner family in the Loire valley. Worth millions, they lovingly grew the grapes and produced the wine unique to the region, muscadet and chenin blanc. El Tigre shattered most of the terrorist stereotypes. He had not been brought up in poverty or nursed in a revolution. He'd been born to the branch of the family that ran the

North African wineries, and while his mother was Moroccan, he'd been raised in the lap of luxury and educated at the Sorbonne. So how had he become an international terrorist, wondered Horst Jaeger, and why? Jaeger did not know the answer to those questions, but he did know that El Tigre had just become a known quantity, and now that they'd identified their man at long last, they could begin to look for him.

On the Mount of Olives side of the Kidron Valley stands the little village of Silwan. It has no claim to fame other than its location next door to Bethany of biblical fame. A poor Palestinian village with the usual mixture of Muslim and Christian influences, Silwan does boast a particularly interesting shop: Alexander the Grape Exporters. The small storefront shop does very little local trade, as there is little call for expensive French wines in this impoverished village. No, this operation serves as a shipping portal to Africa and to the East. Wines are relabeled to avoid the staggering import taxes usually assessed Loire Valley wines.

Early on a crisp and somewhat cool Tuesday morning, an unobtrusive little woman accompanied by a thin tall young man came in through the front door of Alexander the Grape Exporters, list in hand. The surly secretary looked up annoyed, unused to customers before 10:00 in the morning.

"Yes, what can I do for you?" asked the secretary curtly.

"I need to speak with Mr. d'Villiers if you please," said the woman politely. "Please tell him both Monique and her son are here."

El Tigre was indeed on site, napping in his suite in the back of the shop. His quarters conveniently opened to the back lot where he kept his Renault for quick getaways. When the secretary came and disturbed his rest with the news, he immediately came to life. His sometime-lover and the mother of his only child, Monique had been detained, arrested, then incarcerated by the Israelis for aiding and abetting a terrorist operation in Hebron. He hadn't seen her or the boy in some years.

Trembling at the counter, Monique stood supported by her son Pierre. She had been released and allowed to see her son on condition that she would lead Interpol to Jean Jacques. She hated betraying him, but she had little choice if she wanted freedom and a life with Pierre.

Jean Jacques emerged through the curtain that separated the front office from the main part of the warehouse, and sure enough there was Monique and Pierre, with tears in their eyes.

"Monique, mon Dieu, how did you get free, and what in the world are you doing here?"

"Mon cheri, you must flee at once! The police have found out your true identity. I've come to warn you. You must go quickly—NOW!" She kissed him on the cheek and pushed him toward the curtain. He looked her in the eye, terror in his glance, and fled, stopping just long enough to gather his satchel and revolver. Hopping into the front seat of his car and snapping on his seat belt, he thrust the key into the ignition, turned it, and heard nothing but silence. Dead silence.

"Going somewhere, Monsieur d'Villiers?" asked Franz Oberholser, who had accompanied the Israeli SWAT team to this spot. "Why don't you join us since you seem to be having car trouble?" Opening the door, Franz dragged the Frenchman from the car, handing him over to the Israeli police. The clock of the tiger with nine lives had just struck ten.

63

An Answer from Amstutz

THE DAY OF RECKONING had come for Johannes Amstutz—he must either put up or shut up. Mr. al Haq had relentlessly returned again and again with apocalyptic warnings of the doom that awaited him. Johannes had grown tired of seeing the little badger with the gold tooth grin. So, having gone to the bank the previous afternoon, he made his way to the Metropolitan Museum where a man with a sick smile, Mr. Bacon, awaited him at the door.

Had he been a younger man, Amstutz might well have chanced the legal warfare. He had a good lawyer, but he knew now that unless he cut his loses at once, he might cut short not only his freedom but the rest of his life. One did not cheat the Metropolitan Museum of Art. Meek as a lamb, the usually irascible Mr. Amstutz took the now familiar walk down the hall to the curator's office.

"No need to drag this out is there?" said Mr. Bacon. "My time and yours are valuable of course. Here is the release notice saying that we promise not to sue you for misrepresentation, and you in turn are giving us back all that we paid you originally for the ankh, plus 5 percent interest as an aggravation fee to cover our legal costs in dealing with the Egyptian government. They in turn now promise to drop the charges they threatened to file against both you and us. You're ready to sign?"

"What choice do I have?" he said, reaching for his pen. "I should thank you, I suppose, for working this out quietly and discretely, and I do hope you'll consider doing business with me again, if the opportunity arises. I apologize for all the grief and aggravation this has caused you and the museum."

"Let this be a cautionary tale for us all," replied Mr. Bacon, relieved to have the matter almost behind him.

A sobered and somber Mr. Amstutz walked down the marble hallway head down. Simultaneously, the little Egyptian man walked into Mr. Bacon's office. The first words out of his mouth were, "Now about the arrangements to send the ankh back to Cairo at the end of August . . ."

64

Road Trip to Galilee

WHEN IT CAME TO exploring archaeological sites, Art West and Grace Levine were like kids in a candy store. They could not wait to look at one thing after another after another. There was something about seeing the actual sites where Jesus taught or where Paul founded a church, or where John of Patmos received his revelations, that gave them a sense of history unobtainable from any book. Behind big black sunglasses, Grace maneuvered her little red sports car toward Scythopolis, one of the Greek cities of the Decapolis, a Hellenistic city league.

In about 63 BC the Roman general Pompey rebuilt "the city of the Scythians" or Scythopolis, next to the Old Testament city of Beth Shean. Colossians 3:11 attests to this. What is interesting about Scythopolis is that it is the only city of the Decapolis west of the Jordan River. The other nine members of the Decapolis were east of the Jordan; for example, Gerasa (as in the Gerasene demoniac), now modern-day Jerash. Scythopolis became the capital city of the Decapolis, and it grew and prospered throughout the Roman and well into the Byzantine periods until it was destroyed by an earthquake in AD 749.

Art and Grace were both interested in this city because of its first-century history and its Roman connections. They had arranged to meet Professor Lloyd-Jones at 9:30 for a quick tour of the site. Apparently the Pax Romana had favored the city, evidenced by its high-level urban planning and extensive construction, including the best-preserved

Roman theater of ancient Samaria, a hippodrome for racing, and an extensive cardo or marketplace. Mount Gilboa, 7 kilometers (4.3 miles) away, provided dark basalt blocks for construction as well as water via aqueduct.

Located south of the sea of Galilee and next to the Jordan, the excavations had unearthed a full theater, a Roman bath complete with caldarium, tepidarium, and frigidarium (the hot, warm, and cool steam rooms), as well as various streets, shops, and temples. But of late the funding had been thin. Reportedly, an excavator, in haste and in desperation for more funding, had mangled a large Roman altar, cutting it in half with a backhoe. Art and Grace wanted to see this altar.

"Well Grace, here's what I think, in a nutshell," said Art.

"Art, hardly anything you think is small enough to fit into a nutshell!" retorted Grace.

"Fair enough," said Art with a laugh. "But it appears to me that we may find some clues at Scythopolis about the degree of Roman presence in the Holy Land in Jesus and Paul's day, and perhaps some clues about the emperor cult as well, and thus, about those ankhs."

"We live in hope," replied Grace.

As they pulled up to the parking area next to the old Roman theatre in Scythopolis, they saw Professor Lloyd-Jones standing next to the kiosk. "Spot on time. Welcome!"

"Thank you! It's great to see you again. Grace and I can't wait to look around!" said Art enthusiastically.

"Perhaps even more so after I show you something." He led them through the turnstile to what served as the site's café and motioned toward a table. Holding out his right hand, Professor Lloyd-Jones showed them the Nero coin he recently purchased from Kahlil. "Here is the Aureus, the famous Nero gold coin from the end of his reign."

"It's my contention that the gematric value of the Latin inscription 'NERO CAESAR AUGUSTUS' on the front of this coin is indeed 666." He paused dramatically, eyebrows raised. "And now, a little something found right here in Scythopolis." When he opened his other hand, there sat another perfect Aureus. Grace's and Art's eyes got big, but they waited for the professor to finish. He then pulled a folded picture from his pocket.

"This is a photo of a replica coin from earlier in Nero's reign. What do you notice that is different?" asked Lloyd-Jones.

"For a start, the later representation on the Aureus seems to more clearly depict Nero as a god—right?" asked Art.

"Exactly," said Lloyd-Jones. "Notice the top of the head on the Aureus, with the rays of the sun glinting off it. Here is a Nero not afraid to be depicted as a god, even on coins minted in Rome. Look at the obverse side of the Aureus coin. Do you see Nero standing there with toga on and halo in place? Note the ritual plate or patera and the scepter. And his wife is also holding her own patera but also a cornucopia, perhaps symbolizing her fertility. The inscription on the back side reads 'Augustus and Augusta.' Both husband and wife are seen as 'majesty,' but only Nero has the spiky looking hair on the back side depicting that he is a radiant Nero imbued with divine light and power."

Art stared transfixed at the picture. "Wow! I knew Nero was a crazy megalomaniac, but he really did have divine pretensions and intentions didn't he!"

"Indeed he did," said Lloyd-Jones. "And he wanted that depicted on the coins that went right round the Empire. It's interesting that he is depicted as if he and his wife are making an offering, hence the pateras, and so showing his own duty to the gods, but at the same time, showing his divinity through the 'radiate' feature. Let's take a little walk through this magnificent site. I have something else to show you."

Art and Grace followed the professor through the Roman theater, down the main cardo and through the Roman baths, which had been beautifully reconstructed, complete with signs explaining their historic importance. Heading further down the street towards tel Beth Shean, which loomed like a giant hill before them at the end of the site, they examined the shops and the remains of a temple probably dedicated to Zeus, or in Roman times Jupiter Optimus Maximus. At the bottom of the hill Professor Lloyd-Jones took a sharp left turn toward a part of the site still under excavation. Several young diggers sat under a tent, sifting and washing small artifacts. Behind the tent, but under its own canopy, stood in two huge pieces an enormous marble structure that looked like the remains of an altar.

"It came from that mound just over there. Thankfully, they have not tried to move it any further than here." He motioned for them to come closer. "Read the inscription!" The professor sounded almost giddy with delight. Grace and Art bent over to look at the Latin inscription, which, in translation read:

ALTAR DEDICATED TO THE DIVINE AUGUSTUS
AND THE DIVINE CLAUDIUS AND THE DIVINE NERO

"Now we don't know whether there was ever a full temple here or not, but what we do know is that sacrifices would have been offered on this altar to these "gods," as a temple was not required to carve out a sacred spot. All that was needed was an altar and a priest and a sacrifice. In short, my friends, the emperor cult was alive and well right here in the heart of the Holy Land in the first century AD."

Grace interrupted the exuberant professor. "Do you think this was a rather secluded spot? After all, it is the only Decapolis city on this side of the Jordan. Would it have been an anomaly? Or do you think we academics have underestimated how wide the Greek and Roman presence was here before AD 70?"

"I tend to think the latter. Something continued to fire up the resistance from AD 6 until the Jewish war in the 60s. I submit it had something to do with the worship of false gods, perhaps even the worship of a historical human being, a pagan emperor. This made the Jewish Zealots see red. Taxation was bad enough; emperor worship was intolerable!"

"No wonder Jesus talked about the abomination taking place in Jerusalem in the temple itself," said Art.

"No wonder indeed," said Lloyd-Jones.

Art began to fill in more of the details. "Anyone who heard Jesus's apocalyptic discourse knew that, for the most part, he was not talking about events in the far distant future, but about things leading up to the destruction of the temple in Jerusalem in 70, things that could happen in a biblical generation of forty years. And indeed he was a true prophet, because he died in 30 and the temple fell in 70."

"Remarkable," said Lloyd Jones. "I had not yet made that connection."

"Of course, Jesus also refers to his second coming in Mark 13 as well, but without mention of immediately preceding historical events. It occurs to me now that his apocalyptic, eschatological discourse and the later reflections of his followers were ways of critiquing paganism in general, and perhaps the emperor cult in particular. When I recently saw the Priene inscription in Izmir, I was struck again by how much the language was like the Gospel rhetoric regarding the good news of a savior and peace to all humans."

"So maybe," said Grace reflecting, "Christian apocalyptic had as its particular object, talking in coded language about how God would judge the pagan emperors and their cults. Maybe their codes including using symbolic numbers, and though Christians were being persecuted, prosecuted, and executed, they still needed to instill hope in one another that God was in control and would deal with their tormentors."

"Exactly," said Art, "Exactly. They had visions of future redemption from above and talked about them in apocalyptic code."

"Like the prophetic code we find in the Sibylline oracles that are Jewish and/or Christian in origin. Even Jesus has a gematric number—888."

The three scholars enjoyed probing and pursuing the logic of a particular train of thought as they toured the rest of the site. Things were becoming clearer and clearer in Art's mind about this whole matter, and now he realized that there were probably various high-status Christians who wore ankhs in various places in the Empire. The ankhs, inscribed with numbers like 666, were talismans to protect the wearer from the spiritual pollution of idols and the idolatry of emperor worship.

65

Championship in the Balance

THE MORNING OF GAME 5 sizzled not just with anticipation, but with temperatures nearing 100°F. Under the watchful eye of his security detail, Ishmael spent some time at the hotel pool. He considered the loose ends in his life, and realized that Issah's death had led him to question almost everything he had committed himself to as a teen. He decided to have a long talk with Father Abbas about resurrection and Jesus, and being with his brother and mother in eternity. He was no scholar, but he knew enough to know that he did not know enough. He flipped open his phone and placed a call.

"*Salam aleichum*, church office, Assad speaking."

"*Aliechum salam.* This is Ishmael Arafat, how are you?"

"I am fine, but I am also speechless—this is The Cat?"

"It is. And I'd like to speak with Father Abbas if I may."

"Wow. Great job last night! I mean, certainly. Just a moment."

Father Abbas came on the line, his voice soft and gentle. "Yes Ishmael, how can I help?"

"May I please come see you about some personal things that have been troubling me? I'll be back in Bethlehem by this evening, and could come by in the morning."

"Why certainly. Why not come and join me for coffee at, say, 9:30 after the Monday morning mass. You know where my little office is?"

"Yes, just down from the St. Jerome crypt, right?"

"Right. Looking forward to seeing you soon."

"You too, Father, thanks for making some time."

∾

Game 5 started with unparalleled intensity. In the first quarter alone, Ishmael launched nineteen foul shots, making sixteen. It appeared that Eilat's players believed that the way to beat their opponents was to beat them up. With forty seconds to play in the game, Eilat had managed to eke out a one-point lead, and they had the ball. On the inbounds play, Heltman threw the ball two-thirds of the floor to a speedy guard who thought he was heading for a sure layup, until The Cat snuck up behind him and pounced. Soaring over the cylinder, he grabbed the ball before it touched the backboard, and came down holding it in one hand. The referee blew his whistle, but then had no idea what to call. The hometown fans shrieked their pleas for goaltending, but the ref signaled Maccabee ball with twenty-seven seconds left on the clock.

"Rob, get the ball to Ishmael, and everyone else clear out of the way!" Coach Cousey shouted with what was left of his voice. "Take your man under the basket, all of you, and let Ishmael operate. Their guard hasn't matched you yet, Ishmael. Don't make your move until you see the clock is down to about five seconds. Got it? Everyone know what they're supposed to do?"

"Yes coach," they all said in harmony.

"Then since they are not going to give us this victory, let's go out there and TAKE IT!"

When Ishmael got the ball, it almost seemed like he was in a trance. The clock slowly wound down, he faked to the right, he faked to the left, and finally he drove the lane. But suddenly he pulled up for his famous fade away jumper over the outstretched hand of the defender. Just before the play clock expired the ball left his hand and seemed to float for an eternity in the air before it dropped perfectly through the net. The whole Tel Aviv team erupted, and the bench players poured onto the floor. The referees had to shoo them back off the court, as there was still two seconds left on the clock, but the desperation heave by an Eilat player at the buzzer fell well short of its mark. The Maccabees had lived to see Game 6 at home, with a 3–2 lead in the series. As the dejected Eilat fans filed out of the arena, Ishmael looked up into the stands, and could have sworn he saw Issah smiling from the bleachers.

66

Caesarea Philippi and the Gates of Hades

THE JOURNEY NORTH TOOK longer than expected, but gave Grace and Art plenty of time to discuss the gates of Hades reference in Matthew 16 that Jesus made to Peter at Caesarea Philippi.

Grace stared at the gaping hole in the rock wall. "Do you think Jesus really was referring to this cave and the stream? I guess even I could imagine the gates of Hades and the river Styx here in this god-forsaken place!"

"I think Jesus deliberately led his disciples here to talk to them about who he was, and who they thought he was, and yes I do think the setting prompted what Jesus said to Peter here."

"I do too. It just makes too much sense. Jesus is saying that the gates of death and the underworld would not prevail against his community, and he could point over there and they would know immediately what he had in mind—not a statement about hell, but a statement about how his community would endure forever. That is a remarkable statement considering how little his community of followers was in his own day."

"Sure, but look at all these niches carved out of the sheer rock face. Some were for statues of the Greek gods, for example, of Panyas, which was the original name of the city, but some surely were also added when Herod Philip had this city renamed in his own honor, and that of Caesar."

"Are you thinking what I am thinking—that maybe there was statue of Tiberias, the so called 'divine son of Augustus' in one of those niches?"

"Exactly," said Art. "You just read my mind."

"Nope, it's just that great minds think alike," smiled Grace.

"But," said Art, "when Peter confessed Jesus to be the Jewish Messiah, and he accepted that acclamation, he added that he would be that Son of Man figure who would die and rise again. And it seems to me that if Jesus really said such a thing, it would be hard to miss the polemic against the pagan images right there next to them. He would be asserting that he was the one about which good news and divine tales would be chronicled, and not any of those pretenders over there in those niches."

"Well, that's possible," said Grace, "But whatever else you say, this place is a lesson in how texts only have meaning in context, in this case the physical and archaeological context."

"How right you are," replied Art. After examining the niches in the rock face more closely, they headed up the hill to the archaeological dig. Grayson Johnson met them, trowel in hand.

After hugs all around, Grayson said, "It sure is better to see you standing, than lying down in that hospital bed. I see you still have a cast on your hand."

"Yep, but it's on the mend. I don't know how well I'll be able to use it when the cast comes off. Thank God I'm left-handed. Grayson, I know you're eager to show us around. Why don't we start with the inscription?"

Grayson took his friends over to the director's tent and opened the flap hollering, "Scholars in the house!"

Amos Avner, looking tanned and very relaxed, was enjoying some Haifa orange juice. He stood, shook their hands, and offered his guests the folding chairs.

"I'm afraid it's the best I've got to offer, but I do have some wonderful orange juice, fresh squeezed and cold, if you like?"

"Oh, we would like!" said Grace.

As they sat and sipped, Dr. Avner began to tell his tale of the summer dig. "Let me start by saying that I really did not expect to find what we found here at all. I thought perhaps we might find a Greek statue or maybe some later Crusader ruins from up on top of the hill, but I didn't expect to find a Roman inscription! I'll show it to you in a bit, but here is what it says." He handed them a photo. Art quickly translated the Latin: "Auguries for the Emperor were taken by me, Publianus, the pontifex, and were good. He is our lord and our god."

"Which emperor is the immediate question!" exclaimed Art.

"Which emperor indeed, but here's where Grayson's find may add a little clarity. That piece of ankh had an inscription reading '*divi filii . . . Caesaris Augusti.*'"

"And that," urged Art, "surely must be a reference to someone in the Julian, not the Flavian, dynasty. Maybe even Tiberius, don't you think?"

"That seem plausible to me," said Amos, "but you two are the experts in things Roman and Christian, not me. It is true however that the Sea of Galilee at some point came to be called the Sea of Tiberias, named after the city Herod Antipas built there."

Art noticed that Grayson was fidgeting at the edge of the tent, and could barely contain himself. Suddenly he burst out, "But there's more! When I put the little ankh under a microscope I noticed there was something else etched on a part of the cross piece, the letters PUB."

"So you think," said Grace, without hesitation, "that this ankh might have belonged to Publianus, who wore the ankh as a sign that he hoped to be blessed by the divine Caesar, the son of Augustus?"

"Bingo," said Grayson. "I couldn't have put it better, which is why you are the prof, and I am the trowel man."

Art thought about all this for several moments. "If we put this together with the evidence from Scythopolis, and the two Cairo ankhs with Latin inscriptions, I think we've got our proof that the Romans adapted ankhs as talismans, and that Christians and the emperor cult faithful alike wore them for either blessing or protection, or both. It also means that both Julian and Flavian emperors were claiming divine honors, and that the birth of the emperor cult goes back before Nero and in the east was already present here in the time of Jesus."

"So," jumped in the ever-eager Grayson, "Jesus was saying that he was the real deal and these other dead emperors were just parodies, cheap imitations."

"One more thing," mused Art. "The story of Isis and Osiris is a story about a dying and possibly rising god, even though the characters in the story are purely mythical or fictional. Could Jesus have actually been suggesting that those Egyptian stories were just vague foreshadowings of who he would become?"

"Very interesting to consider," offered the host. "Why don't I take you and show you the inscription and ankh themselves."

"Sounds great," they said in unison.

As they left Dr. Avner's tent, Art's mind flashed back to another 'son of man,' Issah, who had given his life for Art. The professor whispered to God, "May he rise again like the first Son of Man."

67

Abbas, Father

THOUGH SMALL AND CRAMPED, especially for a basketball player of Ishmael's height, Father Abbas's office still had an inviting warmth to it. Candles burned in the little stone alcove adorned with a cross, and the room smelled of fresh-brewed coffee. The priest offered Ishmael a cup filled to the brim. The rich dark aroma wafted into Ishmael's nostrils and set him immediately at ease.

"Father, please forgive me in advance if I don't ask my questions quite right," began Ishmael.

"There are no wrong questions here my friend, only two men on a journey towards God," replied Father Abbas.

"Okay, but I guess Issah has already arrived at the end of the journey?"

"Actually no, Ishmael, he hasn't. He's in an in-between state. Right now his spirit is with the Lord, but he awaits the day of resurrection when Christ returns and all true believers are conformed to the resurrected image of God's Son."

"Did Jesus really die on the cross?" asked Ishmael. "Many of the mullahs say no, that God would not allow that to happen to a good man and prophet like Jesus."

"Let me ask you a counter question, though it is a delicate one. Was Issah a good man?"

"Of course! And a far better person than I am!"

"And you have no doubt he went to be with God?"

"None. Of that I feel very sure."

"Good. Then hear me when I say that God allowed him to suffer a horrible death as we all painfully learned. Why should it have been different with Jesus himself?"

Ishmael thought about this for a long while. He sat rubbing his forehead with his large hand, and finally looked at the priest. "I see your point. But then you are saying God reversed that horrible tragedy in Jesus's life by resurrection, and he will do the same for my brother?"

"Exactly, my son, exactly."

"But what if I want to be part of that life of Issah's when the resurrection comes? What if I want to ask his forgiveness and see his smile once more? What must I do to come to that good place and time?"

"Well Ishmael, it is not something you must *do*, it is something you must be. You must be born again and accept Jesus as your savior. As you know, that can be costly, especially in Palestine. We're marked with the sign of the cross, and to many this is seen as a death sentence."

"But one has to die to be raised from the dead, right?"

"Right."

"And we are all going to die some day anyway—right?"

"Right, unless Jesus comes back quite soon."

"Then if I accept that Jesus died and rose, then why should I be afraid of death anymore? Why should I run and hide and make my life decisions on the basis of that sort of fear?"

"Fear of death is a natural thing for a mortal person, but you're right that if you've been given the gift of new birth and with it everlasting life, then you have nothing ultimately to fear. God and his power of life ARE greater than our fear and greater than death."

"Then Father, I'd like to become a follower of that first Issah please, and in due course be baptized. And I wonder about something else. Can I choose a new name, a Christian name, at baptism?"

"Yes, did you have one in mind?"

"I think I'd like the name Yacov, the name of the first brother of Jesus, who did not believe until after Jesus rose from the dead and appeared to him. I know the English is Jacob or even James, but I prefer the biblical name Jacov. That way, I can still be Issah's brother even into eternity, in name as well as in nature."

"So shall it be, my son. When shall we do this?"

"I can't imagine doing this without my mother, and I still have a basketball tournament to win, so how about next Friday? Oh, and one more thing—could we do it at the Jordan instead of in the church, like the original baptisms by Jesus's cousin?"

"Absolutely! I'll make all the arrangements."

Small tears of repentance and joy slid down the cheeks of Israel's most famous basketball player.

"Let me pray now for you," said Father Abbas, placing his hands on Ishmael's head. "Heavenly Father, you alone can give new spiritual life, but I ask today that as Ishmael was once physically born, that even now he might be spiritually reborn into new and everlasting life. We ask that you would place your protection around him especially during this time of transition in his life, and that you would bind up his and his family's wounds as they still mourn the passing of Issah, as do we all. Most of all we ask that next Friday will be a special day, a very special and joyful day on which we welcome a new Christian into the world whose name shall be called Yacov, henceforth."

Ishmael looked up at the priest. "Amen, may it be so." The candles in the room all flickered but did not go out, as if a mighty wind had just blown through the place.

68

The Trial of the Tiger, the Triumph of the Cat

INTERPOL DID NOT NEED extradition papers for El Tigre because he was wanted for murder in the Holy Land. The tricky bit, however, was that he had shot Issah in Bethlehem, though Issah lived in Jerusalem. Here, it was determined that Israeli law must take precedence for any citizen of Jerusalem who paid taxes in Jerusalem and to the state of Israel, as Issah had done. This in some ways made it easier, for Israeli law was in no way lenient or ambiguous when it came to terrorists murdering innocent people.

El Tigre knew he was in a desperate situation, and used his one phone call to contact the family lawyer in Paris. Offering little comfort, his attorney confirmed that he would have to remain in Israeli custody and be tried there. But in an interesting twist, he did promise to file a motion that Jean-Jacques be tried as a French Moroccan, not as a Palestinian or Israeli, in the hopes of more lenient sentencing. The Moroccan embassy, however, wanted nothing to do with El Tigre and refused to file an amicus brief on his behalf. El Tigre had worn out his welcome in Morocco when he had been involved in the murder of a famous professor of world religions at Moulay Slimane University. The professor had dared to say in his classroom that Islam was wrong about the death of Jesus, that Jesus had actually been crucified.

The trial was also expedited to avoid any immediate reprisals from Hamas. The press releases had simply said that a Frenchman named

Jean-Jacques d'Villiers would stand trial for the murder of an unnamed citizen of Jerusalem, unnamed to protect Issah's family. Hamas had no more knowledge of who that was than almost anyone else in Israel, and the trial received no more than a brief mention on the back page of the *Jerusalem Post*. Even to his closest associates in Hamas, El Tigre had never disclosed his real identity. They all thought he was a Moroccan, with a Moroccan name.

The morning of his trial dawned cloudy, but hot, and his basement jail cell provided no comfort. After a careful screening, his clothes had been returned for the trial. El Tigre had rationed his breakfast bottle of water, knowing that he might not see another for hours. Dressed and waiting in his cell, he made sure no one was watching. He removed his left shoe, a simple loafer, and twisted the bottom of the heel until it slid open revealing a small packet of white powder. Relieved, he had a hard time believing that no one had discovered it. Perhaps they had and hoped he would use it thus saving the state of Israel time and money. Quickly pouring the powder into the water and shaking up the bottle, El Tigre drained the bottle to its bottom and then lay down and waited. It did not take long. The strychnine attacked his nervous system within moments, blocking all neural impulses. A series of violent muscle spasms culminated in his death before Inspector Mordecai reached his cell. El Tigre's face was badly contorted into a sick grin, and his form was doubled over in the fetal position. This wild cat would never prowl again.

Ishmael arrived at the practice court in Tel Aviv on Tuesday morning, sporting a face full of stubble and a new air of ease and confidence. For the moment, the sadness had gone. Despite their best efforts, they'd not been able to put away the pesky and persistent Eilat team on Monday. Game 6 had gone down as a mighty defensive struggle, which Eilat won 93–90 in overtime. It was now down to a Game 7, winner take all.

Manny was so nervous, he couldn't eat anything, but he greeted his team with a smile and said, "Tonight, we can make history. Tonight, we will all give everything to become champions."

"Don't worry," said Ishmael. "Don't you know it's the Year of The Cat?" And everyone smiled. It was good to have their superstar back, joking and in a sporting mood.

From the tip-off, it quickly became apparent that the referees were going to let the teams play. They were not going to call a zillion fouls tonight. This strongly favored the more agile Maccabees, especially Rob and Ishmael. They owned the court with their run-and-gun style of play, and by halftime the score rose to an astounding 62–54 lead. The Cat posted twenty points with only one foul. There was so much adrenaline flowing that none of the Tel Aviv players much wanted the halftime rest.

The second half was no different. It was Ishmael from the corner for a three-pointer; Ishmael down the lane for an old-fashioned three points; Ishmael with the thunder dunk over Heltmann; Ishmael with the behind-the-back pass to Rob for the layup. By the fourth quarter, the demoralized Jaguars, down by thirty, would have raised a white flag if they could have. During the last five minutes of the game Coach Cousey substituted liberally, and all the starters joined the crowd singing, "We will, we will rock you" and "We are the champions." When the game was over, and the requisite champagne—ironically from the d'Villiers vineyards—poured over every head, including Mr. Cohen's, the press got their time with The Cat. "And where will you go now? Disney World?" they asked.

"Nope," said Ishmael, "I'm heading to North Carolina." But he refused to elaborate.

Soon after, the commissioner of the Israeli Basketball League presented Ishmael with the MVP trophy. At that precise moment the old Al Stewart classic "The Year of the Cat" poured from the arena speakers. Ishmael's mother Ruth and his sister-in-law Rachel came down from the stands for the presentation, and stood with him for hundreds of jubilant photographs. It was quite a contrast from a week ago when they buried Issah. But what the public did not know is that the Arafats had a double reason to be jubilant—a new Christian was about to be born into the family.

69

An Engaging Conversation

L E JAZZ HOT OVERFLOWED with ecstatic high-society Maccabee fans, and erupted when the owner of their favorite team walked through the doors an hour after the game. Manny was riding high on the wave of congratulatory notes, thrilled with the IBA trophy. But the real prize he wanted more than any other was the hand of Grace Levine in marriage. He had bought a suit, gray with metallic thin blue stripes, which would reflect under the neon light of the restaurant. He was stylin' or at least he thought so.

Grace, on the other hand, had dressed simply in a pale yellow shift. After a light dinner involving some marinated steak kebabs and wine, they joined the other revelers on the dance floor as the DJ heated up the room with some Sade. When they returned to the table, much to Grace's surprise, a vase of her favorite aromatic yellow roses awaited her. She read the attached card, blushed a little, and said, "Can we talk?"

Manny didn't know if he'd ever been this nervous. He had a gigantic diamond burning a hole in his pocket and wondered what there was to talk about.

"Manny dear, is this déjà vu? Haven't we already talked about this? I'm still not quite ready to get married, so before you get down on your knees and embarrass us both, I have a suggestion. Why don't we take the next year to be sure? Not date anyone else. You know, 'go steady,' as they say in the States. No pressure. Then we'll decide."

Manny had never met a woman like Grace who could so take charge of a situation, and he had no vocabulary, nor any plays in his play book to respond to this counter offer. The card had asked her to elope with him to Venice.

After several awkward minutes of silence, Manny finally looked up and said, "Grace, you drive a very hard bargain, to say the least. I do love you and I do want to marry you. Right now, I accept your terms. He pulled the velvet box from his coat pocket, flipping it open. "Let's call this our 'going steady' ring."

Grace knew this was hard on Manny, but she was not ready for the full court press yet. Grace was overwhelmed with the brilliance of the stone. She looked at Manny and realized again how much this all meant to him—and felt truly sorry about her conflicting emotions. "Just kiss me," she said. She did not have to ask twice. The DJ, seeing them kiss, cued Bill Evans' rendition of "Tenderly" and the couple became oblivious to everyone around them, as the kiss seemed to last forever.

70

The Emperor's Old Clothes

Grace invited Art to give a lecture at Hebrew University entitled, "Ankhs, Amulets, and the Emperor's Old Clothes," sharing some of the findings of his summer research in Egypt, Turkey, and Israel. That very morning Art had sent Walid Serwassy in Cairo a fax confirming the authenticity of the stolen ankhs and their importance in reflecting both a positive and a negative reaction to the emperor cult. The matter had been resolved without disgracing anyone, including the curator of the Metropolitan Museum, and Art was glad about that. Too often what happened was that one or another party chose to play the shame and blame game. This time diplomacy and persuasion had triumphed without giving to the world and its media the sort of negative publicity no museum, whether in Cairo or in New York, needed.

Since the lecture was free and open to the public, Kahlil and Hannah closed the shop, Sarah left the café in the care of her new assistant manager, and Camelia, Dr. Avner, and Professor Lloyd-Jones joined them. Even Ishmael and his mother had come.

Worried about effectively conducting the PowerPoint presentation with only one working hand, he accepted Grayson's offer to help. Clad in his lone suit, ponytail and a tie-dyed bow tie, the graduate student stood at the ready, beaming from ear to ear. This was his moment in the "shade" of Doc West so to speak, having been out in the sun all of the last two months digging.

Grace, in her favorite white and black outfit, carefully coiffed hair, and high heels, approached the podium. "Many of you had the pleasure on various occasions to hear one of the world's preeminent New Testament scholars, Dr. Arthur West, who really needs no introduction at this university. This summer we are pleased to have him debut his lecture on Imperial Period ankhs and their function for pagans and Christians. Please give a warm welcome to my friend and colleague, Dr. West."

As the applause rang out, Grace hugged Art as he came across the platform. He caught a glimpse of her hand. "Wow, looks like someone loves you like a rock—to borrow a phrase." Grace cracked up and said, "Go get 'em mister, we'll discuss that later."

"I am especially pleased to have the help today of my assistant, a budding scholar, Grayson Johnson." Grayson loped across the stage feeling very self-conscious under the lights, gave a little anemic wave to the audience, and took the clicker. Art activated the screen and immediately the audience saw ankhs and amulets.

"To the average person today, scarabs and ankhs and amulets are just some sort of ancient jewelry or keepsakes. They may be interesting to look at but they are mute objects with no particular power or spiritual force. This is not, however, how the ancients viewed such objects. Over the course of the last couple of months I've been in Egypt, Turkey, and Israel, and I can tell you it has been a journey of discovery in many ways. One of the most important things I have learned is that even small amulets or ankhs or scarabs can indeed contain a wealth of information about the ancient world and its beliefs.

"The ankh was of course an Egyptian symbol of life. It can be seen in many of the hieroglyphic paintings and draws from before and during the NT era. But some ankhs have more 'life' to them than others, it would appear, and the three I am mainly talking about this morning all have inscriptions on the reverse side, inscriptions in Latin. This is odd, to say the least. Why wouldn't the inscriptions be in hieroglyphics or Greek? Inquiring minds want to know.

"Even more surprising is that the inscriptions read as follows: 'DCLXVI' on one, '*Caesaris . . . Flavianus*' on a second one, and finally, on one only recently discovered by Grayson Johnson himself at the dig at Caesarea Philippi, '*divi filii . . . Caesaris Augustus*.' Two of these ankh inscriptions refer clearly enough to one or another of the emperors.

The third one is the gematric or symbolic number 666. Now that number should ring a bell with you all. It is the symbolic and polemical number used by Christians to refer to an emperor. It is not a number a devotee or underling of the emperor would ever use of the emperor. So now we have a quandary. Are we being told that both followers and opponents of the emperor wore ankhs with inscriptions in them, and if so, why? Here is a clear picture of the now-famous golden ankh, which has the 666 on the back of it. Notice that it is something meant to be worn around the neck, and notice as well it bears a resemblance to the Christian cross. Keep those things in mind.

"Here we need to bring into picture perhaps the most notable or notorious of all the first century emperors; of course, I am referring to the last of the Julian emperors, Nero himself. Here is a very famous coin indeed, the golden Aureus minted between AD 64 and 68.

"Doctor Lloyd-Jones, a classics professor from Durham University, kindly sent me his digital picture of this coin. Notice not merely the image of Nero on the front of the coin but also the golden rays on the top of his head, and if you look at the obverse side Nero is the figure on the left with the apparently punk-rock spiky hair!

"Returning to the subject at hand," said Art with a grin on his face, "the sun rays or 'radiate' indicate that the Emperor is depicting himself as being suffused with divine light and power, indeed, that he should be viewed as amongst the divine. And this brings me to my first major point. Coins and art objects were used as propaganda, specifically for religious propaganda, in antiquity. The Emperor was especially good at using such things, but apparently others did as well.

"At the beginning of my summer explorations I was in the southern part of Egypt at a famous complex that includes a temple built by Romans, but with a portion built for the second-century Emperor Trajan. Here is a picture of the one I have in mind called the Philae Temple.

"There are a lot of reasons to find this temple interesting, but my main focus this morning is on a little graffito which was pointed out to me by my guide. The graffito reads:

> He is many men and no man, towering like the sphinx, dead and alive, but who knows what he thinks? Back from the Styx; 666.

"Now this graffito refers to the famous legend about Nero coming back from the dead to haunt and indeed take over again the Roman Empire. The gematric number has been rightly said by many scholars to be the numerical value of Nero's name written in Latin, or Greek or Hebrew. Nero is Mr. 666, who died mysteriously and then was believed to be coming back from the Styx. There were in fact two or three imposters between AD 68, when Nero died, and 90, all of whom claimed to be Nero, but they were eclipsed by one figure who actually was an emperor, namely Domitian. He was seen as Nero back from the dead first because of his persecution, prosecution, and execution of Christians. But there is a second reason. He demanded that he be called and treated as '*Deus et Dominus Noster*'—'Our Lord and Our God.'

"Yes, two real historical human figures were hailed as gods in the first century: Jesus of Nazareth and at least one of the emperors. So far as I can tell, these two rising religious movements had quite similar messages about a god who walked upon the earth bringing peace and salvation to one and all. Consider for a moment the Priene inscription that I examined while I was in Izmir in Turkey.

> It seemed good to the Greeks of Asia, in the opinion of the high priest Apollonius of Menophilus Azanitus: "Since Providence, which has ordered all things and is deeply interested in our life, has set in most perfect order by giving us Augustus, whom she filled with virtue that he might benefit humankind, sending him as a savior [*sôtêr*], both for us and for our descendants, that he might end war and arrange all things, and since he, Caesar, by his appearance [*phanein*] (excelled even our anticipations), surpassing all previous benefactors, and not even leaving to posterity any hope of surpassing what he has done, and since the birthday of the god Augustus was the beginning of the good tidings for the world that came by reason of him [*êrxen de tôi kosmôi tôn di auton euangeliôn hêgenethlios tou theou*]," which Asia resolved in Smyrna . . .

"Now my concern is with the end of the inscription, which speaks of the birth of Octavian as the birthday of a god. But note especially that this birthday is hailed as the 'beginning of the good news' about a savior who would benefit all humankind and end war. This should sound familiar, because similar claims are made about and for Jesus in the Gospels. In other words, the rhetoric of the emperor cult was in a duel with the rhetoric of the Christian gospel; both were talking about real historical figures now seen as deities and worshiped as such.

"It has been conventional up until now to suggest that the emperor cult really didn't get going, if we are talking about the worship of a living emperor, until the mid-first century AD. Prior to that, the spirit of the deceased Emperor Augustus was venerated or worshipped. It would appear this is not quite correct. For one thing, the Priene inscription is from 9 BC, whilst Octavian was still alive. For another, there is the evidence of the ankh found at Caesarea Philippi. Dr. Avner has rightly deciphered this inscription as follows:

> Auguries for the Emperor were taken by me, Publianus, the pontifex, and were good. He is our lord and our god.

"Notice two things. First, there is the reference to the emperor as lord and god. Secondly, the priest in question is taking auguries as the pontifex in the emperor cult.

"I can only conclude that the emperor cult was right here on the edge of the Holy Land, possibly as early as the first century AD. In addition, the good Professor Lloyd-Jones also showed me a Roman altar found at Scythopolis, on this side of the Jordan. The altar has a clear and large inscription, which reads:

ALTAR DEDICATED TO THE DIVINE AUGUSTUS AND
THE DIVINE CLAUDIUS AND THE DIVINE NERO.

This does not prove there was a whole emperor cult temple there, but an altar indicates that worship was indeed offered to such Roman rulers at least on the periphery of even the Holy Land in the first century. The emperor cult, like Christianity, was on the rise, and competing for some of the same clientele, especially in the Gentile world. So let us return if we may for a moment to the golden ankh with 666 on it.

"This cross-like object, like most amulets or ankhs in antiquity, was believed to have a certain aura or power to bring blessing or ward off curses. The person who wore this had 666 inscribed on it, the same as the number on the Philae Temple, the same as the number found in the book of Revelation. I'm sure that 666 was the code name for either the Emperor Nero or Domitian or both. Remember that Domitian was seen as the second coming of Nero. But what sort of Christian could afford and wear such a golden ankh? Clearly a high-status person—but what else can be said?

"Here we are in the realm of conjecture, but the letter of Paul to the Philippians, probably written from Rome, tells us of Christians who were part of the praetorian guard and part of Caesar's household. We hear of the latter in Romans 16 as well. My suggestion would be that Christians in those high circles might well need protection from the emperor cult's negative spiritual influence, as they might well have been required to attend worship in such a temple. Remember, Gentile Christians were not exempt, as Jews were, from the requirement of worshipping the emperor. It is entirely probable that there were high-status Roman Christians who found themselves in a difficult situation. In fact, we know this happened because Paul, in 1 Corinthians 8–10, warns his audience about going to idol feasts in pagan temples where demons lurked. Some Christians listened better to Paul than others. Some Christians chose to wear protection in the form of an ankh.

"There is one more facet of this subject that should be discussed now. If you look carefully at Christian apocalyptic literature, including Mark 13, 2 Thessalonians 2 and the Book of Revelation, which is to say, teachings of Jesus, Mark, Paul, and John of Patmos, it seems abundantly clear that apocalyptic coded language was used to critique prophetically the emperor cult. Furthermore the 'cult of Jesus,' if we can call it that, in its technical and non-pejorative sense, meaning the worship of Jesus, had a very different spiritual ethos.

"The emperor cult celebrated peace and salvation brought through war and violence. The Jesus cult celebrated peace and salvation through love and forgiveness. Apocalyptic rhetoric in the Christian context furthered this latter good news message, not the former pagan one. It also called Christians to cross bearing, not merely cross wearing, in hopes of protection. This is the literature of suffering and preparation for martyrdom, and calls for leaving justice and vengeance entirely in the hands of God. How very different this is than the message of the good news of the emperor, born to conquer the world with the sword. Still today, many Christians and others mistake the apocalyptic rhetoric of the New Testament as a call to arms. I would suggest just the opposite. The message of apocalyptic in the New Testament is 'a farewell to arms,' an embracing of the gospel of love, non-violence, and forgiveness. It would be my view that what our world needs is the new garments of that gospel, not the blood-stained garments of the emperor's now ancient clothes. Thank you very much!"

The applause was thunderous, with some bravos sprinkled throughout the crowd. Art came stage right and there was Grace waiting for him, beaming: "Your pen is mightier than the sword." But the person most deeply impressed and impacted by the lecture was a brand new Christian named Ishmael, who had already laid down his all too human weapons, and taken up the good news of salvation by grace and with forgiveness.

71

Total Immersion

Dawn came quite early on Friday morning, and Ishmael was already up and getting dressed by 6:30. His mother Ruth had also arisen early, as had Rachel and the children, and everyone hurried into the kitchen for a quick breakfast, for this was no ordinary day. This was a day to remember forever. Eating and finishing dressing, and cramming into the church van with Father Abbas had all transpired by 7:45, and the bus headed down the road to Jericho before 8:00, just as Father Abbas had requested. He had reserved a spot for baptism in the Jordan near Jericho for 9:30, so time was of the essence. Also invited to this joyous occasion was Art West, whom Issah had dearly loved and appreciated over the years. Art was accompanied by Grayson, himself a very committed if unconventional Christian. Grace and Manny had been pleased to be invited and were now curious about what would transpire.

The sun spread its heat and light across the river, and if one looked east, the waters looked like a pure sheet of gold. Father Abbas was wearing a black robe, a huge cross, and his little hat. One of the local children came and tugged on his robe. "Why do you wear a black robe? Aren't you too hot?"

"For my sins, child, for my sins," he kidded. "I am sweating them off."

Walking down the dirt path, the group made its way through the river reeds and past the palm trees until they finally saw the water itself, with the small sandy area beside it. Absolutely everything was quiet and still. Only the occasional sound of a bird or a vehicle in the distance broke the absolute solitude. All eyes focused on the water itself—shimmering, shining, gleaming, gliding down, down to the Dead Sea.

At this time of year the shallow waters moved slowly, requiring Father Abbas and Ishmael to wade out almost to the center of the river. Facing the small party that stood upon the shore, Father Abbas stood behind Ishmael and whispered to him, "I will lower you slowly into the water. Are you ready to hold your breath?"

"Yes Father," said Ishmael, whose pulse was racing.

"Ishmael Arafat, I baptize you this day for the remission of all your sins past and present, and in sure and certain hope of the resurrection, in the name of the Father, and the Son, and the Holy Spirit."

Ishmael felt the cool waters wash over him and Father Abbas's arm supporting him. It was so refreshing Ishmael almost wished to stay under for a while, like a child on an exceedingly hot day who has just jumped into the local fishing pond to cool off. But then he felt the warm rush of the humid day envelope him once more.

"You are now a new creature in Christ. Dwell no more in the past. Jesus has saved you from all that has come before, and the past is dead and gone. As a new creature, receive a new name. Formerly you said, 'Call me Ishmael,' but now we all proclaim, 'You shall be Yacov, named after the brother of the first Issah, Jesus Christ himself.'"

On the shore Grayson shouted, "Hallelujah," and Art with tears in his eyes said, "Praise the Lord, for he is risen, he is risen indeed. And praise God that the brother of Issah who was once lost, now is found, and is forever more Jacob, whom God loves."

If Issah could indeed look down from paradise, he would have seen a small band of human beings embracing one another on that little shore. And the Christians among them were witnessing in song:

> Up from the grave he arose
> With a mighty triumph o'er his foes.
> He arose a victor o'er the dark domain,
> And he lives forever with his saints to reign.
> He arose, he arose, Hallelujah, Christ arose.

THE END

Author's Notes

THE CHARACTERS IN THIS novel and its plot are of course fictional, but the discussions about historical matters are factual, with rare exception, and the exceptions are all possibilities. For example, amulets and ankhs were indeed worn to ward off curses or to obtain blessings, and Christians did wear them, and while no one has yet found an ankh with an imperial cult inscription, it is not impossible that it will happen. Similarly, the graffito at the temple in Philae in our story, though fictional, is possible, if there were Christians this far south early on. I am inclined to think there were, in light of the Ethiopian eunuch story in Acts 8. The story about the pagan altar chopped in half by frantic diggers at Scythopolis is in fact true and bears clear witness to the presence of pagan religion within the historic borders of the Holy Land during the lifetime of Jesus and Paul.

In ch. 14, Art makes reference to an interpretation of the history of the Coptic language from the Coptic Church itself. This reference can be found at "The History of the Coptic Language," The St. Shenouda the Archimandrite Coptic Society website, online: http://www.stshenouda .com/coptlang/copthist.htm. Also in ch. 14 Art distributed a handout printed from a "popular online encyclopedia" article on the *Gospel of Judas*. The content of the handout was taken and adapted slightly from "Gospel of Judas," *Wikipedia, The Free Encyclopedia*, http://en.wikipedia .org/w/index.php?title=Gospel_of_Judas&oldid=276728529 (accessed March 2008).

Chapter 19 contains an excerpt from an article in the May/June 2008 edition of *Biblical Archaeology Review*, "Biblical Views: Forgers and Scholars—Unlikely Bed Fellows." Used by permission.

Chapter 34 contains an article Art has printed from a Web site. This is an actual article (Dan Wooding, "Cairo's garbage dump priest has Cave Cathedral," *BC Christian News*, November 1998, online: http://www .canadianchristianity.com/cgi-bin/bc.cgi?bc/bccn/1198/cairo). Special thanks to Dan Wooding at Assist News and David Dawes at Christian Info Society for kind permission to reprint the article here.